ACCA

PAPER F6

TAXATION (UK)
FA 2007

P
R
A
C
T
I
C
E

&

R
E
V
I
S
I
O
N

K
I
T

In this January 2008 second edition

- We discuss the **best strategies** for revising and taking your ACCA exams

- We show you how to be well prepared for the **June and December 2008 exams**

- We give you **lots of great guidance** on tackling questions

- We show you how you can **build your own exams**

- We provide you with **three** mock exams including the **December 2007 paper**

Our **i-Pass** product also supports this paper.

FOR EXAMS IN JUNE AND DECEMBER 2008

LEARNING MEDIA

Second edition January 2008

First edition March 2007

ISBN 9780 7517 4683 9 ~ OK
(previous edition 9780 7517 3359 4)

British Library Cataloguing-in-Publication Data
A catalogue record for this book is available from the
British Library

Published by

BPP Learning Media Ltd
BPP House, Aldine Place
London W12 8AA

www.bpp.com/learningmedia

Printed in Great Britain by
WM Print
42-47 Frederick Street
Walsall
W Midlands, WS2 9NE

Contents

Question index

The headings in this checklist/index indicate the main topics of questions, but questions often cover several different topics.

Preparation questions, listed in italics, provide you with a firm foundation for attempts at exam-standard questions.

Helping hand questions give tips on how to approach questions which will be helpful if you are unsure where to start.

Questions with analysis show how to annotate questions to highlight key points, as you will need to do in the examination. The answers show the key points your answer should have contained.

Questions set under the old syllabus exam are included in this kit (labelled BTX and the date of the exam) because their style and content are similar to those that appear in the new syllabus exam. The questions have been amended as appropriate to reflect the new syllabus exam format.

BPP LEARNING MEDIA

Mock exam 3 (December 2007)

63	Vanessa Serve and Serene Volley	30	54	247	259
64	Sofa Ltd	25	45	248	263
65	David and Angela Brook	20	36	251	267
66	Edmond Brick	15	27	252	270
67	Samantha Fabrique	10	18	253	272

Planning your question practice

Our guidance from page xxix shows you how to organise your question practice, either by attempting questions from each syllabus area or **by building your own exams** – tackling questions as a series of practice exams.

Topic index

Listed below are the key Paper F6 syllabus topics and the numbers of the questions in this Kit covering those topics.

If you need to concentrate your practice and revision on certain topics or if you want to attempt all available questions that refer to a particular subject, you will find this index useful.

Using your BPP Practice and Revision Kit

Tackling revision and the exam

You can significantly improve your chances of passing by tackling revision and the exam in the right ways. Our advice is based on recent feedback from ACCA examiners.

- We look at the dos and don'ts of revising for, and taking, ACCA exams

- We focus on Paper F6; we discuss revising the syllabus, what to do (and what not to do) in the exam, how to approach different types of question and ways of obtaining easy marks

Selecting questions

We provide signposts to help you plan your revision.

- A full **question index**

- A **topic index** listing all the questions that cover key topics, so that you can locate the questions that provide practice on these topics, and see the different ways in which they might be examined

- **BPP's question plan** highlighting the most important questions and explaining why you should attempt them

- **Build your own exams**, showing how you can practise questions in a series of exams

Making the most of question practice

At BPP we realise that you need more than just questions and model answers to get the most from your question practice.

- Our **Top tips** provide essential advice on tackling questions, presenting answers and the key points that answers need to include

- We show you how you can pick up **Easy marks** on questions, as we know that picking up all readily available marks often can make the difference between passing and failing

- We summarise **Examiner's comments** to show you how students who sat the exam coped with the questions

- We include **Marking guides** to show you what the examiner rewards

- We refer to the **BPP Learning Media Study Text** (Finance Act 2007 edition) for detailed coverage of the topics covered in each question

- A number of questions include **Analysis** and **Helping hands** to show you how to approach them if you are struggling

Attempting mock exams

There are three mock exams that provide practice at coping with the pressures of the exam day. We strongly recommend that you attempt them under exam conditions. **Mock exams 1 and 2** reflect the question styles and syllabus coverage of the exam; **Mock exam 3** is the December 2007 paper. To help you get the most out of doing these exams, we not only provide help with each answer, but also guidance on how you should have approached the whole exam.

Passing ACCA exams

Revising and taking ACCA exams

To maximise your chances of passing your ACCA exams, you must make best use of your time, both before the exam during your revision, and when you are actually doing the exam.

- Making the most of your revision time can make a big, big difference to how well-prepared you are for the exam

- Time management is a core skill in the exam hall; all the work you've done can be wasted if you don't make the most of the three hours you have to attempt the exam

In this section we simply show you what to do and what not to do during your revision, and how to increase and decrease your prospects of passing your exams when you take them. Our advice is grounded in feedback we've had from ACCA examiners. You may be surprised to know that much examiner advice is the same whatever the exam, and the reasons why many students fail don't vary much between subjects and exam levels. So if you follow the advice we give you over the next few pages, you will **significantly** enhance your chances of passing **all** your ACCA exams.

How to revise

☑ Plan your revision

At the start of your revision period, you should draw up a **timetable** to plan how long you will spend on each subject and how you will revise each area. You need to consider the total time you have available and also the time that will be required to revise for other exams you're taking.

☑ Practise Practise Practise

The **more exam-standard questions** you do, the **more likely you are to pass** the exam. Practising full questions will mean that you'll get used to the time pressure of the exam. It is important that you practise questions without looking at the answers. When the time is up, you should note where you've got to and then try to complete the question, giving yourself practice at everything the question tests.

☑ Revise enough

Make sure that your revision covers the breadth of the syllabus, as in most papers most topics could be examined. However it is true that some topics are **key** – they appear in most exams, or are a particular interest of the examiner – and you need to spend sufficient time revising these. Make sure you also know the **basics** – the fundamental calculations, proformas and layouts.

☑ Deal with your difficulties

Difficult areas are topics you find dull and pointless, or subjects that you found problematic when you were studying them. You mustn't become negative about these topics; instead you should build up your knowledge by reading the **Passcards** and using the **Quick quiz** questions in the Study Text to test yourself. When practising questions in the Kit, go back to the Text if you're struggling.

☑ Learn from your mistakes

Having completed a question you must try to look at your answer critically. Always read the **Top tips guidance** in the answers; it's there to help you. Look at **Easy marks** to see how you could have quickly gained credit on the questions that you've done. As you go through the Kit, it's worth noting any traps you've fallen into, and key points in the **Top tips** or **Examiner's comments** sections, and referring to these notes in the days before the exam. Aim to learn at least one new point from each question you attempt, a technical point perhaps or a point on style or approach.

☑ Read the examiners' guidance

We refer throughout this Kit to **Examiner's comments**; some of these are available on ACCA's website. As well as highlighting weaknesses, examiners' reports as often provide clues to future questions, as many examiners will quickly test again areas where problems have arisen. ACCA's website also contains articles by examiners which you **must** read, as they may form the basis of questions on any paper after they've been published.

☑ Complete all three mock exams

You should attempt the **Mock exams** at the end of the Kit under **strict exam conditions**, to gain experience of how to approach the questions, managing your time and producing answers.

How NOT to revise

☒ Revise selectively

Examiners are well aware that some students try to forecast the contents of exams, and only revise those areas that they think will be examined. Examiners try to prevent this by doing the unexpected, for example setting the same topic in successive sittings.

☒ Spend all the revision period reading

You cannot pass the exam just by learning the contents of Passcards, Course Notes or Study Texts. You have to develop your **application skills** by practising questions.

☒ Audit the answers

This means reading the answers and guidance without having attempted the questions. Auditing the answers gives you **false reassurance** that you would have tackled the questions in the best way and made the points that our answers do. The feedback we give in our answers will mean more to you if you've attempted the questions and thought through the issues.

☒ Practise some types of question, but not others

Although you may find the numerical parts of certain papers challenging, you shouldn't just practise calculations. These papers will also contain written elements, and you therefore need to spend time practising written question parts.

☒ Get bogged down

Don't spend a lot of time worrying about all the minute detail of certain topic areas, and leave yourself insufficient time to cover the rest of the syllabus. Remember that a key skill in the exam is the ability to **concentrate on what's important** and this applies to your revision as well.

☒ Overdo studying

Studying for too long without interruption will mean your studying becomes less effective. A five minute break each hour will help. You should also make sure that you are leading a **healthy lifestyle** (proper meals, good sleep and some times when you're not studying).

How to PASS your exam

☑ Prepare for the day

Make sure you set at least one alarm (or get an alarm call), and allow plenty of time to get to the exam hall. You should have your route planned in advance and should listen on the radio for potential travel problems. You should check the night before to see that you have pens, pencils, erasers, watch, calculator with spare batteries, also exam documentation and evidence of identity.

☑ Plan your three hours

You need to make sure that you spend the right length of time on each question – this will be determined by the number of marks available. Each mark carries with it a **time allocation** of **1.8 minutes**. A 25 mark question therefore should be selected, completed and checked in 45 minutes.

☑ Read the questions carefully

To score well, you must follow the requirements of the question, understanding what aspects of the subject area are being covered, and the tasks you will have to carry out. The requirements will also determine what information and examples you should provide. Reading the question scenarios carefully will help you decide what **issues** to discuss, **techniques** to use, **information** and **examples** to include and how to **organise** your answer.

☑ Plan your answers

Five minutes of planning plus twenty-five minutes of writing is certain to earn you more marks than thirty minutes of writing. Consider when you're planning how your answer should be **structured,** **w**hat the **format** should be and **how long** each part should take.

Confirm before you start writing that your plan makes **sense**, covers **all relevant points** and does not include **irrelevant material.**

☑ Show evidence of application of knowledge

Remember that examiners aren't just looking for a display of knowledge; they want to see how well you can **apply** the knowledge you have. Evidence of application will include writing answers that only contain **relevant** material, using the facts to **support** what you say and stating any **assumptions** you make.

☑ Stay until the end of the exam

Use any spare time to **check and recheck** your script. This includes checking you have filled out the candidate details correctly, you have labelled question parts and workings clearly, you have used headers and underlining effectively and spelling, grammar and arithmetic are correct.

How to FAIL your exam

☒ Don't do enough questions

If you don't attempt all the questions on paper F6, you are making it harder for yourself to pass the questions that you do attempt. If for example you don't do a 20 mark question, then you will have to score 50 marks out of 80 marks on the rest of the paper, and therefore have to obtain 63% of the marks on the questions you do attempt. Failing to attempt all of the paper is symptomatic of poor time management.

☒ Include irrelevant material

Markers are given detailed mark guides and will not give credit for irrelevant content. The markers will only give credit for what is **relevant**.

☒ Don't do what the question asks

Failing to provide all the examiner asks for will limit the marks you score.

☒ Present your work poorly

Markers will only be able to give you credit if they can read your writing. There are also plenty of other things that will make it more difficult for markers to reward you. Examples include:

- Not using black or blue ink
- Not showing clearly which question you're attempting
- Scattering question parts from the same question throughout your answer booklet
- Not showing clearly workings or the results of your calculations
- Crossing out workings that are correct. You should never cross your workings out; if the main answer is wrong the examiner wants to give credit for correct workings.

Paragraphs that are too long or which lack headers also won't help markers so won't help you.

Using your BPP Learning Media products

This Kit gives you the question practice and guidance you need in the exam. Our other products can also help you pass:

- **Learning to Learn Accountancy** gives further valuable advice on revision

- **Passcards** provide you with clear topic summaries and exam tips

- **Success CDs** help you revise on the move

- **i-Pass CDs** offer tests of knowledge against the clock

- **Learn Online** is an e-learning resource delivered via the Internet, offering comprehensive tutor support and featuring areas such as study, practice, email service, revision and useful resources

You can purchase these products by visiting www.bpp.com/mybpp.

Visit our website www.bpp.com/acca/learnonline to sample aspects of Learn Online free of charge.

BPP
LEARNING MEDIA

Passing F6

Revising F6

The F6 syllabus is very wide, covering a broad range of taxes. The questions are similar in style to those set in the previous syllabus. The examiner is still David Harrowven. The focus is, however, now mainly on computational aspects rather than written answers, although it is possible that there could be written elements in each question or that an entirely written answer may be required.

All five questions are compulsory and must be attempted. You will find it difficult to pass the exam if you do not attempt all of the questions.

You should therefore not attempt to 'question spot'. Instead ensure that you have covered the entire syllabus, even those areas that you find dull or uninteresting. It is better to have a broad knowledge for this exam than to be specialised in any one area.

Topics to revise

That said, you must have sound knowledge in the following fundamental areas if you are to stand a chance of passing the exam. You should therefore revise the following areas particularly well.

- Income tax computation including the personal allowance and the tax bands and rates.

- The calculation of benefits from employment, such as company car and/or fuel, use of an employer's asset and low cost loans. Make sure you can spot tax free benefits too.

- Capital allowances proforma paying particular attention to the availability of first year allowances. Note particularly the difference in the calculation rules between individuals (sole traders and partners) and companies.

- Calculation of profits chargeable to corporation tax (PCTCT). Be aware that you may need to calculate the various elements that make up the PCTCT such as property business income, interest income, gains and so on.

- Computation of chargeable gains paying attention to whether the disposal is made by an individual or a company, particularly for aspects such as indexation allowance and taper relief.

- How to calculate VAT payable or repayable depending on the type of supply (ie standard rated, zero rated or exempt).

- The different classes of NIC payable by employees and their employers compared to those due from self employed individuals or partners.

Question practice

Question practice under timed conditions is essential, so that you can get used to the pressures of answering exam questions in **limited time** and practise not only the key techniques but allocating your time between different requirements in each question. Our list of recommended questions includes questions of various marks.

Passing the F6 exam

Displaying the right qualities

The examiner expects students to display the following qualities.

Qualities required	
Knowledge development	Questions will test your knowledge of underlying principles and major technical areas of taxation, as they affect the activities of individuals and businesses, across the breadth of the F6 syllabus. You will also be expected to apply this knowledge to the facts of each particular question and also to identify the compliance issues for your client.
Computation skills	Although you will be expected to be able to calculate the tax liability, note that you will also be marked on the methods you use. So, if your numbers are not perfect you will not necessarily lose too many marks so long as your method is correct and you have stated any assumptions you have made.
Ability to explain	Whilst the main focus of the exam is on the computation of tax liabilities, you may also be required to explain rules and conditions, so take care to practise the written elements of the answers also.
Identification capability	You must know who you are calculating tax liabilities for – is the client a company or an individual? Be sure who you are advising as this will seriously impact your answers.

You will not always produce the exact same answer as we have in our answer section. This does not necessarily mean that you have failed the question, but if you do use the suggested proformas and methods you will maximise the number of marks you can achieve.

Avoiding weaknesses

We give details of the examiner's comments and criticisms (based on the previous syllabus, but still relevant to F6) throughout this Kit. These hardly varied over the last few years. His reports always emphasise the need for thorough preparation for the exam, but there are various things you can do on the day of the exam to enhance your chances. Although these all sound basic, the examiner has commented that many scripts don't:

- Make the most of the information given in the question
- Follow the question requirements
- Set out workings clearly

Reading time

You will have 15 minutes reading time for Paper F6. Here are some helpful tips on how to best utilise this time.

- Speed read through the question paper, jotting down any ideas that come to you about any of the questions.

- Decide the order which you're likely to tackle questions (probably easiest questions first, most difficult questions last).

- Spend the remainder of reading time reading the question(s) you'll do first in detail jotting down proformas and plans (any plans or proformas written on the question paper should be reproduced in the answer booklet).

- When you can start writing, get straight on with the question(s) you've planned in detail.

If you have looked at all of the questions during the reading time, this should hopefully mean that you will find it easier to answer the more difficult questions when you come to them, as you will have been generating ideas and remembering facts while answering the easier questions.

Choosing which questions to answer first

There are five compulsory questions, with a larger number of marks awarded for the first two questions.

- Many students prefer to answer the questions with the largest number of allocated marks first. Others prefer to answer a question on their most comfortable topic.

- Whatever the order, make sure you leave yourself **sufficient time** to tackle all the questions. Don't get so bogged down in the calculations in the first question you do, especially if it's your favourite topic, that you have to rush the rest of the paper.

- Allocate your time carefully between different question parts. If a question is split into a number of requirements, use the number of marks available for each to allocate your time effectively.

Tackling questions

You'll improve your chances by following a step-by-step approach along the following lines.

Step 1   Read the requirement

Identify the knowledge areas being tested and see precisely what the examiner wants you to do. This will help you focus on what's important in the question.

Step 2   Check the mark allocation

This helps you allocate time.

Step 3   Read the question actively

You will already know which knowledge area(s) are being tested from having read the requirement so whilst you read through the question underline or highlight key words and figures as you read. This will mean you are thinking about the question rather than just looking at the words blankly, and will allow you to identify relevant information for use in your calculations.

Step 4   Plan your answer

You may only spend five minutes planning your answer but it will be five minutes well spent. Identify the calculations you will need to do and whether you have appropriate proformas to assist in these. If there is a written element to the question, determine whether you can you use bullet points or if you need a more formal format.

Step 5   Write your answer

Stick carefully to the time allocation for each question, and for each part of each question.

Gaining the easy marks

There are two main ways to obtain easy marks in the F6 exam.

Proformas

There will always be basic marks available for straightforward tasks such as putting easy figures into proformas, for example putting the cost figure for an addition into a capital allowances proforma. Do not miss out on these easy marks by not learning your proformas properly. Make it easy for yourself to pick up the easy marks.

Deadlines and dates

An important component of your knowledge of the different taxes is the administrative, or compliance, details such as filing deadlines and tax payment dates. This element of the requirement can often be answered even before you make any calculations, for example stating the submission deadline for an individual's self assessment tax return.

The exam paper

The syllabus is assessed by a three-hour paper-based examination.

The paper will be predominantly computational and will have five questions, all of which will be compulsory.

- Question one will focus on income tax and question two will focus on corporation tax. The two questions will be for a total of 55 marks, with one of the questions being for 30 marks and the other being for 25 marks.

- Question three will focus on chargeable gains (either personal or corporate) and will be for 20 marks.

- Questions four and five will be on any area of the syllabus and will respectively be for 15 marks and 10 marks.

There will always be at a minimum of 10 marks on value added tax. These marks will normally be included within question one or question two, although there might be a separate question on value added tax.

National insurance contributions will not be examined as a separate question, but may be examined in any question involving income tax or corporation tax.

Groups and overseas aspects of corporation tax will only be examined in question two, and will account for no more than one third of the marks available for that question.

Questions one or two might include a small element of chargeable gains.

Any of the five questions might include the consideration of issues relating to the minimisation or deferral of tax liabilities.

Additional information

The Study Guide provides more detailed guidance on the syllabus.

Pilot paper

Below is a breakdown of the contents of the Pilot paper.

Q1   Mark Kett – income tax computation
Q2   Scuba Ltd – corporation tax and VAT
Q3   Paul Opus – capital gains
Q4   Li Fung – change of accounting date
Q5   Loser Ltd – corporation tax losses

The Pilot paper questions are included in this Kit.

Useful websites

The websites below provide additional sources of information of relevance to your studies for *Taxation (UK)*

- www.bpp.com

  Our website provides information about BPP Learning Media products and services, with a link to the ACCA website.

- www.accaglobal.com

  ACCA's website. Includes student section. It is vital that you read any articles written by David Harrowven, the paper F6 examiner. These articles are reproduced on this website. You will also find other articles of relevance to Paper F6 on this website.

Planning your question practice

Planning your question practice

We have already stressed that question practice should be right at the centre of your revision. Whilst you will spend some time looking at your notes and Paper F6 Passcards, you should spend the majority of your revision time practising questions.

We recommend two ways in which you can practise questions.

- Use **BPP's question plan** to work systematically through the syllabus and attempt key and other questions on a section-by-section basis

- **Build your own exams** – attempt questions as a series of practice exams

These ways are suggestions and simply following them is no guarantee of success. You or your college may prefer an alternative but equally valid approach.

BPP's question plan

The BPP plan below requires you to devote a **minimum of 36 hours** to revision of Paper F6. Any time you can spend over and above this should only increase your chances of success.

Step 1   For each section of the syllabus, **review your notes** and the relevant chapter summaries in the Paper F6 **Passcards**.

Step 2   Start by looking at any preparation **questions/questions with helping hands** for some topics. These questions are designed to ease the transition from study to exam standard questions. If you are very confident you may wish just to look through the answers to these questions. However, if you are not completely confident at tax attempt these questions properly.

Step 3   Then do the **key questions** for that section. These are shown in **white boxes** in the table below. Even if you are short of time you must attempt these questions if you want to pass the exam. Try to complete your answers without referring to our solutions.

Step 4   For some questions we have suggested that you prepare **answer plans** rather than full solutions. This means that you should spend about 30% of the time allowance for the questions brainstorming the question and drawing up a list of points to be included in the answer.

Step 5   Once you have worked through all of the syllabus sections attempt **Mock exam 1** under strict exam conditions. Then have a go at **Mock exam 2**, again under strict exam conditions. Just before the exam, if you have time, attempt **Mock exam 3**, again under strict exam conditions. This is the December 2007 paper.

Syllabus section	Passcards chapters	Questions in this Kit	Comments	Done ☑
Revision period 1 Income tax computations				
Preparation question	1, 2, 5	1	This is a useful preparation question but work through alongside the answer if short of time.	☐
Key question	2, 3	2	Work through this question carefully.	☐
Revision period 2 Pensions				
Key question	5	16	Pensions are topical so work through this question very carefully.	☐
Revision periods 3/4 Employees				☐
Question with helping hand		3	The computation of taxable benefits is frequently examined. You may also be required to spot tax free benefits. There are a lot of rules to learn so take your time.	
Key questions	3, 4, 5, 6, 12, 18	4, 5, 6	Useful questions. Answer in full.	☐
Revision periods 5/6 Trading profits and losses for individuals				
Key questions: adjustment of profits	2, 7, 8, 9, 12, 13, 16, 18	7, 8, 9	Key questions that also include basis period rules for an individual. Answer in full. Q8 also covers employment income and is a good comparison with trading income. You should ignore the disposal in Q9 if you are short of time.	☐
Preparation questions: change of accounting date	2, 9	11, 12	This is new to the syllabus. You should be happy with the calculations in these questions.	☐
Key question: basis periods	9, 11	17	This is a past exam question. Attempt this when you are happy with the preparation questions.	☐
Key question: income tax losses	10	10	Losses are a key area so answer this question in full.	☐
Revision period 7 Partnerships				
Key questions: partnerships	5, 7, 8, 11, 12	14, 15, 16	Useful questions. Answer in full.	☐

Syllabus section	Passcards chapters	Questions in this Kit	Comments	Done ☑
Revision period 8 Overseas aspects/ self assessment			You should briefly review the residency rules. Self assessment is a key topic.	
Key question: self assessment	18	13	Useful question. Answer in full.	☐
Revision period 9 NIC				
Key question	2, 12, 13 – 17	25	A question covering a number of taxes. Work through carefully.	☐
Revision period 10 Capital gains			Gains will be tested in a stand alone question and may also be tested in any of the other questions. The gains rules are therefore key for your exam.	
Preparation question	13	18	Useful question. Work through alongside the answer if your time is short.	☐
Key question: basics	13 – 17	22	Useful question. Answer in full.	☐
Revision period 11 Additional aspects of capital gains			The gains rules for shares, chattels and immoveable property, including PPR relief.	
Key questions	13 – 17 19	20, 26, 27	These are key questions. Make sure you understand the calculations, particularly for PPR relief.	☐
		28, 29	Questions 28 and 29 cover gains for a company so you may want to come back to these once you have revised the corporation tax rules.	☐
Revision period 12 Capital gains reliefs				
Key questions	13 – 17	19, 21, 23, 24	It is likely that you will not be able to avoid reliefs for gains in the exam. Note the only relief available to companies is rollover relief.	☐
Revision periods 13/14 Computing corporation tax				
Preparation questions: computing corporation tax	20	30	Useful preparation question to practice the marginal relief rules.	☐
Key questions: comprehensive computation	8, 13 – 17, 19, 20, 24, 25	31, 32, 33, 34 35, 38	Vitally important key questions that you must work through in full. These are similar to the type of question that you could see as Question 2 in the exam. If you run out of time prepare plans for Questions 33 and 38. Question 33 also covers VAT aspects.	☐
		28, 29	Questions 28 and 29 deal with gains for companies.	

Syllabus section	Passcards chapters	Questions in this Kit	Comments	Done ☑
Revision period 15 Corporation tax losses				
Key questions: single company losses	13 – 17, 19, 20, 21	36, 37	Important questions covering a single company's losses. Answer both in full.	☐
Revision period 16 Corporation tax groups				
Preparation question: group losses	22	41	Useful question. Work through alongside the answer if your time is limited.	☐
Key questions: group losses	8, 13, 16, 19, 20, 22, 24	42, 43, 44, 45	Important questions. Group losses are a popular exam question.	☐
Revision period 17 Overseas aspects of corporation tax				
Question with helping hand	20, 23	39	Work through alongside the answer if you feel confident with DTR.	☐
Key question	8, 20, 21, 23	40	Useful question. Answer in full.	☐
Revision period 18 VAT				
Key questions	25, 26	46, 47, 48, 49	Essential questions. There will be at least 10 marks for VAT in your paper so be prepared.	☐

Build your own exams

Having revised with your notes and the BPP Passcards, you can attempt the questions in the Kit as a series of practice exams.

You can make up practice exams, either yourself or using the mock exams that we have listed below.

	Practice exams					
	1	*2*	*3*	*4*	*5*	*6*
1	4	5	9	15	6	7
2	36	33	40	34	38	35
3	19	28	24	21	22	29
4	42	17	12	13	14	11
5	49	16	47	48	46	37

Whichever practice exams you use, you must attempt **Mock exams 1, 2 and 3** at the end of your revision.

Questions

1 Preparation question: personal tax computation

Roger Thesaurus has the following income and outgoings for the tax year 2007/08.

		£	
(a)	Share of partnership profits	57,000	
(b)	Interest on a deposit account with the Scotia Bank	2,197	(net)
(c)	Interest paid on a loan taken out to purchase an interest in the partnership of which Mr Thesaurus is a partner.	6,000	(amount paid)
(d)	Personal pension contributions. Roger joined a personal pension scheme on 6 April 2007.	9,360	(amount paid)
(e)	Dividends received on UK shares	900	(amount received)

Required

(a) Calculate the income tax payable by Mr Thesaurus for 2007/08.

(b) Explain how you have dealt with the personal pension contribution and the interest paid on the loan to purchase a share in the partnership.

Guidance notes

1 The major part of this question requires you to calculate an individual's overall tax position. You should start by heading your answer and laying it out: non-savings, savings and dividend income. Next show deductible interest, net income and the personal allowance. It will then be more difficult to overlook anything.

2 Start with non-savings income and any deductions made specifically from it.

3 Insert the types of savings and dividend income, remembering that amounts are always included gross in the tax computation even if the amounts are actually received net.

4 Deduct any deductible interest. Firstly from non-savings income, then from savings income and lastly from dividend income.

5 Total income less deductible interest is net income.

6 After deducting the personal allowance to find the taxable income, you need to calculate tax payable. Don't forget to extend the basic rate band by the gross amount of the pension contributions paid.

2 Brad and Lauren

27 mins

(a)   Brad, an advertising executive, and his wife Lauren, an IT consultant, have one son. Having made a large gain on the sale of a property when they got married, they have acquired a considerable number of investments. They now require assistance in preparing their taxation returns for 2007/08 and have listed out their income and expenditure:

Lauren

	£
Salary	45,000
ISA account – dividends	350
– interest	125
Dividend received on Virgin plc shares	2,250
Building society interest (Joint account – total interest credited)	4,400 (net)
Interest received on 2008 10% Treasury Stock (received gross)	2,000
Gift Aid payment to Dogs Trust	1,000

Brad

	£
Salary	41,500
Premium Bond winnings	5,000
Interest received on National Savings & Investments Certificates	300
Building society interest (Joint account – total interest credited)	4,400 (net)

Required

Calculate Brad and Lauren's income tax liability for 2007/08. **(10 marks)**

(b)   Lauren's father, Tom, a widower, who is 69, has the following income for 2007/08.

	£
State retirement pension	4,226
Pension from former employer	14,355
Building society interest	6,348

Tom gave £3,900 to Oxfam (a registered charity) on 21 September 2007 under Gift Aid.

Required

Calculate Tom's income tax liability for 2007/08. **(5 marks)**

(Total = 15 marks)

3 Rita

27 mins

Rita, who is a fashion designer for Daring Designs Limited, was relocated from London to Manchester on 6 April 2007. Her annual salary is £48,000. She was immediately provided with a house with an annual value of £4,000 for which her employer paid an annual rent of £6,000. Rita was reimbursed relevant relocation expenditure of £12,000. Daring Designs Limited provided ancillary services for the house in 2007/08 as follows.

	£
Electricity	700
Gas	1,200
Water	500
Council tax	1,300
Property repairs	3,500

The house has been furnished by Daring Designs Limited prior to Rita's occupation at a cost of £30,000. On 6 October 2007 Rita bought all of the furniture from Daring Designs Ltd for £20,000 when its market value was £25,000.

Daring Designs Limited had made an interest free loan to Rita in 2006 of £10,000. The loan is not being used for a 'qualifying purpose'. No part of the loan has been repaid.

Rita was provided with a company car. It had a list price of £18,500 and a CO_2 emissions figure of 144g/km. Daring Designs Limited paid for the petrol for all the mileage done by Rita until 5 December 2007. On 5 December 2007 the company discontinued the company car scheme and sold the car to Rita for £5,000, its market value on that date.

Required

Calculate the total amount chargeable to income tax as employment income on Rita for the year 2007/08.

(15 marks)

Helping hand

1   There are five benefits to calculate in this question. Set up a proforma to summarise these and then deal with each separately.

2   There is only a basic accommodation benefit here based on the higher of annual value and rent paid.

3   Rita has use of the furniture for only part of the year so you will need to pro-rate the benefit.

4   She also only has use of the car for part of the year so again you will need to pro-rate the benefit. Is there private fuel supplied?

---

4 Vigorous plc (BTX 12/03)   45 mins

Vigorous plc runs a health club. The company has three employees who received taxable benefits during 2007/08, and it therefore needs to prepare forms P11D for them. Each of the three employees is paid an annual salary of £35,000. The following information is relevant:

Andrea Lean

(1)   Andrea was employed by Vigorous plc throughout 2007/08.

(2)   Throughout 2007/08 Vigorous plc provided Andrea with a petrol powered company motor car with a list price of £19,400. The official CO_2 emission rate for the motor car is 265 grams per kilometre. Vigorous plc paid for all of the motor car's running costs of £6,200 during 2007/08, including petrol used for private journeys. Andrea pays £150 per month to Vigorous plc for the use of the motor car.

(3)   Vigorous plc has provided Andrea with living accommodation since 1 November 2005. The property was purchased on 1 January 2003 for £130,000. The company spent £14,000 improving the property during March 2003, and a further £8,000 was spent on improvements during May 2007. The value of the property on 1 November 2005 was £170,000, and it has an annual value of £7,000. The furniture in the property cost £6,000 during November 2005. Andrea personally pays for the annual running costs of the property amounting to £4,000.

(4)   Throughout 2007/08 Vigorous plc provided Andrea with a mobile telephone costing £500. The company paid for all business and private telephone calls.

Ben Slim

(1)   Ben commenced employment with Vigorous plc on 1 July 2007.

(2)   On 1 July 2007 Vigorous plc provided Ben with an interest free loan of £120,000 so that he could purchase a new main residence. He repaid £20,000 of the loan on 1 October 2007.

(3)   During 2007/08 Vigorous plc paid £9,300 towards the cost of Ben's relocation. His previous main residence was 125 miles from his place of employment with the company. The £9,300 covered the cost of disposing of Ben's old property and of acquiring his new property.

5

(4)   During the period from 1 October 2007 until 5 April 2008 Vigorous plc provided Ben with a new diesel powered company motor car which has a list price of £11,200. The official CO_2 emission rate for the motor car is 131 grams per kilometre. Ben reimburses Vigorous plc for all the diesel used for private journeys.

Chai Trim

(1)   Chai was employed by Vigorous plc throughout 2007/08.

(2)   During 2007/08 Vigorous plc provided Chai with a two-year old company van, although the van was unavailable during the period 1 August to 30 September 2007. No fuel was provided for private journeys.

(3)   Vigorous plc has provided Chai with a television for her personal use since 6 April 2005. The television cost Vigorous plc £800 in April 2005. On 6 April 2007 the company sold the television to Chai for £150, although its market value on that date was £250.

(4)   Throughout 2007/08 Vigorous plc provided Chai with free membership of its health club. The normal annual cost of membership is £800. This figure is made up of direct costs of £150, fixed overhead costs of £400 and profit of £250. The budgeted membership for the year has been exceeded, but the health club has surplus capacity.

(5)   On 6 April 2007 Vigorous plc provided Chai with a new computer costing £1,900. She uses the computer at home for personal study purposes.

Required

(a)   Explain what is meant by the term 'P11D employee'.   **(3 marks)**

(b)   Calculate the taxable benefit figures that Vigorous plc will have to include on the forms P11D for Andrea, Ben, and Chai for 2007/08.   **(19 marks)**

(c)   Explain how the income tax liability in respect of taxable benefits is collected by HMRC.   **(3 marks)**

(Total = 25 marks)

5 Bryan Thompson   **54 mins**

Bryan Thompson (age 48) is a full-time director of Watnot Ltd.

During 2007/08 he was paid a salary of £75,000 and had the private use of a car provided by his employer. The car had a list price of £25,000 when new in January 2006 and had an emissions rating (petrol) of 160g/km.

In September 2007, the company offered to replace his car with a more expensive model. Bryan declined the offer and instead on 5 October 2007 the company purchased a car with a list price of £7,500 and an emissions rating (petrol) of 140g/km for use by his wife. Bryan pays for all petrol used in his car with the company credit card. His wife pays for the petrol for use in the car provided for her use personally.

Bryan pays 10% of his salary (excluding his benefits) into his employer's occupational pension scheme. His employer matches his contribution.

Since March 2007, the company has paid £100 a month medical insurance to cover Bryan and his family. In January 2008, his son had a minor operation on his leg costing £1,800 which was paid for by the insurance company.

During August 2007, Bryan attended an international business conference in Florida. His wife went with him for a holiday. They stayed for five nights and the cost of the double room was £100 per night upgraded from £75 per night for the single room originally booked for Bryan. The return air fares were £1,000 each. All costs were paid by the company.

In December 2007, Bryan was transferred to the new head office 200 miles from his original office which necessitated moving house. The company paid the following expenses in connection with his move:

	£
Agents' fees	4,500
Removal costs	750
Stamp Duty Land Tax	10,500
Legal fees	1,800

Bryan and his wife also receive income from a furnished house they jointly own. During 2007/08 the income and expenses were:

	£
Rental income	20,000
Caretaker's wages	2,600
Heat and light	1,400
Interest on loan to purchase property	6,000

In February 2008 Bryan received net interest of £3,200 from a two year high interest savings account which had matured. He received a dividend of £1,800 from Adams plc, a UK company in June 2007.

Required

(a)	Calculate Bryan's net assessable income and tax liability for 2007/08.	**(25 marks)**
(b)	Calculate Bryan's NIC due for 2007/08.	**(5 marks)**

(Total = 30 marks)

6 Mark Kett (Pilot paper)   45 mins

On 31 December 2007 Mark Kett ceased trading as a marketing consultant. He had been self-employed since 6 April 2002, and had always made his accounts up to 5 April. On 1 January 2008 Mark commenced employment as the marketing manager of Sleep-Easy plc. The company runs a hotel. The following information is available for the tax year 2007/08:

Self-employment

(1) Mark's tax adjusted trading profit for the nine-month period ended 31 December 2007 is £20,700. This figure is before taking account of capital allowances.

(2) The tax written down values for capital allowances purposes at 6 April 2007 were as follows:

	£
General pool	13,800
Expensive motor car	14,600

The expensive motor car was used by Mark, and 40% of the mileage was for private purposes.

(3) On 15 June 2007 Mark had purchased office furniture for £1,900. All of the items included in the general pool were sold for £18,800 on 31 December 2007. On the cessation of trading Mark personally retained the expensive motor car. Its value on 31 December 2007 was £11,800.

Employment

(1) Mark is paid a salary of £3,250 (gross) per month by Sleep-Easy plc, from which income tax of £620 per month has been deducted under PAYE.

(2) During the period from 1 January 2008 to 5 April 2008 Mark used his private motor car for business purposes. He drove 2,500 miles in the performance of his duties for Sleep-Easy plc, for which the company paid an allowance of 16 pence per mile. The relevant HM Revenue & Customs authorised mileage rate to be used as the basis of an expense claim is 40 pence per mile.

7

(3)   On 1 January 2008 Sleep-Easy plc provided Mark with an interest free loan of £64,000 so that he could purchase a new main residence.

(4)   During the period from 1 January 2008 to 5 April 2008 Mark was provided with free meals in Sleep-Easy plc's staff canteen. The total cost of these meals to the company was £400.

Property income

(1)   Mark let out a furnished property throughout the tax year 2007/08. He received gross rents of £8,600, 5% of which was paid to a letting agency. During December 2007 Mark spent £540 on replacing dilapidated furniture and furnishings.

(2)   From 6 April 2007 to 31 December 2007 Mark let out a spare room in his main residence, receiving rent of £350 per month.

Investment income

(1)   During the tax year 2007/08 Mark received dividends of £2,880, interest from government stocks (gilts) of £1,900, and interest of £430 from an individual savings account (ISA). These were the actual cash amounts received.

(2)   On 3 May 2007 Mark received a premium bond prize of £100.

Other information

(1)   On 15 December 2007 Mark made a gift aid donation of £780 (net) to a national charity.

(2)   Mark's payments on account of income tax in respect of the tax year 2007/08 totalled £11,381.

Required

(a)   Compute the income tax payable by Mark for the tax year 2007/08, and the balancing payment or repayment that will be due for the year. **(22 marks)**

(b)   Advise Mark as to how long he must retain the records used in preparing his tax return for the tax year 2007/08, and the potential consequences of not retaining the records for the required period. **(3 marks)**

(Total = 25 marks)

7 Clayton Delaney

45 mins

Clayton Delaney had been a self-employed electrician for many years. His business was centred on a shop from which he sold electrical goods to the public and to the electrical trade. He also carried out electrical work himself for his customers.

Because of deteriorating health his wife could no longer look after the shop in Clayton's absence and she retired aged 60 on 31 March 2007. She had no source of income thereafter. Clayton decided to permanently cease trading on 30 June 2007 and on 1 July 2007 commenced working for a firm of electrical contractors.

His summarised accounts for the year ended 30 June 2007 are as follows.

Profit and loss account

		£		£
Telephone	(1)	240	Gross profits on sales	19,645
Repairs	(2)	1,180	Bank interest received	
Depreciation		1,350	December 2006	
Buildings insurance	(3)	600	(Note (3) of other relevant	
Lighting and heating	(3)	420	information)	300
Car expenses	(4)	1,750	Profit on sale of shop fittings	20
Impairment losses	(5)	950	Work done for customers	16,000
Rates	(6)	1,850		
Wages and national insurance contributions:				
Mrs Delaney	(7)	5,000		
Wages and national insurance contributions:				
Mr Delaney		11,850		
Bank interest paid	(8)	630		
General expenses	(9)	1,995		
Net profit		8,150		
		35,965		35,965

Figures in brackets refers to notes to the accounts.

Notes to the accounts

(1)   Telephone: one-fifth of the charge is for private calls.

(2)   Repairs were as follows (see also note (3)).

	£
Roof repairs	650
Redecorating bedroom	230
Replacing floor tiles in shop	300
	1,180

(3)   Clayton and his wife live on the shop premises. HMRC have agreed that two-thirds of the household expenditure is in respect of the living accommodation.

(4)   Car expenses: the total mileage in the year was 16,000 of which half was private. This was the same fraction as in earlier years.

(5)   **Irrecoverable debts (impairment loss)**

A loan of £500 to a neighbour was written off during the year. The remaining £450 relates to trade debts written off.

(6) **Rates**

	£
Business rates	1,200
Council tax	650
	1,850

(7) Mrs Delaney's wages: Mrs Delaney looked after the shop in Mr Delaney's absence and ran the clerical side of the business.

(8) Bank interest paid: the interest was paid on the business account overdraft.

(9) **General expenses**

	£
Accountancy	600
Legal costs in defending claim for allegedly faulty work	200
Printing, stationery and postage	220
Gifts to trade customers: one Christmas hamper each, costing £30	900
Donation of prize in local carnival (a free advertisement was provided in the programme)	50
Donation to a national charity (not paid under the gift aid scheme)	25
	1,995

(10) Overlap profits on commencement of trade were £1,200.

In addition Clayton had taken stock from the shop for personal use. The cost price of these items was £600 and the average gross profit margin was 20%. No payment had been made for the goods by Clayton, and no adjustment had been made in the accounts.

The tax written-down values at 1 July 2006 of business assets were as follows.

Car	£5,700
Pool	£490

On 31 December 2006 Clayton traded in his car for £4,500 and purchased a new one costing £9,000.

On 30 June 2007 the items in the pool were sold for £400 (all less than original cost) and the car had a market value of £3,500.

Other relevant information is as follows.

(1) Since commencing employment, Clayton earned £1,500 gross per month, payable on the last day of the month in arrears. Because he was expected to travel around in his employment he was provided with a company car by his employer.

(2) The car had a diesel engine and had a list price of £10,000 when new. Its CO_2 emissions were 147g/km. Clayton's employer agreed to provide fuel for the first 5,000 miles of his private motoring during 2007/08.

(3) Clayton has an investment account with the Halifax Bank. Interest of £395 was credited on 31 December 2007.

(4) Clayton had purchased £8,000 of 5% Treasury stock during 2004.

Required

(a) Calculate the amount of the taxable profits for 2007/08. **(18 marks)**

(b) Calculate the amount of Clayton's income tax payable for 2007/08. **(7 marks)**

(Total = 25 marks)

8 Noel and Liam Wall (BTX 06/07)   45 mins

Noel and Liam Wall are brothers. Noel has more income than Liam, so he is surprised that for the tax year 2007/08 his total income tax liability and national insurance contributions were much lower than Liam's. The following information is available for the tax year 2007/08:

Noel Wall

(1)   Noel is a self-employed musician. His profit and loss account for the year ended 5 April 2008 was as follows:

	£	£
Fee income		86,240
Depreciation	1,980	
Motor expenses (note 2)	5,600	
Professional fees (note 3)	2,110	
Repairs and renewals (note 4)	2,360	
Telephone (note 5)	830	
Travelling and entertaining (note 6)	960	
Other expenses (note 7)	2,050	
		(15,890)
Net profit		70,350

(2)   During the year ended 5 April 2008 Noel drove a total of 8,400 miles, of which 7,560 were for business journeys.

   Noel's motor car had a tax written down value of £32,800 at 6 April 2007.

(3)   The figure for professional fees consists of £840 for accountancy fees, £510 for personal tax advice in respect of the tax year 2006/07, and £760 for legal fees in connection with the defence of Noel's business internet domain name.

(4)   The figure for repairs and renewals consists of £1,900 for a new guitar, and £460 for repairing this guitar when it was damaged.

(5)   Noel uses his mobile telephone to make business telephone calls. The total cost of the mobile telephone is included in the profit and loss account as an expense, although £160 of this cost relates to private telephone calls.

(6)   The figure for travelling and entertaining includes £370 for entertaining clients, and £120 for parking fines.

(7)   The figure for other expenses includes £100 for a donation to a political party, £230 for a trade subscription to the Institute of Musicians, and £625 for Noel's golf club membership fee.

(8)   In addition to his self-employed income, Noel received dividends of £7,560 during the tax year 2007/08. This was the actual cash amount received.

Liam Wall

(1)   Liam is employed as a music producer by Forever Ltd. The company runs a recording studio. During the tax year 2007/08 he was paid a gross annual salary of £65,000.

(2)   Throughout the tax year 2007/08 Forever Ltd provided Liam with a diesel powered motor car which has a list price of £32,400. The official CO_2 emission rate for the motor car is 221 grams per kilometre. The company also provided Liam with fuel for private journeys.

(3)   On 6 July 2007 Forever Ltd provided Liam with a new computer costing £1,800. He uses the computer at home for personal internet browsing.

(4)   On 6 August 2007 Forever Ltd provided Liam with a mobile telephone costing £350. This is the only mobile telephone that has been provided to Liam by Forever Ltd.

(5)   On 1 December 2007 Forever Ltd paid a golf club membership fee of £580 for the benefit of Liam.

11

(6)   On 1 January 2008 Liam paid a professional subscription of £220 to the Guild of Producers, a HM Revenue & Customs' approved professional body.

(7)   In addition to his employment income, Liam received building society interest of £6,640 during the tax year 2007/08. This was the actual cash amount received.

Required

(a)   Calculate Noel's income tax liability and national insurance contributions for the tax year 2007/08.

(15 marks)

(b)   Calculate Liam's income tax liability and national insurance contributions for the tax year 2007/08.

(10 marks)

(Total = 25 marks)

9 Tony Note (BTX 06/06)

45 mins

Tony Note is self-employed running a music shop. His profit and loss account for the year ended 5 April 2008 is as follows:

	£	£
Gross profit		198,000
Expenses:		
Depreciation	2,640	
Motor expenses (1)	9,800	
Professional fees (2)	4,680	
Repairs and renewals (3)	670	
Travelling and entertaining (4)	4,630	
Wages and salaries (5)	77,200	
Other expenses (6)	78,780	
		(178,400)
Net profit		19,600

(1)   Motor expenses

During the year ended 5 April 2008 Tony drove a total of 20,000 miles, of which 2,500 were driven when he went on holiday to Europe. The balance of the mileage is 20% for private journeys and 80% for business journeys.

(2)   Professional fees

The figure for professional fees consists of £920 for accountancy, £620 for personal financial planning advice, £540 for debt collection, and £2,600 for fees in connection with an unsuccessful application for planning permission to enlarge Tony's freehold music shop.

(3)   Repairs and renewals

The figure for repairs and renewals consists of £270 for a replacement hard drive for the shop's computer, and £400 for a new printer for this computer.

(4)   Travelling and entertaining

The figure for travelling and entertaining consists of £3,680 for Tony's business travelling expenses, £480 for entertaining suppliers, and £470 for entertaining employees.

(5)   Wages and salaries

The figure for wages and salaries includes a salary of £16,000 paid to Tony's wife. She works in the music shop as a sales assistant. The other sales assistants doing the same job are paid a salary of £12,000 p.a.

(6)   Other expenses

The figure for other expenses includes £75 in respect of a wedding present to an employee, £710 for Tony's health club subscription, £60 for a donation to a political party, and £180 for a trade subscription to the Guild of Musical Instrument Retailers.

(7)   Use of office

Tony uses one of the six rooms in his private house as an office for when he works at home. The total running costs of the house for the year ended 5 April 2008 were £4,320.

(8)   Private telephone

Tony uses his private telephone to make business telephone calls. The total cost of the private telephone for the year ended 5 April 2008 was £680, and 25% of this related to business telephone calls. The cost of the private telephone is not included in the profit and loss account expenses of £178,400.

(9)   Goods for own use

During the year ended 5 April 2008 Tony took goods out of the music shop for his personal use without paying for them, and no entry has been made in the accounts to record this. The goods cost £600, and had a selling price of £950.

(10)   Plant and machinery

The tax written down values for capital allowances purposes at 6 April 2007 were as follows:

	£
General pool	7,400
Expensive motor car	16,200

The expensive motor car is used by Tony.

Disposal of freehold music shop

On 10 November 2007 Tony sold his freehold music shop for £320,000. The shop had been purchased on 8 August 2003 for £188,000, and was always used by Tony for business purposes. Tony has claimed to roll over the gain arising on the music shop against the cost of a new freehold music shop that he purchased on 4 October 2007 for £210,000.

Required

(a)   Calculate Tony's tax adjusted trading profit for the year ended 5 April 2008.   **(16 marks)**

(b)   Calculate Tony's income tax and capital gains tax liabilities for the tax year 2007/08.   **(6 marks)**

(c)   Advise Tony as to how long he must retain the records used in preparing his tax return for 2007/08, and the potential consequences of not retaining the records for the required period.   **(3 marks)**

(Total = 25 marks)

10 Malcolm   27 mins

(a)   Malcolm started in business as a self-employed builder on 1 August 2006. His adjusted trading results, after capital allowances, were:

	£
Period ended 30 November 2006	(10,000) Loss
Year ended 30 November 2007	(20,000) Loss
Year ended 30 November 2008	15,000 Profit

Prior to being self-employed Malcolm was employed as a builder when his earnings were:

	£
2006/07 (to 31 July 2006)	5,650
2005/06	8,000
2004/05	NIL

He received annual building society interest income of £3,040 (net) from 2005/06 onwards. In 2006/07 he realised a capital gain on the disposal of a non-business asset of £9,400 after indexation but before the annual exemption. Taper relief was not available on the disposal of this non-business asset.

Required

Show how Malcolm's trading losses can be utilised most effectively, giving your reasoning.

You may assume the 2007/08 rates and allowances apply to all years relevant to this question.   **(12 marks)**

(b)   You are required to state by what date(s) the claims you are proposing in part (a) should be submitted.

(3 marks)

(Total = 15 marks)

Helping hand

1   Work out what the losses are first. You need to use the opening year rules to do this so jot down the dates of each basis period first, then apportion the loss accordingly. Remember you can only use a loss once.

2   Now consider what loss reliefs are available. There are three choices here:

   •   Relief against general income of the current year/previous year (including a claim against gains if relevant)

   •   Relief against general income of the three years preceding the loss-making year.

   •   Relief by carry forward against future profits of the same trade

3   Check the effect of loss relief on the personal allowance – will it be lost if a loss is used in the same year or deferred back?

4   Don't forget to do part (b). Even if you get stuck on part (a), there are three easy marks for time limits in part (b).

---

11 Li Fung (Pilot paper)   27 mins

Li Fung commenced in self-employment on 1 October 2003. She initially prepared accounts to 30 June, but changed her accounting date to 31 March by preparing accounts for the nine-month period to 31 March 2007. Li's trading profits since she commenced self-employment have been as follows:

	£
Nine-month period ended 30 June 2004	18,600
Year ended 30 June 2005	24,900
Year ended 30 June 2006	22,200
Nine-month period ended 31 March 2007	16,800
Year ended 31 March 2008	26,400

Required

(a)   State the qualifying conditions that must be met for a change of accounting date to be valid.   **(3 marks)**

(b)   Compute Li's trading income assessments for each of the five tax years 2003/04, 2004/05, 2005/06, 2006/07 and 2007/08.   **(9 marks)**

(c)   Advise Li of the advantages and disadvantages for tax purposes of changing her accounting date from 30 June to 31 March.   **(3 marks)**

(Total = 15 marks)

12 Robert Sax

27 mins

Robert Sax commenced trading on 1 June 2000 drawing up accounts to 30 September. His adjusted profits were as follows:

	£
1.6.00 – 30.9.01	30,000
y/e 30.9.02	40,000
y/e 30.9.03	50,000
y/e 30.9.04	60,000
y/e 30.9.05	55,000

He decided to change his accounting date to 31 December. Profits were as follows:

	£
1.10.05 – 31.12.06	75,000
y/e 31.12.2007	40,000

He decided to retire on 31 March 2008. His profits of his final 3 months of trade were £12,000.

Calculate the assessments for all years. **(15 marks)**

13 Vera Old (BTX 06/05)

27 mins

Vera Old has been a self-employed antiques dealer since 1997. Her tax liabilities for 2006/07 and 2007/08 are as follows:

	2006/07	2007/08
	£	£
Income tax liability	8,240	4,770
Tax suffered at source	(810)	(640)
Income tax payable	7,430	4,130
Class 4 national insurance contributions	1,660	1,230
	9,090	5,360
Capital gains tax liability	1,820	700
	10,910	6,060

Required

(a)   Assuming that Vera does not make a claim to reduce the payments on account, prepare a schedule of her payments on account and balancing payment or repayment for 2007/08. Your answer should show the relevant due dates of each payment/repayment. **(3 marks)**

(b)   (i)   Advise Vera of the claim that she should make to reduce her payments on account for 2007/08.
(2 marks)

         (ii)   State the implications if Vera were to instead make a claim to reduce her payments on account for 2007/08 to nil. **(2 marks)**

(c)   Advise Vera of the latest date by which her self-assessment tax return for 2007/08 should be submitted, and the implications if it is submitted three months late. **(3 marks)**

(d)   (i)   Assuming that her self-assessment tax return for 2007/08 is submitted on time, state the date by which HMRC will have to notify Vera if they intend to enquire into the return, and the possible reasons why such an enquiry would be made. **(3 marks)**

         (ii)   State the circumstances in which HMRC would be entitled to raise a discovery assessment in respect of Vera's self-assessment tax return for 2007/08. **(2 marks)**

(Total = 15 marks)

14 Roger and Brigitte

27 mins

Roger and Brigitte commenced in business on 1 October 2003 as hotel proprietors, sharing profits equally.

On 1 October 2005 their son Xavier joined the partnership and from that date each of the partners was entitled to one-third of the profits.

The profits of the partnership adjusted for income tax, are:

	£
Period ended 30 June 2004	30,000
Year ended 30 June 2005	45,000
Year ended 30 June 2006	50,000
Year ended 30 June 2007	60,000

Required

(a)   Calculate the assessable profits on each of the partners for all relevant years from 2003/04 to 2007/08.

(11 marks)

(b)   Calculate the overlap profits for each of the partners.

(4 marks)

(Total = 15 marks)

15 Xio, Yana and Zoe (BTX 12/04)

54 mins

Xio, Yana and Zoe have been in partnership since 6 April 2000 as marketing consultants.

Until 30 June 2007 profits were shared 50% to Xio, 30% to Yana and 20% to Zoe. This was after paying an annual salary of £6,000 to Xio. On 30 June 2007 Zoe resigned as a partner, and from that date profits were shared equally between Xio and Yana. No salaries were paid after this date.

The partnership's profit and loss account for the year ended 5 April 2008 is as follows:

	£	£
Gross profit		200,600
Expenses		
Depreciation	12,600	
Motor expenses (note 1)	19,000	
Professional fees (note 2)	5,300	
Repairs and renewals (note 3)	7,500	
Other expenses (note 4)	120,200	
		(164,600)
Net profit		36,000

Notes

(1)   *Motor expenses*

The figure for motor expenses is in respect of mileage undertaken by the partners, of which 40% is for private purposes.

(2)   *Professional fees*

The figure for professional fees consists of £600 for accountancy, £2,600 for legal fees in connection with the defence of the partnership's internet domain name, and £2,100 for legal fees in connection with the grant of a new five-year lease of parking spaces for employees' motor cars.

(3)   *Repairs and renewals*

The figure for repairs and renewals consists of £2,800 for decorating the partnership offices, and £4,700 for constructing a new wall in order to split one large office room into two smaller rooms.

BPP
LEARNING MEDIA

(4)   *Other expenses*

The figure of £120,200 for other expenses includes £5,060 for entertaining customers, £460 for entertaining employees, and £600 in respect of gifts to customers. The gifts were hampers of food costing £60 each. The remaining expenses are all allowable.

(5)   *Plant and machinery*

The tax written down values of the partnership's assets for capital allowances purposes at 6 April 2007 were as follows:

	£
General pool	17,000
Xio's motor car	16,500
Yana's motor car	7,000
Zoe's motor car	15,000

The partners' motor cars are all owned by the partnership, and in each case 40% of the mileage is for private purposes.

Zoe retained her motor car when she resigned from the partnership on 30 June 2007. On that date her motor car was valued at £12,400.

Other income

(1)   Xio received building society interest of £800 during 2007/08. This was the actual cash amount received.

(2)   Yana sold some investments during 2007/08, and this resulted in capital gains of £32,800. This figure is after taking account of indexation allowance and taper relief.

(3)   Zoe was appointed as the sales director of Aardvark plc on 1 July 2007, and was paid director's remuneration of £28,000 during 2007/08. She also received dividends of £10,800 during 2007/08. This was the actual cash amount received.

Required

(a)   Calculate the partnership's tax adjusted trading profit for the year ended 5 April 2008.   **(11 marks)**
(b)   Calculate the trading income assessments of Xio, Yana and Zoe for 2007/08.   **(6 marks)**
(c)   Calculate for 2007/08:

(i)   Xio's income tax liability and national insurance contributions.   **(4 marks)**
(ii)   Yana's income tax liability, national insurance contributions and capital gains tax liability.   **(6 marks)**
(ii)   Zoe's income tax liability.   **(3 marks)**

(Total = 30 marks)

16 Wright & Wong   18 mins

Geoff Wright and Sam Wong are in partnership running a design studio, with profits being shared in the ratio 4:1. They both wish to start saving for their retirement and would like to make maximum contributions to a pension. They have heard that the rules have recently changed. The partnership's trading profit for 2007/08 is £175,000. Neither Geoff or Sam has any other income.

Required

(a)   Advise Geoff and Sam of the maximum amount they can each contribute in 2007/08 to obtain tax relief.

(4 marks)

(b)   Explain the method by which Geoff and Sam will be given tax relief for their pension contributions and show their income tax liability.   **(5 marks)**

(c)   Explain how they will be able to continue to contribute to their pensions if the partnership ceases trading on 5 April 2008 and they no longer have earnings.   **(1 mark)**

(Total = 10 marks)

17 Amy Bwalya (BTX 06/06)   27 mins

(a)   Amy Bwalya commenced in self-employment on 1 August 2005, preparing accounts to 31 May. Her trading profits for the first two periods of trading were as follows:

	£
Ten-month period ended 31 May 2006	38,500
Year ended 31 May 2007	52,800

Required

Calculate the amount of trading profits that will have been assessed on Amy for the tax years 2005/06, 2006/07 and 2007/08. Your answer should show the amount of overlap profits.   **(5 marks)**

(b)   Cedric Ding and Eli Fong commenced in partnership on 6 April 2003, preparing accounts to 5 April. Cedric resigned as a partner on 31 December 2007, and Gordon Hassan joined as a partner on 1 January 2008. The partnership's trading profit for the year ended 5 April 2008 is £90,000. Profits were shared as follows:

(1)   Eli was paid an annual salary of £6,000.

(2)   Interest was paid at the rate of 10% on the partners' capital accounts, the balances on which were:

	£
Cedric	40,000
Eli	70,000
Gordon (from 1 January 2008)	20,000

Cedric's capital account was repaid to him on 31 December 2007.

(3)   The balance of profits were shared:

	Cedric	Eli	Gordon
	%	%	%
6 April 2007 to 31 December 2007	60	40	
1 January 2008 to 5 April 2008		70	30

Required

Calculate the trading income assessments of Cedric, Eli and Gordon for the tax year 2007/08.   **(5 marks)**

(c)   Ivan Jha ceased trading on 31 December 2007. He had commenced in self-employment on 1 October 2000, initially preparing accounts to 30 September. His overlap profits for the period 1 October 2000 to 5 April 2001 were £4,500. Ivan subsequently changed his accounting date to 30 June by preparing accounts for the nine month period to 30 June 2006. His trading profits for the final four periods of trading were as follows:

	£
Year ended 30 September 2005	36,000
Nine-month period ended 30 June 2006	23,400
Year ended 30 June 2007	28,800
Six-month period ended 31 December 2007	10,800

Required

Calculate the amount of trading profits that will have been assessed on Ivan for the tax years 2005/06, 2006/07 and 2007/08.   **(5 marks)**

(Total = 15 marks)

CHARGEABLE GAINS FOR INDIVIDUALS AND COMPANIES

CHARGEABLE GAINS FOR INDIVIDUALS AND COMPANIES

Questions 18 to 29 cover the taxation of chargeable gains for both individuals and companies, the subject of Part B of the BPP Study Text for Paper F6.

18 Preparation question: gains

Emily made the following disposals in 2007/08:

(1) Factory

Acquired 1 July 2003 for £150,000. Emily let out the factory to Teds R Us Ltd, a soft toy manufacturer. The factory was sold for £225,000 on 10 July 2007.

(2) Painting

This had been acquired by Emily's husband Arthur on 1 March 1996 for £50,000. Arthur had given the painting to Emily on 1 July 2002 when it was worth £60,000. Emily sold the painting for £73,000 on 2 May 2007. The indexation factor for March 1996 to April 1998 is 0.073.

(3) Vase

Emily had acquired this asset on 10 August 1988 for £40,000. She sold it on 1 December 2007 for £19,000.

Emily's net income for 2007/08 is £32,000. She has no other income. She made a donation to charity of £780 in August 2007.

Required

Calculate Emily's CGT liability for 2007/08.

19 Irene Cutter   36 mins

Irene disposed of the following assets in 2007/08:

(1) In September 2007 she gifted a building worth £90,000 to her daughter. The building had been used in Irene's business since it was purchased for £40,940 in June 2002. A joint claim was made for any gain arising on the gift to be held over under the gift relief rules.

(2) In February 2008, she sold an antique vase for £6,300. She had purchased the vase for £2,800 in December 2003.

(3) She sold 8,000 shares in Rightway plc (a quoted company) for £82,000 on 1 September 2007. She had acquired 6,000 shares in the company for £12,000 in August 1986. The company made a 1 for 3 rights issue on 1 September 1999 for £5 per share. Irene took up her full entitlement. The indexed value of the 1985 pool on 5 April 1998 was £19,947.

(4) On 21 November 2007 Irene sold five acres of land for £78,000. This represented part of a 12-acre plot purchased in March 2001 for £45,750 as an investment. On 21 November 2007, the remaining seven acres were valued at £104,000.

(5) In March 2008 Irene sold a vintage motor car, which had been purchased on 24 September 1999 for £12,000. The car was sold for £24,000.

Irene had capital losses brought forward at 6 April 2007 of £14,000. She had no taxable income in 2007/08 due to losses in her trade.

Required

(a)   Calculate Irene's Capital Gains Tax liability for 2007/08 and state by when this should be paid.   **(18 marks)**

(b)   State Irene's daughter's base cost of the building gifted to her in September 2007 and state by when the claim for gift relief must be made.   **(2 marks)**

(Total = 20 marks)

20 Stephanie Wood   36 mins

Details of Stephanie's capital disposals in 2007/08 are given below:

(1)   Shares in North Seaton Ltd

Stephanie sold 3,000 shares (a 30% holding) on 27 July 2007 for £16,800. She had bought 2,000 shares in January 1992 for £1,200 and a further 1,000 shares on 4 August 1999 for £1,400. In December 1999 there was a 1:2 rights issue at £2 per share which Stephanie took up in full. North Seaton Ltd is an unlisted manufacturing company in the north of England. The indexed value of the 1985 pool on 5 April 1998 was £1,439.

(2)   96 Burnside Close

Sold on 31 August 2007 for £150,000 (before estate agents fees of £1,750). She had bought the house on 28 February 1987 for £25,000 and had lived there until 27 August 1995 when she moved in with her boyfriend Steve. The house was redecorated then let out from 1 March 1997 until sale. The indexation factor from February 1987 to April 1998 is 0.620 and from February 1987 to August 2007 is 1.065.

(3)   Painting

Stephanie sold an oil painting in October 2007 for £2,800 at auction. Costs of disposal were £280. She had originally purchased the painting in August 1997 for £8,000.

(4)   Land

Stephanie sold a one acre plot of land in March 2008 for £19,000. She had bought a 7 acre site in January 2000 for £12,000. The value of the remaining 6 acres in March 2008 was £125,000. The land had never been used for business purposes.

(5)   Vase

On 16 April 2007 Stephanie sold a large vase for £9,000. She had acquired the vase for £4,400 on 16 April 1999.

Stephanie is self employed and a higher rate tax payer. She had capital losses of £1,833 brought forward from 2006/07.

Required

Calculate Stephanie's CGT liability for 2007/08, claiming all available reliefs.   **(20 marks)**

21 Anita Patel

36 mins

Anita Patel had the following capital transactions during 2007/08.

Disposal date

9 August 2007	She sold an antique painting which had cost her £4,000 in July 1996 for £10,000. The £10,000 was after deducting selling costs of £200. The indexation factor from July 1996 to April 1998 is 0.067 and from July 1996 to August 2007 is 0.360.
1 September 2007	Anita had purchased a necklace in June 2003 for £10,000. She lost it in June 2007 and received insurance proceeds of £12,000 on 1 September 2007. She purchased a replacement necklace later that month, which cost £12,000. She claimed to rollover the gain.
22 December 2007	Her dad is a hunt jockey and he had given her a valuable racing horse for her 18th birthday in August 1998. Its market value at the time was £50,000. The horse has won many races since and she sold him for £125,000.
3 February 2008	She sold a warehouse for £246,000. She had bought the warehouse on 17 April 1999 for £172,000. The factory has always been used in Anita's sole trade business. Anita purchased a new warehouse on 12 January 2008 for £236,000 and has claimed to rollover the gain. The new warehouse is also used in Anita's business.
19 March 2008	Anita sold 6 acres of a 10 acre field that she bought as an investment in August 1997 for £10,000. Proceeds were £30,000 and she turned down an offer of £20,000 for the remaining 4 acres. The indexation factor from August 1997 to April 1998 is 0.026 and from August 1997 to March 2008 is 0.339.
29 March 2008	She sold a Thimble collection inherited from her grandmother in January 2001, when it was worth £8,000, for £5,000.

Anita has capital losses brought forward of £4,000. Her father pays her £15,000 a year for exercising his horses and she makes profits of £10,000 pa from her business. She suffered PAYE on the income for exercising the horse of £3,769.

Required

Calculate the income and capital gains tax payable and state the respective due dates. **(20 marks)**

22 Jack Chan

36 mins

Jack Chan has been in business as a sole trader since 1 May 2001. On 28 February 2008 he transferred the business to his daughter Jill, at which time the following assets were sold to her:

(1) Goodwill with a market value of £60,000. The goodwill has been built up since 1 May 2001, and has a nil cost. Jill paid Jack £50,000 for the goodwill.

(2) A freehold office building with a market value of £130,000. The office building was purchased on 1 July 2007 for £110,000, and has always been used by Jack for business purposes. Jill paid Jack £105,000 for the office building.

(3) A freehold warehouse with a market value of £140,000. The warehouse was purchased on 1 September 2005 for £95,000, and has never been used by Jack for business purposes. Jill paid Jack £135,000 for the warehouse.

(4) A motor car with a market value of £25,000. The motor car was purchased on 1 November 2005 for £23,500, and has always been used by Jack for business purposes. Jill paid Jack £20,000 for the motor car.

Where possible, Jack and Jill have elected to hold over any gains arising.

Jack also made the following disposals during the year.

(5)   On 1 May 2007 he sold a picture for £30,000 – he had acquired this for £10,000 in June 1995. The indexation factor from June 1995 to April 1998 is 0.085 and from June 1995 to May 2007 is 0.370.

(6)   He sold his entire holding of 12,000 ordinary shares in Coleman plc for £16,000 on 1 June 2007. He had purchased 10,000 shares in January 2002 for £8,000. In December 2003 there was a 1:5 bonus issue. The shares were non business assets.

(7)   He sold three acres of a twelve acre plot of land for £45,600 on 1 November 2007. He had acquired the original plot of land for £125,000 in May 2002. He refused an offer of £250,000 for the remaining nine acres. The land had never been used for business purposes.

Jack's taxable income for 2007/08 is £25,500. He has unused capital losses of £6,100 brought forward from 2006/07.

Required

Calculate Jack's capital gains tax liability for 2007/08, and advise him by when this should be paid.   **(20 marks)**

23 Chandra Khan   **36 mins**

Chandra Khan disposed of the following assets during 2007/08:

(a)   On 15 June 2007 Chandra sold 10,000 £1 ordinary shares (a 30% shareholding) in Universal Ltd, an unquoted trading company, to her daughter for £75,000. The market value of the shares on this date was £110,000. The shareholding was purchased on 10 July 2003 for £38,000. Chandra and her daughter have elected to hold over the gain as a gift of a business asset.

(b)   On 8 November 2007 Chandra sold a freehold factory for £146,000. The factory was purchased on 3 January 1997 and had an indexed cost at 6 April 1998 of £72,000. 75% of the factory has been used in a manufacturing business run by Chandra as a sole trader. However, the remaining 25% of the factory has never been used for business purposes. Chandra has claimed to rollover the gain on the factory against the replacement cost of a new freehold factory that was purchased on 10 November 2007 for £156,000. The new factory is used 100% for business purposes by Chandra.

(c)   On 8 March 2008 Chandra incorporated a wholesale business that she has run as a sole trader since 1 May 2006. The market value of the business on 8 March 2008 was £250,000. All of the business assets were transferred to a new limited company, with the consideration consisting of 200,000 £1 ordinary shares valued at £200,000 and £50,000 in cash. The only chargeable asset of the business was goodwill, and this was valued at £100,000 on 8 March 2008. The goodwill has a nil cost.

(d)   On 1 December 2007 Chandra sold her main residence for £350,000. She had purchased the house on 1 December 1989 for £100,000 and lived in it until 1 December 1992. She then went travelling for five years and returned to the house on 1 December 1997. She only stayed in the house for one year until 1 December 1998 at which time she moved into her fiancé's apartment. She let out the house from that date. The indexation factor from December 1989 to April 1998 is 0.369 and from December 1989 to December 2007 is 0.769.

Required

Calculate the chargeable gains arising from Chandra's disposals during 2007/08.   **(20 marks)**

Helping hand

1   This question has distinct parts – deal with them separately then summarise your findings.

2   A gift is deemed to be at market value so you will need to use this as the proceeds figure in part (a). Some of the gain will be immediately chargeable as this is a sale at undervalue.

3   In part (b) you need to separate out the business and non-business elements of the gain. Only the business element can have rollover relief.

4   Incorporation relief applies in part (c). You need to calculate the proportion of the consideration that applies to the shares. Only this proportion will gain relief.

5   In part (d) you are dealing with PPR relief. You will find it easier to determine the periods of actual, deemed and non-occupation if you produce a summary table explaining why you have treated periods in a particular way. Do not forget the rules for lettings relief.

24 Sophia Tang (BTX 12/05)   36 mins

Sophia Tang, a widow aged 78, has been in business as a sole trader since 1 April 1986. On 31 March 2008 she transferred the business to her daughter Wong, at which time the following assets were sold to Wong:

(1)   A freehold shop with a market value of £260,000. The shop had been purchased on 1 July 2002 for £113,000, and has always been used by Sophia for business purposes. Wong paid Sophia £160,000 for the shop.

(2)   A freehold warehouse with a market value of £225,000. The warehouse had been purchased on 1 April 1986 for £70,000, and has never been used by Sophia for business purposes. Wong paid Sophia £100,000 for the warehouse. The indexation allowance from April 1986 to April 1998 is £50,100, and from April 1986 to March 2008 it is £117,262.

Where possible, Sophia and Wong have elected to hold over any gains arising.

Sophia also made the following unconnected disposals during the year.

(3)   On 10 September 2007 she sold 500 shares in Gum plc, a quoted company, for £6,000. In February 2008 she sold another 700 shares for £9,800. She had acquired 400 shares in July 1992 at £3 per share and another 1,000 shares on 1 September 1999 at £6 per share. The indexed value of the 1985 pool on 6 April 1998 was £1,405.

(4)   In June 2007 she sold a house for £350,000. The house had been acquired in June 1987 for £35,000. Sophia used the house as her main residence until June 1991 when she moved into the house owned by her husband and her house was let up to the date of sale. The indexation factor from June 1987 to April 1998 is 0.596 and from June 1987 to June 2007 is 1.021.

Sophia is a higher rate taxpayer.

She made no other capital disposals in the 2007/08 tax year and has losses brought forward of £12,350.

Required

Calculate Sophia's capital gains tax liability for the tax year 2007/08 and state when it is due.   **(20 marks)**

25 Carolyn Kraft

45 mins

Carolyn Kraft is aged 34. She is employed as a buyer for a large retail group of companies. She is married to Mike. They have no children.

In the tax year 2007/08, Carolyn was paid a salary of £32,600 (PAYE £5,366). Carolyn also received bank interest of £8,000 in 2007/08. On 14 November 2007 Carolyn made a one off donation under Gift Aid to Cancer Research UK of £780.

Mike undertakes a business from home. His accounts for the year ended 31 December 2007 show an adjusted profit of £53,400. He is also entitled to capital allowances of £1,600. Mike had owned a freehold shop which he had used in his business. He had acquired the shop on 10 April 2006 for £53,300 and sold it for £85,000 in August 2007. He is considering acquiring another shop to replace this one.

Mike also received dividends of £9,000 in 2007/08 and makes a contribution of £260 each month to his personal pension.

Carolyn bought a flat in August 2005 for £180,000. Carolyn arranged for renovation work to be undertaken, which cost £30,000 in January 2007. Carolyn sold the flat for £250,000 in December 2007. The flat was unoccupied between the date of purchase and the date of sale.

Required

(a)   Calculate both Carolyn and Mike's income tax due for 2007/08 and state when it is due.   **(11 marks)**

(b)   Calculate the amount of national insurance contributions payable by both Carolyn and Mike for 2007/08.
(4 marks)

(c)   Calculate Carolyn and Mike's 2007/08 capital gains tax liability stating the due date. Assume Mike does not acquire another shop.   **(8 marks)**

(d)   Briefly explain the relief available to Mike if he does acquire another shop.   **(2 marks)**

(Total = 25 marks)

26 Peter Shaw

36 mins

Peter, aged 67, made the following disposals in 2007/08:

(1)   He purchased a building for £200,000 on 1 January 2001 which he let commercially as offices to an unquoted company. On 10 April 2007 he sold the building for £600,000.

(2)   He held 20,000 shares in Forum Follies plc which he purchased in May 1998 for £50,000. In March 2008, Exciting Enterprises plc acquired all the share capital of Forum Follies plc. Under the terms of the take-over for every two shares previously held in Forum Follies plc shareholders received three ordinary shares in Exciting Enterprises plc plus £1 cash. Immediately after the take-over the ordinary shares in Exciting Enterprises plc were quoted at £3 each. None of the shares are business assets for taper relief purposes.

(3)   Peter purchased shares in Dassau plc, a quoted company, as follows.

	No of shares	Cost £
December 1984	1,000	2,000
April 2000 1 for 2 rights issue		£2 per share

In November 2007 he sold 1,200 shares for £9,500. The shares are not business assets.

The indexed value of the FA 1985 pool at 6 April 1998 was £3,580.

(4)   He sold the following items on 1 August 2007:

(a)   A Ming vase bought in September 2000 for £2,000. The sales proceeds were £8,000.

(b)   A Leonardo cartoon bought in March 1984 for £7,200 and sold for £5,500. The Indexation allowance for March 1984 to April 1998 is 0.859.

(c)   An item of plant bought for use in his business in March 2000 which cost £5,300. The sales proceeds were £8,500. Peter had claimed capital allowances on this asset.

Peter had capital losses brought forward from 2006/07 of £6,400.

Peter's income for the year consists of bank interest of £6,000 (net) and dividends of £10,800 (net).

Required

Calculate the CGT payable by Peter for 2007/08 and state when it is due.   **(20 marks)**

27 Paul Opus (Pilot paper)   **36 mins**

Paul Opus disposed of the following assets during the tax year 2007/08:

(1)   On 10 April 2007 Paul sold 5,000 £1 ordinary shares in Symphony Ltd, an unquoted trading company, for £23,600. He had originally purchased 40,000 shares in the company on 23 June 2005 for £110,400.

(2)   On 15 June 2007 Paul made a gift of his entire shareholding of 10,000 £1 ordinary shares in Concerto plc to his daughter. On that date the shares were quoted on the Stock Exchange at £5.10–£5.18, with recorded bargains of £5.00, £5.15 and £5.22. Paul's shareholding had been purchased on 29 April 1992 for £14,000. The shareholding is less than 1% of Concerto plc's issued share capital, and Paul has never been employed by Concerto plc. The indexation factor from April 1992 to April 1998 is 0.170, and from April 1992 to June 2007 it is 0.483.

(3)   On 9 August 2007 Paul sold a motor car for £16,400. The motor car had been purchased on 21 January 2004 for £12,800.

(4)   On 4 October 2007 Paul sold an antique vase for £8,400. The antique vase had been purchased on 19 January 2007 for £4,150.

(5)   On 31 December 2007 Paul sold a house for £220,000. The house had been purchased on 1 April 2001 for £114,700. Paul occupied the house as his main residence from the date of purchase until 30 June 2004. The house was then unoccupied until it was sold on 31 December 2007.

(6)   On 16 February 2008 Paul sold three acres of land for £285,000. He had originally purchased four acres of land on 17 July 2006 for £220,000. The market value of the unsold acre of land as at 16 February 2008 was £90,000. The land has never been used for business purposes.

(7)   On 5 March 2008 Paul sold a freehold holiday cottage for £125,000. The cottage had originally been purchased on 28 July 2006 for £101,600 by Paul's wife. She transferred the cottage to Paul on 16 November 2007 when it was valued at £114,800. The cottage is not a business asset for taper relief purposes.

Paul's taxable income for the tax year 2007/08 is £15,800.

Required

Compute Paul's capital gains tax liability for the tax year 2007/08, and advise him by when this should be paid.

(20 marks)

28 Cube Ltd (BTX 06/06)

36 mins

Cube Ltd sold the following shareholdings during the year ended 31 March 2008:

(a)   On 10 May 2007 4,000 50 pence ordinary shares in Parallel plc were sold for £46,500. Cube Ltd had purchased 22,000 shares in Parallel plc on 1 November 2001 for £101,200. The retail prices index (RPI) for November 2001 was 173.6, and for May 2007 it was 209.4.

(b)   On 31 July 2007 10,000 £1 ordinary shares in Rectangle plc were sold for £38,000. Cube Ltd had originally purchased 15,000 shares in Quadrangle plc on 1 July 2007 for £96,000. On 15 July 2007 Quadrangle plc was taken over by Rectangle plc. Cube Ltd received one £1 ordinary share and one £1 preference share in Rectangle plc for each £1 ordinary share held in Quadrangle plc. Immediately after the takeover each £1 ordinary share in Rectangle plc was quoted at £4·50 and each £1 preference share was quoted at £1·50.

(c)   On 12 August 2007 a thoroughbred racehorse was sold for £35,000. Cube Ltd had purchased the horse on 5 July 2004 for £26,000.

(d)   On 31 October 2007 8,000 £1 ordinary shares in Square plc were sold for £26,850. Cube Ltd had purchased 12,000 shares in Square plc on 1 October 2007 for £60,000. On 16 October 2007 Square plc made a 1 for 3 bonus issue.

(e)   On 24 January 2008 an office, used in the business, was sold for £335,760. Cube Ltd had originally purchased the office on 1 April 2000 for £126,000. Cube Ltd had acquired another office on 1 September 2007 for £340,000. The retail prices index (RPI) for April 2000 was 170.1, and for January 2008 it was 210.8.

(f)   On 31 March 2008 12,000 £1 ordinary shares in Triangle plc were sold for £57,800. Cube Ltd had purchased 8,000 shares in Triangle plc on 1 March 2008 for £28,800. On 15 March 2008 Triangle plc made a 1 for 1 rights issue. Cube Ltd took up its allocation under the rights issue in full, paying £3·20 for each new share issued.

Cube Ltd's only other income for the year ended 31 March 2008 was a trading profit of £90,000. There are no associated companies.

Required

Calculate Cube Ltd's corporation tax liability for the year ended 31 March 2008 assuming all available reliefs are claimed. **(20 marks)**

29 Forward Ltd (BTX 12/04)

36 mins

Forward Ltd sold the following assets during the year ended 31 March 2008:

(1)   On 31 May 2007 Forward Ltd sold a freehold office building for £290,000. The office building had been purchased on 15 July 1993 for £148,000. The retail prices index (RPI) for July 1993 was 140.7, and for May 2007 it was 205.2.

Forward Ltd purchased a replacement freehold office building on 1 June 2007 for £250,000.

(2)   On 30 November 2007 Forward Ltd sold 5,000 £1 ordinary shares in Backward plc for £62,500. Forward Ltd had originally purchased 9,000 shares in Backward plc on 20 April 1989 for £18,000, and purchased a further 500 shares on 30 November 2007 for £6,500. The retail prices index for April 1989 was 114.3, and for November 2007 it was 209.4.

Forward Ltd purchased 10,000 £1 ordinary shares in Sideways plc on 1 December 2007 for £65,000.

(3)   On 3 February 2008 the company received £155,000 from an insurance company in respect of a painting that had been destroyed in a flood in December 2007. The company had purchased the painting in August 1999 for £100,000. Forward Ltd immediately spent all of the insurance proceeds on a replacement painting, costing £200,000. The retail prices index for August 1999 was 165.5, for December 2007 it was 210.1 and for February 2008 it was 211.5.

Where possible, Forward Ltd has claimed to rollover any gains arising.

Forward Ltd's only other income for the year ended 31 March 2008 is its trading income of £75,000. There are no associated companies.

Required

(a)   Calculate Forward Ltd's corporation tax liability for the year ended 31 March 2008, and state by when this should be paid. Your answer should clearly identify the amount of any gains that have been rolled over. Capital allowances should be ignored.   **(16 marks)**

(b)   Explain how Forward Ltd's rollover relief claim would have altered if on 1 June 2007 it had acquired a leasehold office building on a 15-year lease for £300,000, rather than purchasing the freehold office building for £250,000.   **(4 marks)**

(Total = 20 marks)

TAXATION OF COMPANIES

Questions 30 to 45 cover corporate businesses, the subject of Part C of the BPP Study Text for Paper F6.

30 Preparation question: corporation tax computation

Abel Ltd, a UK trading company, produced the following results for the year ended 31 March 2008.

	£
Income	
Adjusted trading profit	245,000
Rental income	115,000
Bank deposit interest accrued (non-trading investment)	4,000
Capital gains: 25 September 2007	35,000
28 March 2008	7,000
(There were capital losses of £40,000 brought forward at 1 April 2007.)	
Trading losses brought forward at 1 April 2007	20,000
Expenditure	
Gift Aid donation	7,000

Required

Compute the corporation tax (CT) payable by Abel Ltd for the above accounting period.

Guidance notes

1   In working out a company's profits chargeable to corporation tax (PCTCT), we must bring together all taxable profits, including gains. You must therefore start by drawing up a working, and picking out from the question all relevant profit figures.

2   Once you have found the PCTCT, you can consider the rate of tax. You should find that marginal relief applies. If you do not, look carefully to see whether you have missed anything.

31 Unforeseen Ultrasonics Limited   45 mins

Unforeseen Ultrasonics Limited (UUL) is a United Kingdom resident company which manufactures accessories for telecommunication systems. It has no associated companies.

The company's results for the year ended 31 December 2007 were as follows.

	£
Trading profits (adjusted for taxation but before capital allowances) (note 1)	2,300,000
Bank interest receivable (non-trading investment)	1,500
Debenture interest received (non-trading investment) (note 4)	80,000
Payment under the gift aid scheme to a national charity (paid September 2007)	5,000

The company has traded in a purpose built unit since 1 January 2001. The total cost of the unit was made up as follows:

	£
Freehold land	50,000
Manufacturing area	240,000
Canteen	30,000
Design office	90,000
General office	70,000
	480,000

On 1 July 2007 an extension to the general office was completed costing £60,000.

On 1 January 2007 the tax written-down values of plant and machinery were as follows.

	£
Pool	190,000
Short-life asset	4,000

The short-life asset was purchased on 1 December 2002 and was sold on 31 July 2007 for £10,000.

On 1 August 2007 a new car (not low emission) costing £18,000 was purchased for the managing director. The car previously used by him had cost £10,000 in April 2004 and was sold for £8,000. A new precision engineering machine was purchased on 1 August 2007 for £56,251.

On 1 September 2007, Unforeseen Ultrasonics Limited sold a piece of land for £69,874. The land had been acquired as an investment in July 1991 for £27,000.

Notes

(1)   In arriving at the adjusted trading profit an adjustment had been made for small capital additions in May 2007 totalling £24,375 which the company had written off as repairs but which HMRC had insisted were added back.

(2)   On 1 January 2007 the company had capital losses brought forward of £30,000.

(3)   On 1 January 2007 the company had trading losses brought forward of £600,000.

(4)   The debentures were acquired on 1 April 2007. All amounts accrued in the nine months to 31 December 2007 were received in the period.

(5)   The company paid corporation tax at the full rate in its accounting period ended 31 December 2006.

(6)   The company is a small enterprise for capital allowance purposes.

Required

Calculate the corporation tax payable for the year ended 31 December 2007 and state the due date(s) for payment of this amount and the amount of any losses carried forward.

Assume indexation factor July 1991 – September 2007 is 0.555.

(25 marks)

32 Arable Ltd (BTX 06/04)   54 mins

Arable Ltd commenced trading on 1 April 2007 as a manufacturer of farm equipment, preparing its first accounts for the nine-month period ended 31 December 2007. The following information is available:

Trading income

The trading income profit is £284,600. This figure is before taking account of capital allowances and any deduction arising from the premiums paid in respect of leasehold property.

Industrial building

Arable Ltd had a new factory constructed at a cost of £400,000 that the company brought into use on 1 May 2007.

The cost was made up as follows:

	£
Land	120,000
Site preparation	14,000
Professional fees	6,000
Drawing office serving the factory	40,000
Showroom	74,000
Factory	146,000
	400,000

Plant and machinery

Arable Ltd purchased the following assets in respect of the nine-month period ended 31 December 2007:

		£
15 February 2007	Machinery	29,150
18 February 2007	Building alterations necessary for the installation of the machinery	3,700
20 April 2007	Lorry	19,000
12 June 2007	Motor car (1)	11,200
14 June 2007	Motor car (2)	14,600
17 June 2007	Motor car (3)	13,000
29 October 2007	Computer	4,400

Motor car (3), purchased on 17 June 2007, is a low emission motor car (CO_2 emission rate of less than 120 grams per kilometre). Arable Ltd is a medium-sized company as defined by the Companies Acts.

Leasehold property

On 1 April 2007 Arable Ltd acquired two leasehold office buildings. In each case a premium of £75,000 was paid for the grant of a fifteen-year lease.

The first office building was used for business purposes by Arable Ltd throughout the period ended 31 December 2007.

The second office building was empty until 30 September 2007, and was then sub-let to a tenant. On that date Arable Ltd received a premium of £50,000 for the grant of a five-year lease, and annual rent of £14,800 which was payable in advance.

Loan interest received

Loan interest of £6,000 was received on 30 September 2007, and £3,000 was accrued at 31 December 2007. The loan was made for non-trading purposes.

Dividends received

During the period ended 31 December 2007 Arable Ltd received dividends of £18,000 from Ranch plc, an unconnected UK company. This figure was the actual cash amount received.

Profit on disposal of shares

On 5 December 2007 Arable Ltd sold 10,000 £1 ordinary shares in Ranch plc for £37,457. Arable Ltd had originally purchased 15,000 shares in Ranch plc on 10 June 2006 for £12,000. A further 5,000 shares were purchased on 20 August 2006 for £11,250. The relevant indexation factors are as follows:

June 2006	198.5
August 2006	199.2
December 2007	210.1

Other information

Arable Ltd has two associated companies.

Required

(a) Calculate Arable Ltd's corporation tax liability for the period ended 31 December 2007. **(27 marks)**

(b) State the date by which Arable Ltd's corporation tax return for the period ended 31 December 2007 should be submitted and explain how the company can correct the return if it is subsequently found to contain an error or mistake. **(3 marks)**

(Total = 30 marks)

33 Scuba Ltd (Pilot paper)

54 mins

(a) Scuba Ltd is a manufacturer of diving equipment. The following information is relevant for the year ended 31 December 2007:

Operating profit

The operating profit is £170,400. The expenses that have been deducted in calculating this figure include the following:

	£
Depreciation and amortisation of lease	45,200
Entertaining customers	7,050
Entertaining employees	2,470
Gifts to customers (diaries costing £25 each displaying Scuba Ltd's name)	1,350
Gifts to customers (food hampers costing £80 each)	1,600

Leasehold property

On 1 April 2007 Scuba Ltd acquired a leasehold office building that is used for business purposes. The company paid a premium of £80,000 for the grant of a twenty-year lease.

Purchase of industrial building

Scuba Ltd purchased a new factory from a builder on 1 July 2007 for £240,000, and this was immediately brought into use. The cost was made up as follows:

	£
Drawing office serving the factory	34,000
General offices	40,000
Factory	98,000
Land	68,000
	240,000

Plant and machinery

On 1 January 2007 the tax written down values of plant and machinery were as follows:

	£
General pool	47,200
Expensive motor car	22,400

The following transactions took place during the year ended 31 December 2007:

		Cost (Proceeds) £
3 January 2007	Purchased machinery	18,020
29 February 2007	Purchased a computer	1,100
4 May 2007	Purchased a motor car	10,400
18 August 2007	Purchased machinery	7,300
15 November 2007	Sold a lorry	(12,400)

The motor car purchased on 4 May 2007 for £10,400 is used by the factory manager, and 40% of the mileage is for private journeys. The lorry sold on 15 November 2007 for £12,400 originally cost £19,800.

Scuba Ltd is a small company as defined by the Companies Acts.

Property income

Scuba Ltd lets a retail shop that is surplus to requirements. The shop was let until 31 December 2006 but was then empty from 1 January 2007 to 30 April 2007. During this period Scuba Ltd spent £6,200 on decorating the shop, and £1,430 on advertising for new tenants. The shop was let from 1 May 2007 to 31 December 2007 at a quarterly rent of £7,200, payable in advance.

Interest received

Interest of £430 was received from HM Revenue & Customs on 31 October 2007 in respect of the overpayment of corporation tax for the year ended 31 December 2006.

Other information

Scuba Ltd has no associated companies, and the company has always had an accounting date of 31 December.

Required

(i)   Compute Scuba Ltd's tax adjusted trading profit for the year ended 31 December 2007. You should ignore value added tax (VAT);   **(15 marks)**

(ii)   Compute Scuba Ltd's corporation tax liability for the year ended 31 December 2007.

(4 marks)

(b)   Scuba Ltd registered for value added tax (VAT) on 1 April 2005. The company's VAT returns have been submitted as follows:

Quarter ended	VAT paid (refunded) £	Submitted
30 June 2005	18,600	One month late
30 September 2005	32,200	One month late
31 December 2005	8,800	On time
31 March 2006	3,400	Two months late
30 June 2006	(6,500)	One month late
30 September 2006	42,100	On time
31 December 2006	(2,900)	On time
31 March 2007	3,900	On time
30 June 2007	18,800	On time
30 September 2007	57,300	Two months late
31 December 2007	9,600	On time

Scuba Ltd always pays any VAT that is due at the same time that the related return is submitted.

During February 2008 Scuba Ltd discovered that a number of errors had been made when completing its VAT return for the quarter ended 31 December 2007. As a result of these errors the company will have to make an additional payment of VAT to HM Revenue & Customs.

Required

(i)   State, giving appropriate reasons, the default surcharge consequences arising from Scuba Ltd's submission of its VAT returns for the quarter ended 30 June 2005 to the quarter ended 30 September 2007 inclusive.   **(8 marks)**

(ii)   Explain how Scuba Ltd can voluntarily disclose the errors relating to the VAT return for the quarter ended 31 December 2007, and state whether default interest will be due, if (1) the net errors in total are less than £2,000, and (2) the net errors in total are more than £2,000.   **(3 marks)**

(Total = 30 marks)

34 Unforgettable Units Limited

45 mins

Unforgettable Units Limited (UUL) is a United Kingdom resident company which manufactures self-assemble furniture. It has no associated companies and has always made accounts up to 31 August. In the year ended 31 August 2007 the company's profit was £817,875 which was arrived at *after* charging and crediting the following items.

		£
Expenditure		
Gift aid donations paid		58,000
Legal expenses	(note 2)	10,000
Income		
Debenture interest	(note 3)	64,000
Bank interest	(note 4)	5,000
Dividend	(note 5)	11,250

Notes

(1) Unforgettable Units Limited is a medium-sized company with a turnover in the year ended 31 August 2007 of £4,000,000. The average number of employees during the accounting period was 160.

(2) Legal expenses incurred were:

Fine for not fitting saws with protective guards	£10,000

(3) *Debenture interest receivable*

	£		£
1.9.06 b/f	–	30.4.07 received	61,000
Profit and loss account	64,000	31.8.07 c/f	3,000
	64,000		64,000

The interest was non-trading income.

(4) *Bank interest*

The £5,000 was credited to the company's bank account on 31 July 2007. The interest is non-trading interest.

(5) On 1 December 2006 Unforgettable Units Limited received a dividend from another UK company of £11,250. This amount represents the actual amount received without any adjustment for tax credits.

(6) *Plant and machinery*

On 1 September 2006 the tax written down value of plant and machinery was:

	£
Main pool	100,000

New machinery, which is not to be treated either a 'short-life' asset or a 'long-life' asset, costing £35,000 was purchased on 31 January 2007. On 1 May 2007 a car that had cost £7,500 in 2003 was sold for £2,000 and replaced with one costing £13,000 (not a low emission car).

(7) *Industrial buildings allowance*

On 1 June 2007 Unforgettable Units Limited purchased a factory for £300,000 from Cape Capsules Limited whose accounting date was 31 March. The factory was built for Cape Capsules Limited at a cost of £250,000 and had been brought into use on 1 August 2000. Maximum industrial buildings allowances had been claimed by Cape Capsules Limited. The factory has not been used for non-trading purposes.

Required

Calculate the corporation tax payable by Unforgettable Units Limited for the year ended 31 August 2007.

(25 marks)

35 Thai Curry Ltd (BTX 06/06)

54 mins

Thai Curry Ltd is a manufacturer of ready to cook food. The following information is available in respect of the year ended 30 September 2007:

Trading loss

The trading loss is £32,800. This figure is before taking account of capital allowances.

Plant and machinery

On 1 October 2006 the tax written down values of plant and machinery were as follows:

	£
General pool	10,600
Expensive motor car	16,400
Short-life asset	2,900

The following transactions took place during the year ended 30 September 2007:

		Cost/ (Proceeds) £
1 November 2006	Sold equipment	(12,800)
15 December 2006	Sold the short-life asset	(800)
8 January 2007	Purchased equipment	7,360
14 January 2007	Sold the expensive motor car	(9,700)
26 February 2007	Purchased motor car (1)	15,800
19 May 2007	Purchased motor car (2)	9,700
20 September 2007	Purchased a new freehold office building	220,000

The equipment sold on 1 November 2006 for £12,800 originally cost £27,400. Motor car (2), purchased on 19 May 2007, is a low emission motor car (CO_2 emission rate of less than 120 grams per kilometre).

The cost of the new freehold office building purchased on 20 September 2007 included £8,500 for the central heating system, £7,200 for sprinkler equipment and the fire alarm system, £10,700 for the electrical and lighting systems, and £7,050 for the ventilation system.

Thai Curry Ltd is a small company as defined by the Companies Acts.

Industrial building

On 1 May 2007 Thai Curry Ltd purchased a second-hand factory for £360,000 (excluding the cost of land). The factory was originally constructed at a cost of £345,000 (excluding the cost of land), and was first brought into use for industrial purposes on 1 May 2002. The previous owner of the factory prepared accounts to 31 March.

Income from property

Thai Curry Ltd lets out two warehouses that are surplus to requirements.

The first warehouse was let from 1 October 2006 until 31 May 2007 at a monthly rent of £2,200. On that date the tenant left owing two months rent which Thai Curry Ltd was not able to recover. During August 2007 £8,800 was spent on painting the warehouse. The warehouse was not re-let until 1 October 2007.

The second warehouse was empty from 1 October 2006 until 31 January 2007, but was let from 1 February 2007. On that date Thai Curry Ltd received a premium of £60,000 for the grant of a four-year lease, and the annual rent of £18,000 which is payable in advance.

Loan interest received

Loan interest of £8,000 was received on 30 June 2007, and £3,500 was accrued at 30 September 2007. The loan was made for non-trading purposes.

Dividends received

During the year ended 30 September 2007 Thai Curry Ltd received dividends of £36,000 from African Spice plc, an unconnected UK company. This figure was the actual cash amount received.

Profit on disposal of shares

On 28 July 2007 Thai Curry Ltd sold 10,000 £1 ordinary shares in African Spice plc, making a capital gain of £152,300 on the disposal.

Other information

Thai Curry Ltd has three associated companies.

Required

(a) Calculate Thai Curry Ltd's tax adjusted trading loss for the year ended 30 September 2007. You should assume that the company claims the maximum available capital allowances. **(13 marks)**

(b) Assuming that Thai Curry Ltd claims relief for its trading loss against total profits against total profits, calculate the company's corporation tax liability for the year ended 30 September 2007. **(11 marks)**

(c) (i) State the date by which Thai Curry Ltd's self-assessment corporation tax return for the year ended 30 September 2007 should be submitted, and advise the company of the penalties that will be due if the return is not submitted until 31 May 2009. **(3 marks)**

(ii) State the date by which Thai Curry Ltd's corporation tax liability for the year ended 30 September 2007 should be paid, and advise the company of the interest that will be due if the liability is not paid until 31 May 2009. **(3 marks)**

(Total = 30 marks)

36 Spacious Ltd (BTX 12/03)   54 mins

Spacious Ltd is a UK resident company that commenced trading on 1 July 2006 as a manufacturer of engineering equipment. The company's summarised profit and loss account for the year ended 31 March 2008 is as follows:

	£	£
Gross profit		101,180
Operating expenses		
Depreciation	54,690	
Patent royalties (note 1)	9,400	
Professional fees (note 2)	22,500	
Repairs and renewals (note 3)	27,700	
Other expenses (note 4)	149,490	
		(263,780)
Operating loss		(162,600)
Profit from sale of fixed assets		
Disposal of office building (note 5)		54,400
Income from investments		
Bank interest (note 6)		7,000
		(101,200)
Interest payable (note 7)		(23,000)
Loss before taxation		(124,200)

Notes

(1) *Patent royalties*

Patent royalties of £3,900 were paid on 30 September 2007, with a further £5,500 being paid on 31 March 2008. These relate to the year ended 31 March 2008.

(2) *Professional fees*

Professional fees are as follows:

	£
Accountancy and audit fee	3,600
Legal fees in connection with the issue of share capital	8,800
Legal fees in connection with the issue of debentures (see note 7)	6,900
Legal fees in connection with the defence of the company's internet domain name	2,300
Legal fees in connection with a court action for not complying with health and safety legislation	900
	22,500

(3) *Repairs and renewals*

The figure of £27,700 for repairs includes £9,700 for constructing a new wall around the company's premises and £5,400 for replacing the roof of a warehouse because it was in a bad state of repair.

(4) *Other expenses*

Other expenses include £1,800 for entertaining customers, £600 for entertaining employees and a donation of £1,000 made to a national charity under the Gift Aid scheme.

(5) *Disposal of office building*

The profit of £54,400 is in respect of a freehold office building that was sold on 30 June 2007 for £380,000. The indexed cost of the building on 30 June 2007 was £345,400. The building has always been used by Spacious Ltd for trading purposes. The company has claimed to rollover the gain arising on the office building against the cost of a new factory that was purchased on 1 July 2007 for £360,000 (see note 8). The new factory is used 100% for trading purposes by Spacious Ltd.

(6) *Bank interest received*

The bank interest was received on 31 March 2008. The bank deposits are held for non-trading purposes.

(7) *Interest payable*

Spacious Ltd raised a debenture loan on 1 October 2007, and this was used for trading purposes. Interest of £23,000 in respect of the first six months of the loan was paid on 31 March 2008.

(8) *Industrial building*

Spacious Ltd purchased a new factory from a builder on 1 July 2007 for £360,000 and this was immediately brought into use. The figure of £360,000 includes £135,000 for land, £61,500 for general offices and £54,000 for a drawing office.

(9) *Long-life asset*

On 1 September 2007 Spacious Ltd installed a new overhead crane costing £110,000 in the new factory. The crane is a long-life asset.

(10) *Plant and machinery*

On 1 April 2007 the tax written down values of plant and machinery were as follows:

	£
General pool	28,400
Expensive motor car	14,800

The following transactions took place during the year ended 31 March 2008:

		Cost/(Proceeds) £
10 April 2007	Purchased equipment	30,200
5 February 2008	Sold the expensive motor car	(9,800)
5 February 2008	Purchased a motor car	13,600
20 March 2008	Sold a lorry	(17,600)
31 March 2008	Purchased a motor car	9,400

The lorry sold on 20 March 2008 for £17,600 originally cost £18,200. The motor car purchased on 31 March 2008 for £9,400 is used by the sales manager, and 20% of the mileage is for private journeys.

Spacious Ltd is a small company as defined by the Companies Acts.

(11) *Other information*

Spacious Ltd has no associated companies.

The company's results for the nine-month period ended 31 March 2007 were as follows:

	£
Trading income profit	183,200
Interest income profit	5,200
Capital loss	(4,900)
Gift aid donation	(800)

Spacious Ltd's profits chargeable to corporation tax for the year ended 31 March 2009 are expected to be £475,000, of which £450,000 represents trading income profit.

Required

(a) Calculate Spacious Ltd's trading loss for the year ended 31 March 2008. Your answer should commence with the loss before taxation figure of £124,200. You should assume that the company claims the maximum available capital allowances. **(19 marks)**

(b) Assuming that Spacious Ltd claims relief for its trading loss against total profits, calculate the company's profits chargeable to corporation tax for the nine-month period ended 31 March 2007 and the year ended 31 March 2008. **(8 marks)**

(c) Explain why it would probably have been beneficial for Spacious Ltd to have carried its trading loss forward, rather than making the claim against total profits. **(3 marks)**

(Total = 30 marks)

37 Loser Ltd (Pilot paper)

18 mins

Loser Ltd's results for the year ended 30 June 2005, the nine month period ended 31 March 2006, the year ended 31 March 2007 and the year ended 31 March 2008 are as follows:

	Year ended 30 June 2005 £	Period ended 31 March 2006 £	Year ended 31 March 2007 £	Year ended 31 March 2008 £
Trading profit/(loss)	86,600	(25,700)	27,300	(78,300)
Property business profit	–	4,500	8,100	5,600
Gift aid donations	(1,400)	(800)	(1,200)	(1,100)

Loser Ltd does not have any associated companies.

Required

(a) State the factors that will influence a company's choice of loss relief claims. You are not expected to consider group relief. **(3 marks)**

(b) Assuming that Loser Ltd claims relief for its losses as early as possible, compute the company's profits chargeable to corporation tax for the year ended 30 June 2005, the nine month period ended 31 March 2006, the year ended 31 March 2007 and the year ended 31 March 2008. Your answer should clearly identify the amount of any losses that are unrelieved. **(5 marks)**

(c) Explain how your answer to (b) above would have differed if Loser Ltd had ceased trading on 31 March 2008. **(2 marks)**

(Total = 10 marks)

38 Unforeseen Upsets Limited

54 mins

Unforeseen Upsets Limited (UUL) is a United Kingdom resident company which has been manufacturing lifeboats for many years. It has no associated companies. The company has previously made up accounts to 31 December but has now changed its accounting date to 31 March.

The company's results for the 15 month period to 31 March 2008 are as follows.

	£
Trading profits (as adjusted for taxation but before capital allowances)	1,125,000
Bank interest receivable (note 4)	20,000
Debenture interest receivable (note 5)	17,500
Chargeable gain (notes 6 and 7)	30,000
Gift aid donation paid (note 8)	20,000
Dividends received from UK companies (note 9)	6,300

Notes

(1) UUL is a small company with a turnover in the period of account ended 31 March 2008 of £2,000,000. The company has 30 employees.

(2) *Capital allowances – plant and machinery*

On 1 January 2007 the tax written-down values of plant and machinery were:

	£
Pool	142,000

Sales during the accounting period were:

		£
31.7.07	3 cars (not low emission)	15,000
30.9.07	Plant and machinery	12,000

Additions during the accounting period were:

		£
1.6.07	1 car (not low emission)	14,000
1.8.07	3 cars (£8,000 each) (not low emission)	24,000
30.11.07	Plant and machinery	92,000
28.2.08	Computer equipment	2,400

(3) On 1 January 2007 the company had trading losses brought forward of £600,000.

(4) *Bank interest receivable*

	£
31.3.07 received	3,000
30.6.07 received	4,000
30.9.07 received	5,000
31.12.07 received	8,000
	20,000

All interest was received at the end of the quarter for which accrued. The bank interest was non trading income.

(5) *Debenture interest receivable (gross amounts)*

	£
30.9.07 received	10,500
31.3.08 received	7,000
	17,500

(a) The loan was made on 1 July 2007.
(b) £1,500 was accrued at 31 December 2007. There was no accrual at 31 March 2008.
(c) The interest was non-trading income.
(d) The interest was received gross from another UK company.

(6) The chargeable gain was realised on 1 July 2007.

(7) On 1 January 2007 the company had capital losses brought forward of £50,000.

(8) Gift Aid donations paid

	£
31.5.07	7,000
31.10.07	4,000
28.2.08	9,000
	20,000

(9) Dividends received

	£
28.2.08	£6,300

Required

(a)   Calculate the corporation tax payable for the fifteen month period of account.   **(20 marks)**

(b)   State the date(s) by which the company must pay its corporation tax liability, the date by which it must file return(s) and the penalties due if returns are not filed by the due date.   **(9 marks)**

(c)   State what unrelieved amounts are carried forward at 31 March 2008.   **(1 mark)**

(Total = 30 marks)

39 B and W Ltd   27 mins

B Ltd acquired 80% of the voting rights of W Ltd in December 2007. Both companies are resident in the United Kingdom. B Ltd has, for several years, owned 5% of the voting capital of P Inc, a company resident abroad.

The following information relates to B Ltd for its twelve-month accounting period ended 31 March 2008.

	£
Income	
Adjusted trading profits	296,000
Capital gains	30,000
Dividend from P Inc (net of 20% overseas tax)	1,600
Debenture interest received 30 November 2007 (non-trading investment)	8,000
FII (inclusive of tax credit) received in May 2007	32,000
Payments	
Gift Aid to charity	18,000

W Ltd also made up accounts for the twelve months to 31 March 2008 and its only taxable income consisted of trading profits of £6,000.

There were no accruals of debenture interest at the beginning or end of the year. The debenture interest was received gross from another UK company.

Required

Compute the corporation tax payable by both B Ltd and W Ltd for the above accounting period, assuming all appropriate claims are made.

Show clearly your treatment of double tax relief.   **(15 marks)**

Helping hand

1   The first thing to do is to work out the PCTCT for B Ltd and W Ltd and, if relevant, the 'profits' figure.

2   This will then lead you to consider the rate of corporation tax payable. Are B Ltd and W Ltd associated companies? If so, this will affect the limits for small companies' marginal relief.

3   Once you have done your basic CT calculation, move on to the DTR. You need to separate out the UK and overseas income and remember that it is beneficial to set a Gift Aid payment where possible against UK income. DTR is the lower of UK tax and the overseas tax.

---

40 Sirius Ltd (BTX 12/03)

54 mins

Sirius Ltd is a manufacturing company with no associated companies. The profit and loss account for the year ended 31 March 2008 show a trading loss of £125,000. This figure includes the following items:

	£
Director's fees	47,000
Depreciation	42,750
Loss on disposal of computer equipment	5,260
Loss on sale of factory	39,500
Bank overdraft interest charged	10,000
Gift Aid donation to Oxfam paid on 15 November 2007	25,000
Dividend paid on 27 January 2008	21,000
Dividend received on 15 March 2008	18,000

Notes

(1)   The written down values of plant and equipment at 1 April 2007 were as follows.

	£
Plant and machinery	42,000
Expensive car	13,000
Short life asset (computer system)	3,600

On 1 June 2007 a new computer system was purchased for £12,000. The existing system, which had cost £9,600 three years earlier, was sold for £250.

On 5 November 2007 a new van was purchased at a cost of £21,680 for the sole use of the transport manager, whose mileage was 75% business and 25% private. The company is small sized for capital allowances purposes.

(2)   In July 2007 a freehold factory was sold for £1,750,000, including land of £1 million. It had been bought new in September 1998 for £85,000, including land of £15,000, and immediately brought into use. As at 1 April 2007 the company had capital losses brought forward of £41,405.

(3)   The profits chargeable to corporation tax for the year ended 31 March 2007 were £3 million, and the budgeted figure for the year ended 31 March 2009 is £105,000.

Future plans

Sirius is planning to set up an overseas operation next year, but is unsure whether to operate overseas through a permanent establishment or a 100% subsidiary. A subsidiary would be resident overseas. Regardless of the type of business structure chosen, the overseas operation is expected to make a tax adjusted trading profit of £200,000 for the year ended 31 March 2009. The overseas corporation tax on these profits will be £40,000.

If the overseas operation is set up as a permanent establishment then profits of £80,000 will be remitted to the UK during the year ended 31 March 2009. These remittances will not be subject to any withholding tax. If the overseas operation is set up as a 100% subsidiary then gross dividends of £80,000 will be paid to Sirius Ltd during the year ended 31 March 2009. These dividends will be subject to withholding tax at the rate of 15% in the overseas country.

All of the above figures are in pounds Sterling.

Required

(a)   (i)   Calculate the corporation tax due for the year ended 31 March 2008 assuming that the trading loss is set off so as to obtain relief as early as possible. The RPI for September 1998 is 164.4 and in July 2007 is 206.6.   **(10 marks)**

         (ii)   State when the corporation tax payment is due and when the company's tax return must be submitted.   **(2 marks)**

(iii)   State any alternative ways in which the company may set off its trading loss for the year ended 31 March 2008, ignoring any profit from overseas sources in the future.   **(3 marks)**

(b)   Explain the taxation factors that should be considered when deciding whether to operate overseas through a permanent establishment or a 100% subsidiary. You are not expected to discuss double taxation relief.

(4 marks)

(c)   Calculate Sirius Ltd's UK corporation tax liability for the year ended 31 March 2009 if the overseas operation is set up as:

(i)   A permanent establishment;   **(4 marks)**
(ii)   A 100% subsidiary company.   **(7 marks)**

You should assume that Sirius Ltd has no other income or expenditure in the year and that the FY2007 corporation tax rates continue to apply in the future.

(Total = 30 marks)

41 Preparation question: group relief

P Ltd owns the following holdings in ordinary shares in other companies, which are all UK resident.

Q Ltd   83%
R Ltd   77%
S Ltd   67%
M Ltd   80%

The ordinary shares of P Ltd are owned to the extent of 62% by Mr C, who also owns 70% of the ordinary shares of T Ltd, another UK resident company. In each case, the other conditions for claiming group relief, where appropriate, are satisfied. No dividends were paid by the companies during the year in question.

The following are the results of the above companies for the year ended 31 March 2008.

	M Ltd £	P Ltd £	Q Ltd £	R Ltd £	S Ltd £	T Ltd £
Income						
Trading income	10,000	0	64,000	260,000	0	70,000
Trading loss	0	223,000	0	0	8,000	0
Property business income	0	6,000	4,000	0	0	0
Payments						
Gift Aid donation	4,000	4,500	2,000	5,000	0	0

Required

(a)   Compute the CT payable for the above accounting period by each of the above companies, assuming group relief is claimed, where appropriate, in the most efficient manner.

(b)   Advise the board of P Ltd of the advantages of increasing its holding in S Ltd, a company likely to sustain trading losses for the next two years before becoming profitable.

Guidance notes

1   Group relief questions nearly always require you to show the most efficient use of relief. You must work out the profits of each company involved, and consider the marginal tax rate of each company. Any company with small companies' marginal relief will have a marginal rate (for FY 2007) of 32.5%.

2   Before working out the rates of tax, you must find the lower and upper limits for small companies' rate and marginal relief. These depend on the number of companies under common control.

3   You must also remember that eligibility for group relief depends not on common control, but on a 75% effective interest.

42 A Ltd

27 mins

On 1 July 2007 A Ltd, a manufacturing company resident in the United Kingdom, acquired 100% of the share capital of B Ltd, also a manufacturing company. B Ltd makes up accounts each year to 30 June. For its year ended 30 June 2008, it sustained a trading loss of £68,000 and had no other chargeable income. A Ltd produced the following information in relation to its nine-month period of accounts to 31 December 2007.

INCOME

	£
Trading income	342,000
Rents receivable	13,000
Loan interest receivable (received gross) (including £2,000 accrued at 31 December 2007)	8,000
Bank interest receivable (including £3,000 accrued at 31 December 2007: £2,000 received 30 June 2007)	5,000
Franked investment income (FII) (including tax credit; received August 2007)	1,000
PAYMENTS	
Gift Aid payment (paid September 2007)	17,000

A Ltd did not pay an dividends to individual shareholders in the above accounting period.

Required

Compute the final taxation position of A Ltd for the above accounting period, assuming maximum group relief is claimed by A Ltd in respect of B Ltd's trading loss.

State the due date for payment of the corporation tax and the date by which A Ltd must file a corporation tax return in respect of the above period. **(15 marks)**

43 Gold Ltd (BTX 06/04)

54 mins

Gold Ltd owns 100% of the ordinary share capital of Silver Ltd. Gold Ltd has an accounting date of 31 December, whilst Silver Ltd has an accounting date of 30 June. The results of Gold Ltd are as follows:

	Year ended 31 December	
	2006	2007
	£	£
Trading income	177,000	90,000
Property business income	5,000	–
Capital gain	–	12,000
Gift Aid donation	(2,000)	(2,000)

For the year ended 30 June 2006 Silver Ltd had profits chargeable to corporation tax of £260,000. Information for the year ended 30 June 2007 is as follows.

	£
Operating loss (note 1)	(167,464)
Income from investments	
Dividends (note 2)	116,514
Loss before taxation	(50,950)

Notes

(1) *Operating loss*

Depreciation of £37,560 has been deducted in arriving at the operating loss of £167,464.

(2) *Dividends received*

The dividends were all received from unconnected UK companies. The figure shown is the actual cash amount received.

(3)   *Plant and machinery*

On 1 July 2006 the tax written down values of plant and machinery were as follows:

	£
General pool	18,225
Expensive motor car (1)	11,750
Short-life asset	2,700

The following transactions took place during the year ended 30 June 2007:

		Cost/ (proceeds) £
1 July 2006	Purchased equipment	3,360
5 July 2006	Sold the expensive motor car (1)	(18,700)
31 August 2006	Purchased motor car (2)	23,250
7 October 2006	Sold a van	(12,220)
12 November 2006	Purchased motor car (3)	9,500
16 April 2007	Sold the short-life asset	(555)

The expensive motor car sold on 5 July 2006 originally cost £31,240. The van sold on 7 October 2006 originally cost £11,750.

Silver Ltd is a small company for capital allowances purposes.

(4)   *Industrial building*

On 1 June 2007 Silver Ltd purchased a second-hand factory for £295,000 (including £85,000 for the land and £62,750 for general offices). The factory was originally constructed at a cost of £215,000 (including £55,000 for the land and £32,000 for general offices). The factory was first brought into use on 1 December 2000. It has always been used for industrial purposes. The original owner prepared accounts to 31 March.

No information is available regarding the year ended 30 June 2008.

Gold Ltd has no other associated companies.

Required

(a)   Calculate Silver Ltd's trade loss for the year ended 30 June 2007.   **(15 marks)**

(b)   Assuming that the maximum possible claim for group relief is made in respect of Silver Ltd's trading loss, calculate Gold Ltd's corporation tax liabilities for the year ended 31 December 2006 and the year ended 31 December 2007.   **(8 marks)**

(c)   Explain how loss relief should be allocated within a group of companies in order to maximise the potential benefit of the relief for the group as a whole.   **(4 marks)**

(d)   Based on the information available, advise Silver Ltd of the most beneficial way of relieving its trading loss of £140,000.   **(3 marks)**

(Total = 30 marks)

44 Apple Ltd

36 mins

You should assume that today's date is 30 November 2008.

Apple Ltd has owned 80% of the ordinary share capital of Bramley Ltd and 85% of the ordinary share capital of Cox Ltd since these two companies were incorporated on 1 April 2006. Cox Ltd acquired 80% of the ordinary share capital of Delicious Ltd on 1 April 2007, the date of its incorporation.

The tax adjusted trading profits/(losses) of each company for the years 31 March 2007, 2008 and 2009 are as follows.

	Year ended 31 March		
	2007	2008	2009 (forecast)
	£	£	£
Apple Ltd	620,000	250,000	585,000
Bramley Ltd	(64,000)	52,000	70,000
Cox Ltd	83,000	(58,000)	40,000
Delicious Ltd	n/a	90,000	(15,000)

The following information is also available.

(1)   Apple Ltd sold a freehold office building on 10 March 2008 for £380,000, and this resulted in a capital gain of £120,000.

(2)   Apple Ltd sold a freehold warehouse on 5 October 2008 for £365,000, and this resulted in a capital gain of £80,000.

(3)   Cox Ltd purchased a freehold factory on 20 September 2008 for £360,000.

(4)   Delicious Ltd is planning to sell a leasehold factory building on 15 February 2009 for £180,000, and this will result in a capital loss of £44,000.

(5)   None of the companies has paid dividends since 1 April 2007.

Because each of the subsidiary companies has minority shareholders, the managing director of Apple Ltd has proposed that:

(1)   Trading losses should initially be carried back and relieved against profits of the loss making company, with any unrelieved amount then being carried forward.

(2)   Chargeable assets should not be transferred between group companies, and rollover relief should only be claimed where reinvestment is made by the company that incurred the chargeable gain.

Required

(a)   (i)   Explain the factors that should be taken into account by the Apple Ltd group when deciding which group companies the trading losses should be surrendered to.   **(2 marks)**

       (ii)   Explain why it may be beneficial for all of the eligible subsidiary companies to elect that their chargeable assets were transferred to Apple Ltd prior to being disposed of outside the group.

                                                                                                        (2 marks)

(b)   (i)   Assuming that the managing director's proposals are followed, calculate the profits chargeable to corporation tax for each of the companies in the Apple Ltd group for the years ended 31 March 2007, 2008 and 2009 respectively.   **(5 marks)**

       (ii)   Advise the Apple Ltd group of the amount of corporation tax that could be saved for the years ended 31 March 2007, 2008 and 2009 if reliefs were instead claimed in the most beneficial manner.

                                                                                                        (11 marks)

Assume that Finance Act 2007 rates apply throughout.

(Total = 20 marks)

45 Tock-Tick Ltd (BTX 06/05)   **54 mins**

Tock-Tick Ltd is a clock manufacturer. The company's summarised profit and loss account for the year ended 31 March 2008 is as follows:

	£	£
Gross profit		822,280
Operating expenses		
Impairment losses (note 1)	9,390	
Depreciation	99,890	
Gifts and donations (note 2)	3,090	
Professional fees (note 3)	12,400	
Repairs and renewals (note 4)	128,200	
Other expenses (note 5)	426,920	
		679,890
Operating profit		142,390
Profit from sale of fixed assets		
Disposal of office building (note 6)		78,100
Income from investments		
Loan interest (note 7)		12,330
		232,820
Interest payable (note 8)		48,600
Profit before taxation		184,220

Notes

(1)   *Impairment losses*

Impairment losses are as follows:

	£
Trade debts recovered from previous years	(1,680)
Trade debts written off	4,870
Non-trade debts written off	6,200
	9,390

(2)   *Gifts and donations*

Gifts and donations are as follows:

	£
Gifts to customers (pens costing £45 each displaying Tock-Tick Ltd's name)	1,080
Gifts to customers (food hampers costing £30 each)	720
Long service award to an employee	360
Donation to a national charity (made under the gift aid scheme)	600
Donation to a national charity (not made under the gift aid scheme)	250
Donation to a local charity (Tock-Tick Ltd received free advertising in the charity's magazine)	80
	3,090

(3)   *Professional fees*

Professional fees are as follows:

	£
Accountancy and audit fee	5,400
Legal fees in connection with the issue of share capital	2,900
The cost of registering the company's trademark	800
Legal fees in connection with the renewal of a 35-year property lease	1,300
Debt collection	1,100
Legal fees in connection with a court action for not complying with health and safety legislation	900
	12,400

(4)   *Repairs and renewals*

The figure of £128,200 for repairs and renewals includes £41,800 for replacing the roof of an office building, which was in a bad state of repair, and £53,300 for extending the office building.

(5)   *Other expenses*

Other expenses include £2,160 for entertaining suppliers; £880 for counseling services provided to two employees who were made redundant; and the cost of seconding an employee to a charity of £6,400. The remaining expenses are all fully allowable.

(6)   *Disposal of office building*

The profit of £78,100 is in respect of a freehold office building that was sold on 20 February 2008 for £276,000. The office building was purchased on 18 November 1997 for £197,900. The indexation allowance from November 1997 to April 1998 was £11,200, and from November 1997 to February 2008 it is £39,900.

The building has always been used by Tock-Tick Ltd for trading purposes.

(7)   *Loan interest received*

The loan interest is in respect of a loan that was made on 1 July 2007. Interest of £8,280 was received on 31 December 2007, and interest of £4,050 was accrued at 31 March 2008. The loan was made for non-trading purposes.

(8)   *Interest payable*

The interest payable is in respect of a debenture loan that is used for trading purposes. Interest of £24,300 was paid on 30 September 2007 and again on 31 March 2008.

(9)   *Plant and machinery*

On 1 April 2007 the tax written down values of plant and machinery were as follows:

	£
General pool	12,200
Expensive motor car	20,800
Short-life asset	3,100

The following transactions took place during the year ended 31 March 2008:

		Cost/(Proceeds)
		£
28 May 2007	Sold the expensive motor car	(34,800)
7 June 2007	Purchased a motor car	14,400
1 August 2007	Sold the short-life asset	(460)
15 August 2007	Purchased equipment	6,700

The expensive motor car sold on 28 May 2007 for £34,800 originally cost £33,600. The motor car purchased on 7 June 2007 is a low emission motor car (CO_2 emission rate of less than 120 grams per kilometre). Tock-Tick Ltd has made an election to treat the equipment purchased on 15 August 2007 as a short-life asset. Tock-Tick Ltd is a small company as defined by the Companies Acts.

Required

(a) Calculate Tock-Tick Ltd's tax adjusted trading income for the year ended 31 March 2008. Your computation should commence with the profit before taxation figure of £184,220. **(19 marks)**

(b) Calculate Tock-Tick Ltd's profits chargeable to corporation tax for the year ended 31 March 2008. **(5 marks)**

(c) State the effect on Tock-Tick Ltd's profits chargeable to corporation tax for the year ended 31 March 2008 if Tock-Tick Ltd had:

   (i) For capital allowances purposes been a large-sized company as defined by the Companies Acts rather than a small company; **(2 marks)**

   (ii) Claimed the maximum possible group relief from a 100% owned subsidiary company that had made a trading loss of £62,400 for the year ended 31 December 2007; **(2 marks)**

   (iii) Made a claim to rollover the gain arising on the sale of the office building (see note 6) against the cost of a new freehold office building that was purchased on 15 April 2008 for £260,000. The new office building is to be used 100% for trading purposes by Tock-Tick Ltd. **(2 marks)**

(Total = 30 marks)

VAT

Questions 46 to 49 cover the VAT rules for both corporate and unincorporated businesses, the subject of Part D of the BPP Study Text for Paper F6.

46 Lithograph Ltd (BTX 06/06)

18 mins

Lithograph Ltd runs a printing business, and is registered for VAT. Because its annual taxable turnover is only £250,000, the company uses the annual accounting scheme so that it only has to prepare one VAT return each year. The annual VAT period is the year ended 31 December.

Year ended 31 December 2006

The total amount of VAT payable by Lithograph Ltd for the year ended 31 December 2006 was £10,200.

Year ended 31 December 2007

The following information is available:

(1)   Sales invoices totalling £250,000 were issued to VAT registered customers, of which £160,000 were for standard rated sales and £90,000 were for zero-rated sales.

(2)   Purchase invoices totalling £45,000 were received from VAT registered suppliers, of which £38,000 were for standard rated purchases and £7,000 were for zero-rated purchases.

(3)   Standard rated expenses amounted to £28,000. This includes £3,600 for entertaining customers.

(4)   On 1 January 2007 Lithograph Ltd purchased a motor car costing £18,400 for the use of its managing director. The manager director is provided with free petrol for private mileage, and the cost of this is included in the standard rated expenses in note (3). The relevant annual scale charge is £1,385. Both figures are inclusive of VAT.

(5)   During the year ended 31 December 2007 Lithograph Ltd purchased machinery for £24,000, and sold office equipment for £8,000. Input VAT had been claimed when the office equipment was originally purchased.

(6)   On 31 December 2007 Lithograph Ltd wrote off £4,800 due from a customer as a bad debt. The debt was in respect of an invoice for a standard rated supply that was due for payment on 31 May 2007.

Unless stated otherwise all of the above figures are exclusive of VAT.

Required

(a)   Calculate the monthly payments on account of VAT that Lithograph Ltd will have made in respect of the year ended 31 December 2007, and state in which months these will have been paid.   **(3 marks)**

(b)   (i)   Calculate the total amount of VAT payable by Lithograph Ltd for the year ended 31 December 2007.
(5 marks)

      (ii)   Based on your answer to part (i) above, calculate the balancing payment that would have been paid with the annual VAT return, and state the date by which this return was due for submission.
(2 marks)

(Total = 10 marks)

47 Tardy Ltd (BTX 06/05)

18 mins

Tardy Ltd registered for value added tax (VAT) on 1 July 2005. The company's VAT returns have been submitted as follows:

Quarter ended	Submitted	VAT paid/ (refunded) £
30 September 2005	One month late	18,600
31 December 2005	One month late	32,200
31 March 2006	On time	8,800
30 June 2006	Two months late	3,400
30 September 2006	One month late	(6,500)
31 December 2006	On time	42,100
31 March 2007	On time	(2,900)
30 June 2007	On time	3,900
30 September 2007	On time	18,800
31 December 2007	Two months late	57,300
31 March 2008	On time	9,600

Tardy Ltd always pays any VAT that is due at the same time that the related return is submitted.

During May 2008 Tardy Ltd discovered that a number of errors had been made when completing its VAT return for the quarter ended 31 March 2008. As a result of these errors the company will have to make an additional payment of VAT.

Required

(a) State, giving appropriate reasons, the default surcharge consequences arising from Tardy Ltd's submission of its VAT returns for the quarter ended 30 September 2005 to the quarter ended 31 December 2007 inclusive.

(7 marks)

(b) Explain how Tardy Ltd can voluntarily disclose the errors relating to the VAT return for the quarter ended 31 March 2008, and state whether default interest will be due, if:

(i) The net errors in total are less than £2,000;
(ii) The net errors in total are more than £2,000.

(3 marks)

(Total = 10 marks)

48 Ram-Rom Ltd (BTX 12/05)   18 mins

Ram-Rom Ltd commenced trading as a manufacturer of computer equipment on 1 July 2007. The company registered for value added tax (VAT) on 1 March 2008. Its inputs for each of the months from July 2007 to February 2008 are as follows:

		Goods purchased £	Services incurred £	Fixed assets £
2007	July	12,300	1,400	42,000
	August	11,200	5,100	–
	September	12,300	7,400	–
	October	16,400	6,300	14,400
	November	14,500	8,500	–
	December	18,800	9,000	–
2008	January	18,500	9,200	–
	February	23,400	8,200	66,600

During February 2008 Ram-Rom Ltd sold all of the fixed assets purchased during October 2007 for £12,000.

On 1 March 2008 £92,000 of the goods purchased were still in stock.

The above figures are all exclusive of VAT. Ram-Rom Ltd's sales are all standard rated.

The following is a sample of the new sales invoice that Ram-Rom Ltd is going to issue to its customers:

SALES INVOICE

Ram-Rom Ltd
123 The High Street
London WC1 2AB
Telephone 0207 100 1234

Customer: XYZ Computers plc
Address: 99 The Low Road
Glasgow G1 2CD

Invoice Date and Tax Point: 1 March 2008

Item Description	Quantity	Price £
Hard Drives	5	220.00
Motherboards	2	100.00
Total Amount Payable (Including VAT)		320.00

Directors: Y Ram & Z Rom
Company Number: 1234567
Registered Office: 123 The High Street, London WC1 2AB

Ram-Rom Ltd pays for all of its inputs one month after receiving the purchase invoice. However, many customers are not paying Ram-Rom Ltd until four months after the date of the sales invoice. In addition, several customers have recently defaulted on the payment of their debts. In order to encourage more prompt payment, Ram-Rom Ltd is considering offering all of its customers a 5% discount if they pay within one month of the date of the sales invoice. No discount is currently offered.

Required

(a)   Explain why Ram-Rom Ltd was able to recover input VAT totalling £43,610 in respect of inputs incurred prior to registering for VAT on 1 March 2008.   **(5 marks)**

(b)   State what alterations Ram-Rom Ltd will have to make to its new sales invoices in order for them to be valid for VAT purposes.   **(3 marks)**

(c)   Explain the VAT implications of Ram-Rom Ltd offering all of its customers a 5% discount for prompt payment.   **(2 marks)**

(Total = 10 marks)

49 Sandy Brick (BTX 06/04)

18 mins

Sandy Brick has been a self-employed builder since 2003. He registered for value added tax (VAT) on 1 January 2008, and is in the process of completing his VAT return for the quarter ended 31 March 2008. The following information is relevant to the completion of this VAT return:

(1) Sales invoices totalling £44,000 were issued to VAT registered customers in respect of standard rated sales. Sandy offers his VAT registered customers a 5% discount for prompt payment.

(2) Sales invoices totalling £16,920 were issued to customers that were not registered for VAT. Of this figure, £5,170 was in respect of zero-rated sales with the balance being in respect of standard rated sales. Standard rated sales are inclusive of VAT.

(3) On 10 January 2008 Sandy received a payment on account of £5,000 in respect of a contract that was completed on 28 April 2008. The total value of the contract is £10,000. Both of these figures are inclusive of VAT at the standard rate.

(4) Standard rated materials amounted to £11,200, of which £800 were used in constructing Sandy's private residence.

(5) Since 1 December 2006 Sandy has paid £120 per month for the lease of office equipment. This expense is standard rated.

(6) During the quarter ended 31 March 2008 £400 was spent on mobile telephone calls, of which 30% relates to private calls. This expense is standard rated.

(7) On 20 February 2008 £920 was spent on repairs to a motor car. The motor car is used by Sandy in his business, although 20% of the mileage is for private journeys. This expense is standard rated.

(8) On 15 March 2008 equipment was purchased for £6,000. The purchase was partly financed by a bank loan of £5,000. This purchase is standard rated.

Unless stated otherwise all of the above figures are exclusive of VAT.

Required

Calculate the amount of VAT payable by Sandy for the quarter ended 31 March 2008. **(10 marks)**

50 Question with analysis: Carolyn Kraft

45 mins

Approaching the answer

You should read through the requirement before working through and annotating the question. This means that you will be aware of the things you are looking for.

Carolyn Kraft is aged 34. She is employed as a buyer for a large retail group of companies. She is married to Mike. They have no children.

In the tax year 2007/08, Carolyn was paid a salary of £32,600 (PAYE £5,366). Carolyn also received bank interest of £8,000 in 2007/08. On 14 November 2007 Carolyn made a one off donation under Gift Aid to Cancer Research UK of £780.

Mike undertakes a business from home. His accounts for the year ended 31 December 2007 show an adjusted profit of £53,400. He is also entitled to capital allowances of £1,600. Mike had owned a freehold shop which he had used in his business. He had acquired the shop on 10 April 2006 for £53,300 and sold it for £85,000 in August 2007. He is considering acquiring another shop to replace this one.

Mike also received dividends of £9,000 in 2007/08 and makes a contribution of £260 each month to his personal pension.

Carolyn bought a flat in August 2005 for £180,000. Carolyn arranged for renovation work to be undertaken, which cost £30,000 in January 2007. Carolyn sold the flat for £250,000 in December 2007. The flat was unoccupied between the date of purchase and the date of sale.

Required

(a)   Calculate both Carolyn and Mike's income tax due for 2007/08 and state when it is due.   **(11 marks)**

(b)   Calculate the amount of national insurance contributions payable by both Carolyn and Mike for 2007/08.
(4 marks)

(c)   Calculate Carolyn and Mike's 2007/08 capital gains tax liability stating the due date. Assume Mike does not acquire another shop.   **(8 marks)**

(d)   Briefly explain the relief available to Mike if he does acquire another shop.   **(2 marks)**

(Total = 25 marks)

50 Question with analysis: Carolyn Kraft

45 mins

Approaching the answer

You should read through the requirement before working through and annotating the question. This means that you will be aware of the things you are looking for.

Look for details of her employment package	Carolyn Kraft is aged 34. She is **employed** as a buyer for a large retail group of companies. She is married to Mike. They have no children.
Extends basic rate band	In the tax year 2007/08, Carolyn was paid a salary of £32,600 (PAYE £5,366). Carolyn also received bank interest of £8,000 in 2007/08. On 14 November 2007 Carolyn made a one off **donation under Gift Aid** to Cancer Research UK of £780.
Self-employment	Mike undertakes a **business from home**. His accounts for the year ended 31 December 2007 show an adjusted profit of £53,400. He is also entitled to capital allowances of £1,600. Mike had owned a freehold shop which he had used in his business. He had acquired the shop on 10 April 2006 for £53,300 and sold it for £85,000 in August 2007. He is considering **acquiring another shop** to replace this one.
Looks like rollover relief	Mike also received dividends of £9,000 in 2007/08 and makes a contribution of £260 each month to his personal pension.
Enhancement expenditure	Carolyn bought a flat in August 2005 for £180,000. Carolyn arranged for **renovation work** to be undertaken, which cost £30,000 in January 2007. Carolyn **sold the flat** for £250,000 in December 2007. The **flat was**
No PPR	**unoccupied** between the date of purchase and the date of sale.

CGT

Required

(a) Calculate both Carolyn and Mike's income tax due for 2007/08 and **state when it is due**. **(11 marks)**

Easy marks

(b) Calculate the amount of national insurance contributions payable by both Carolyn and Mike for 2007/08.   **(4 marks)**

(c) Calculate Carolyn and Mike's 2007/08 capital gains tax liability **stating the due date**. Assume Mike does not acquire another shop.   **(8 marks)**

(d) **Briefly** explain the relief available to Mike if he does acquire another shop.   **(2 marks)**

Follow instructions

(Total = 25 marks)

BPP
LEARNING MEDIA

51 Question with analysis: Unforeseen Upsets Limited 54 mins

Approaching the answer

You should read through the requirement before working through and annotating the question as we have done. This will mean that you are aware of the things you are looking for.

Unforeseen Upsets Limited (UUL) is a United Kingdom resident company which has been manufacturing lifeboats for many years. It has no associated companies. The company has previously made up accounts to 31 December but has now changed its accounting date to 31 March.

The company's results for the 15 month period to 31 March 2008 are as follows.

	£
Trading profits (as adjusted for taxation but before capital allowances)	1,125,000
Bank interest receivable (note 4)	20,000
Debenture interest receivable (note 5)	17,500
Chargeable gain (notes 6 and 7)	30,000
Gift aid donation paid (note 8)	20,000
Dividends received from UK companies (note 9)	6,300

Notes

1   UUL is a small company with a turnover in the period of account ended 31 March 2008 of £2,000,000. The company has 30 employees.

2   *Capital allowances – plant and machinery*

On 1 January 2007 the tax written-down values of plant and machinery were:

	£
Pool	142,000

Sales during the accounting period were:

		£
31.7.07	3 cars (not low emission)	15,000
30.9.07	Plant and machinery	12,000

Additions during the accounting period were:

		£
1.6.07 1 car (not low emission)		14,000
1.8.07	3 cars (£8,000 each) (not low emission)	24,000
30.11.07	Plant and machinery	92,000
28.2.08	Computer equipment	2,400

3   On 1 January 2007 the company had trading losses brought forward of £600,000.

4   *Bank interest receivable*

	£
31.3.07 received	3,000
30.6.07 received	4,000
30.9.07 received	5,000
31.12.07 received	8,000
	20,000

All interest was received at the end of the quarter for which accrued. The bank interest was non trading income.

5   Debenture interest receivable (gross amounts)

		£
30.9.07 received		10,500
31.3.08 received		7,000
		17,500

(a)   The loan was made on 1 July 2007.
(b)   £1,500 was accrued at 31 December 2007. There was no accrual at 31 March 2008.
(c)   The interest was non-trading income.
(d)   The interest was received gross from another UK company.

6   The chargeable gain was realised on 1 July 2007.

7   On 1 January 2007 the company had capital losses brought forward of £50,000.

8   Gift aid donations paid

	£
31.5.07	7,000
31.10.07	4,000
28.2.08	9,000
	20,000

9   Dividends received
           28.2.08   £6,300

Required

(a)   Calculate the corporation tax payable for the fifteen month period of account.   **(20 marks)**

(b)   State the date(s) by which the company must pay its corporation tax liability, the date by which it must file return(s) and the penalties due if returns are not filed by the due date.   **(9 marks)**

(c)   State what unrelieved amounts are carried forward at 31 March 2008.   **(1 mark)**

(Total = 30 marks)

51 Question with analysis: Unforeseen Upsets Limited 54 mins

Approaching the answer

You should read through the requirement before working through and annotating the question as we have done. This will mean that you are aware of the things you are looking for.

Unforeseen Upsets Limited (UUL) is a United Kingdom resident company which has been manufacturing lifeboats for many years. It has no associated companies. The company has previously made up accounts to 31 December but has now changed its accounting date to 31 March.

Long period of account

The company's results for the **15 month period** to 31 March 2008 are as follows.

	£
Trading profits (as adjusted for taxation but before capital allowances)	1,125,000
Bank interest receivable (note 4)	20,000
Debenture interest receivable (note 5)	17,500
Chargeable gain (notes 6 and 7)	30,000
Gift aid donation paid (note 8)	20,000
Dividends received from UK companies (note 9)	6,300

Important for FYAs, payment of CT

Notes

1   UUL is a **small company** with a turnover in the period of account ended 31 March 2008 of £2,000,000. The company has 30 employees.

2   *Capital allowances – plant and machinery*

On 1 January 2007 the tax written-down values of plant and machinery were:

	£
Pool	142,000

Sales during the accounting period were:

		£
31.7.07	3 cars (not low emission)	15,000
30.9.07	Plant and machinery	12,000

Additions during the accounting period were:

Expensive car

		£
1.6.07	1 car (not low emission)	**14,000**
1.8.07	3 cars (£8,000 each) (not low emission)	24,000
30.11.07	Plant and machinery	92,000
28.2.08	Computer equipment	2,400

Addition in p/e 31.3.08

Set against trading income

3   On 1 January 2007 the company had **trading losses** brought forward of £600,000.

4   *Bank interest receivable*

	£
31.3.07 received	3,000
30.6.07 received	4,000
30.9.07 received	5,000
31.12.07 received	8,000
	20,000

Interest is taxed in the period for which it accrues

All interest was received at the end of the quarter for which accrued. The bank interest was **non trading income**.

5   *Debenture interest receivable (gross amounts)*

		£
30.9.07 received		10,500
31.3.08 received		7,000
		17,500

Need to include – accruals basis

(a)   The loan was made on 1 July 2007.

(b)   £1,500 was **accrued** at 31 December 2007. There was no accrual at 31 March 2008.

Interest income

(c)   The interest was **non-trading income**.

(d)   The interest was received gross from another UK company.

Set off capital loss v gain

6   The chargeable gain was realised on 1 July 2007.

7   On 1 January 2007 the company had **capital losses brought forward** of £50,000.

Charges on income

8   **Gift aid donations paid**

		£
31.5.07		7,000
31.10.07		4,000
28.2.08		9,000
		20,000

Gross up to arrive at FII

9   **Dividends received**

28.2.08		£6,300

Required

(a)   Calculate the corporation tax payable for the fifteen month period of account.   **(20 marks)**

(b)   State the date(s) by which the company must pay its corporation tax liability, the date by which it must file return(s) and the penalties due if returns are not filed by the due date.   **(9 marks)**

(c)   State what unrelieved amounts are carried forward at 31 March 2008.   **(1 mark)**

(Total = 30 marks)

52 Question with analysis: A Ltd

27 mins

Approaching the answer

You will not get a 15 mark question examining corporation tax groups in the exam. However this is a good question to practice to ensure your understanding of the area. You should read through the requirement before working through and annotating the question. This means that you will be aware of the things you are looking for.

On 1 July 2007 A Ltd, a manufacturing company resident in the United Kingdom, acquired 100% of the share capital of B Ltd, also a manufacturing company. B Ltd makes up accounts each year to 30 June. For its year ended 30 June 2008, it sustained a trading loss of £68,000 and had no other chargeable income. A Ltd produced the following information in relation to its nine-month period of accounts to 31 December 2007.

INCOME

	£
Trading income	342,000
Rents receivable	13,000
Loan interest receivable (received gross)	8,000
(including £2,000 accrued at 31 December 2007)	
Bank interest receivable (including £3,000	5,000
accrued at 31 December 2007: £2,000 received 30 June 2007)	
Franked investment income (FII)	1,000
(including tax credit; received August 2007)	
PAYMENTS	
Gift Aid payment (paid September 2007)	17,000

A Ltd did not pay an dividends to individual shareholders in the above accounting period.

Required

Compute the final taxation position of A Ltd for the above accounting period, assuming maximum group relief is claimed by A Ltd in respect of B Ltd's trading loss.

State the due date for payment of the corporation tax and the date by which A Ltd must file a corporation tax return in respect of the above period. **(15 marks)**

52 Question with analysis: A Ltd

27 mins

> **Approaching the answer**
>
> You will not get a 15 mark question examining corporation tax groups in the exam. However this is a good question to practice to ensure your understanding of the area. You should read through the requirement before working through and annotating the question. This means that you will be aware of the things you are looking for.

Date company joins group

On **1 July 2007** A Ltd, a manufacturing company resident in the United Kingdom, acquired 100% of the share capital of B Ltd, also a manufacturing company. B Ltd makes up accounts each year to 30 June. For its

Need to work out corresponding

year ended **30 June 2008**, it sustained a trading loss of £68,000 and had no other chargeable income. A Ltd produced the following information in relation to its **nine-month period of accounts to 31 December 2007**.

Short accounting period

INCOME

	£
Trading income	342,000
Rents receivable	13,000
Loan interest receivable (received gross)	8,000

Need to include – accruals basis

(including £2,000 accrued at 31 December 2007)

Bank interest receivable (including £3,000 accrued at 31 December 2007: £2,000 received 30 June 2007)	5,000

Include in calculation of 'profits'.

Franked investment income (FII) (including tax credit; received August 2007)	1,000

PAYMENTS

Gift Aid payment (paid September 2007)	17,000

A Ltd did not pay an dividends to individual shareholders in the above accounting period.

Required

Compute the final taxation position of A Ltd for the above accounting period, assuming maximum **group relief** is claimed by A Ltd in respect of B Ltd's trading loss.

Don't forget this – easy marks!

State the **due date for payment of the corporation tax** and the **date by which A Ltd must file a corporation tax return** in respect of the above period.

(15 marks)

Answers

1 Preparation question: personal tax computation

Text references. Chapters 2 and 5 required for this question.

Top tips. It is essential to separate all the various types of income in the correct layout.

(a) **Income tax computation**

	Non-savings £	Savings £	Dividend £	Total £
Trading income	57,000			
Dividend £900 × 100/90			1,000	
Bank interest £2,197 × 100/80		2,746		
Total income	57,000	2,746	1,000	
Less: deductible interest	(6,000)			
Net income	51,000	2,746	1,000	54,746
Less personal allowance	(5,225)			
Taxable income	45,775	2,746	1,000	49,521

	£
Tax on non-savings income	
£2,230 × 10%	223
£32,370 × 22%	7,121
£11,175 (extended band) × 22%	2,458
Tax on savings income	
£825 (extended band) × 20%	165
£1,921 × 40%	768
Tax on dividend income	
£1,000 × 32.5%	325
Tax liability	11,060
Less tax suffered on bank interest £2,746 × 20%	(549)
tax credit on dividends £1,000 × 10%	(100)
Tax payable	10,411

(b) Contributions up to the amount of earnings qualify for tax relief, therefore the full amount of £9,360 grossed up provide relief.

As Roger is a higher rate tax payer, his basic rate band is extended by the gross amount of the premium actually paid, £12,000 (£9,360 × $^{100}/_{78}$) ie £12,000 + £34,600 = £46,600.

The interest paid on the loan to purchase a share in a partnership is eligible interest which qualifies for tax relief as deductible interest. It is therefore deducted in the computation of net income.

2 Brad and Lauren

Text references. Chapters 2 and 3.

Top tips. Note that the question asked for the tax liability and not the tax due – the tax liability is **before** deduction of any tax credits such as PAYE.

Marking scheme

		Marks
(a)	**Brad**	
	Employment income	½
	Interest	½
	PA	½
	Tax bands	1
	Tax rates	1
	Exempt income	1
	Lauren	
	Interest	½
	Treasury stock (gross)	½
	Dividends	½
	PA	½
	Gift Aid – extend BRB	1
	Tax bands	1
	Tax rates	1½
	ISA – exempt income	10
(b)	**Tom**	
	Pensions	½
	Building society interest	½
	Gift Aid	1
	PAA	1
	Tax bands	1
	Tax rates	1
		5
		15

(a) **Brad: Income Tax Computation 2007/08**

	Non-savings £	Savings £	Total £
Employment income	41,500		
BSI (2,200 × 100/80)		2,750	
Net income	41,500	2,750	44,250
Less PA	(5,225)		
Taxable income	36,275	2,750	39,025

Tax

	£
On non savings income	
£2,230 @ 10%	223
£32,370 @ 22%	7,121
£1,675 @ 40%	670
On savings income	
£2,750 @ 40%	1,100
	9,114

Income tax liability = £9,114

Note. Premium Bond winnings and interest on National Savings & Investments Certificates are exempt income.

Lauren: Income Tax Computation 2007/08

	Non-savings £	Savings £	Dividend £	Total £
Employment income	45,000			
BSI (2,200 × 100/80)		2,750		
Treasury stock		2,000		
Dividends (2,250 × 100/90)			2,500	
Net income	45,000	4,750	2,500	52,250
Less PA	(5,225)			
Taxable income	39,775	4,750	2,500	47,025

Tax

	£
On Non-savings Income	
£2,230 @ 10%	223
£32,370 @ 22%	7,121
£1,282 @ 22% (note)	282
£3,893 @ 40%	1,557
On Savings Income	
£4,750 @ 40%	1,900
On Dividend Income	
£2,500 @ 32.5%	813
Income tax liability	11,896

Note. The basic rate band is extended by the gross amount of the Gift Aid payment. £34,600 + (1,000 × 100/78) = £35,882. Dividends and interest received from an ISA are exempt.

(b) **Tom: Income Tax Computation 2007/08**

	Non-savings £	Savings £	Total £
State pension	4,226		
Employment pension	14,355		
BSI (6,348 × 100/80)		7,935	
Net income	18,581	7,935	26,516
Less age allowance (W)	(7,242)		
Taxable income	11,339	7,935	19,274

Tax

		£
On Non-savings income		
£2,230 @ 10%		223
£9,109 @ 22%		2,004
On Savings income		
£7,935 @ 20%		1,587
Income tax liability		3,814

Working

Age enhanced personal allowance

	£	£
PAA > 65		7,550
Net income	26,516	
Less Gift Aid £3,900 × 100/78	(5,000)	
	21,516	
Less limit	(20,900)	
	616	
÷ 2		(308)
PAA		7,242

Note. The grossed up value of the Gift Aid payment is deducted from net income when calculating the age allowance.

3 Rita

Text references. Chapters 3 and 4 on employees.

Top tips. Always take care to apportion car and fuel benefits correctly. The CO_2 emissions figure for the car is rounded down to the nearest five below. 140g/km is the baseline figure at which the taxable percentage is 15%. The percentage is increased by 1% for each 5g/km by which the CO_2 emissions figure exceeds 140g/km.

		Marks
Salary	1	
Higher of annual value and rent	1	
Ancillary services	2	
Relocation	1	
Use of furniture	1	
Purchase of furniture (W2)	2	
Loan	2	
Car	3	
Fuel	2	
		15

	£
Salary	48,000
Accommodation (W1)	23,200
Relocation (£12,000 − £8,000)	4,000
Loan (£10,000 × 6.25%)	625
Car (£18,500 × 15% × 8/12)	1,850
Fuel benefit (£14,400 × 15% × 8/12)	1,440
Employment income	79,115

Workings

1   *Accommodation*

	£
Rent paid (higher than annual value)	6,000
Electricity	700
Gas	1,200
Water	500
Council tax	1,300
Repairs	3,500
Furniture (20% × £30,000 × 6/12)	3,000
Purchase (W2)	7,000
	23,200

2   *Purchase of furniture*

Benefit is the higher of:

			£
(a)	Cost		30,000
	Less taxed		(3,000)
			27,000
	Less amount paid		(20,000)
			7,000
(b)	Market value		25,000
	Less amount paid		(20,000)
			5,000

ie £7,000

4 Vigorous plc

Text references. Chapters 3 and 4 cover employee taxation.

Top tips. The tests for being a P11D employee are the same as deciding that an employee is not an excluded employee for the purposes of the benefits code.

Easy marks. Car and fuel benefits should provide easy marks and stating the exempt benefit of a mobile phone was worth ½ mark.

Examiner's comments. This question was answered quite badly. In part (a) the majority of candidates appreciated that a P11D employee is one earning £8,500 per year or more, but very few mentioned this figure includes benefits. In part (b) very few candidates correctly calculated the benefit arising from the beneficial loan. However, quite a few candidates correctly calculated the benefit arising from the sale at an under-value of a second-hand asset. Part (c) was not answered particularly well, with few candidates mentioning more than one way in which the income tax liability in respect of benefits is collected.

Marking scheme

			Marks
(a)	Earnings limit	1	
	Test – cash and benefits	1	
	Directors	<u>1</u>	
			3
(b)	**Andrea**		
	Car benefit – %	1	
	– contributions	1	
	– calculations	½	
	Fuel benefit	1	
	Living accommodation – annual value	½	
	– additional benefit	2	
	– furniture	1	
	Mobile phone	½	
	Ben		
	Loan – average method	1½	
	– strict method	2	
	Relocation	1	
	Car benefit – %	1	
	– calculation	1	
	Chai		
	Van	1	
	Television – current MV calculation	1	
	– original MV calculation	1½	
	Health club	1	
	Computer	<u>½</u>	
			19
(c)	PAYE code	1	
	Self assessment	1	
	Other collection methods	<u>1</u>	
			<u>3</u>
			<u><u>25</u></u>

(a) A P11D employee is one who is an employee earning at least £8,500 per annum or a director (in most cases).

In deciding whether an employee earns £8,500, add together the total earnings and benefits that would be taxable if the employee was a P11D employee.

A director is not a P11D employee if he does not have a material interest in the company (control of more than 5% of the ordinary share capital) and is either a full time working director of the company or the company is non-profit making or is established for charitable purposes only.

(b) **Andrea**

Car benefit

Amount by which CO_2 emissions exceed base line:

$(265 - 140) = 125 \div 5 = 25$

Add to 15% = 40% − but maximum taxable % is 35%

	£
£19,400 × 35%	6,790
Less contribution for private use £150 × 12	(1,800)
Taxable benefit for P11D	4,990

Fuel benefit

£14,400 × 35% = £5,040

Living accommodation

Annual value: £7,000

Additional benefit

	£
Cost of property	130,000
Improvements before 6 April 2007	14,000
	144,000
Less de minimis	(75,000)
	69,000

× 6.25% (official rate of interest) = £4,313

Furniture

20% × £6,000 = £1,200

Mobile phone

Exempt benefit

Ben

Taxable cheap loan

Average method $\dfrac{120,000 + 100,000}{2}$ = £110,000 × 6.25% × 9/12 =   £5,156

Strict method

	£
1 July − 30 September	
£120,000 × 6.25% × 3/12	1,875
1 October − 31 March	
£100,000 × 6.25% × 6/12	3,125
	5,000

Ben should elect for the strict method.

Note. This was the answer that the examiner expected. However, strictly speaking Vigorous Plc would enter the average method figure of £5,156 on the P11D and then it would have been up to the employee to elect for the strict method.

Relocation costs

First £8,000 − exempt

Excess is taxable benefit £(9,300 − 8,000) = £1,300

Car benefit

Round down CO_2 emissions to nearest 5 ie 130

Below baseline so the taxable % is 15 + 3% (for diesel car) = 18%

Taxable benefit for P11D

18% × £11,200 × 6/12 = £1,008

Chai

Van benefit

Scale charge

£3,000 × 10/12 = £2,500

Television

		£
Greater of:		
(i)	Current market value	250
	Less price paid by employee	(150)
		100
	And	
		£
(ii)	Market value when first provided	800
	Less benefit 2005/06 (20% × £800)	(160)
	benefit 2006/07 (20% × £800)	(160)
		480
	Less price paid	(150)
		330

Taxable benefit for P11D: £330

Health club membership

Cost to employer (marginal cost so limited to direct costs): £150

Computer

Benefit for private use £1,900 × 20% = £380

(c) Income tax on benefits provided for more than one year will usually be collected in future years by adjusting the employee's PAYE code. Alternatively tax will be collected through the self assessment system.

However tax up to £2,000 can be collected by adjusting the PAYE code for the employee.

Tax on minor benefits may be paid by the employer under an employees' PAYE settlement agreement.

5 Bryan Thompson

Text references. Chapter 2 on tax computation. Chapters 3 and 4 on employees. Chapter 6 on property income. Chapter 12 on NIC.

Top tips. Be methodical and work through each item in a separate working. You can then summarise the results in the tax computation.

Marking scheme

		Marks	
(a)	*Employment income*		
	Salary	½	
	Company Car	2	
	Fuel	1	
	Wife's car	2	
	Wife's fuel	1	
	Pension contribution – Bryan	1	
	– Employer	1	
	PMI	2	
	Overseas trip	2	
	Relocation expenses	2	
	Property business – Income	½	
	– Expenses	½	
	– Wear and tear	1	
	– Joint income	1	
	Interest	1	
	Dividends	1	
	PA	1	
	Tax bands	2½	
	Tax rates	2	
			25
(b)	NIC – Class 1	4	
	– No Class 1A (employer only)	1	
			5
			30

(a) Income tax

	Non-savings £	Savings £	Dividend £
Employment income (W1)	87,424		
Rental income (W4)	4,000		
Dividends (1,800 × 100/90)			2,000
Bank interest (3,200 × 100/80)		4,000	
	91,424	4,000	2,000
Personal allowance	(5,225)		
	86,199	4,000	2,000

		£
Income tax		
£2,230 @ 10%		223
£32,370 @ 22%		7,121
£51,599 @ 40%		20,640
Savings income		
£4,000 × 40%		1,600
Dividends		
£2,000 @ 32.5%		650
Tax liability		30,234

Workings

1 Employment income

	£
Salary	75,000
Car benefit: £25,000 @ ((160 − 140)/5 + 15% =) 19%	4,750
Fuel £14,400 @19%	2,736
Car for wife (note 1) £7,500 @ 15% = 1,125 × 6/12	563
Medical insurance (note 2)	1,200
Trip (W2)	1,125
Removal costs (W3)	9,550
Total	94,924
Less occupational pension contribution (note 3)	
10% × £75,000	(7,500)
Employment income	87,424

2 Trip to Florida

	£	£
Wife's flight		1,000
Hotel charge	100	
Single charge	(75)	
Extra re wife	25 × 5	125
		1,125

3 Removal expenses

	£
Agents fees	4,500
Removal costs	750
Stamp duty	10,500
Legal fees	1,800
	17,550
Less allowed	(8,000)
Assessable	9,550

4 Rental income

	£	£
Rent		20,000
Caretaker	2,600	
Heat and Light	1,400	
Interest	6,000	
Wear and tear 10% × £20,000	2,000	
		(12,000)
		8,000

£8,000 × ½ = £4,000

Notes

(1)   Wife's fuel is not a taxable benefit as she pays for all of her private fuel.

(2)   Son's medical costs already covered by Private Medical Insurance which is taxable on Bryan as a taxable benefit.

(3)   Bryan's pension contribution is deducted directly from his salary at source. The contribution paid by his employer is not a taxable benefit.

(b)   NIC

Bryan will pay Class 1 NICs on his salary only.

			£
(34,840 – 5,225)	=	29,615 @ 11% =	3,258
(75,000 – 34,840)	=	40,160 @ 1% =	402
Class 1 NIC due			3,660

No Class 1A is due in respect of the benefits as this is due from the employer only.

6 Mark Kett

Text references. Chapters 2, 6 to 9 and 18.

Top tips. Set out your proformas in the correct layout to assist the marker to award you maximum marks.

Easy marks. You cannot avoid administration questions in the exam so make sure you learn the rules as they gain you easy marks.

Marking scheme

		Marks
(a)	Trading profit	½
	Capital allowances – Pool	2
	– Motor car	2
	Salary	1
	Beneficial loan	1
	Staff canteen	½
	Expense claim	1½
	Property business profit	2
	Furniture and furnishings	½
	Rent-a-room scheme	1
	Interest from government stocks	1
	Dividends	1
	Individual savings account	½
	Premium bond prize	½
	Personal allowance	½
	Extension of basic rate band	1
	Income tax	2½
	Tax suffered at source – PAYE	1
	– Dividends	1
	Balancing repayment	1

22

(b)

Business records	1
Other records	1
Penalty	1
	3
	25

(a) **Mark Kett income tax computation 2007/08**

	Non-savings income £	Savings income £	Dividend income £	Total £
Trading income (W1)	22,120			
Employment income (W3)	10,150			
Property income (W6)	7,310			
Gilt interest (received gross)		1,900		
Dividends × 100/90			3,200	
Net income	39,580	1,900	3,200	44,680
Less PA	(5,225)			(5,225)
Taxable income	34,355	1,900	3,200	39,455

Tax

	£
£2,230 @ 10%	223
£32,125 @ 22%	7,068
£245 @ 20%	49
£1,000 @ 20% (W8)	200
£655 @ 40%	262
£3,200 @ 32.5%	1,040
	8,842
Less tax credits	
PAYE (3 × £620)	(1,860)
Dividends	(320)
Tax payable	6,662
Less POAs	(11,381)
Repayment due from HMRC	(4,719)

Note. Both the ISA interest and premium bond winnings are exempt from tax.

Workings

1   *Trading income*

	£
Trading profit	20,700
Balancing charge (W2)	1,420
	22,120

2   *Capital allowances*

	Pool £	Exp car (60%) £	CAs £
TWDV b/f	13,800	14,600	
Additions	1,900		
	15,700	14,600	
Disposal	(18,800)	(11,800)	
Balancing charge	(3,100)		(3,100)
Balancing allowance		2,800 @ 60%	1,680
No WDA in year of cessation			
Balancing charge			(1,420)

3   *Employment income*

	£
Salary (1.1.08 – 5.4.08)	9,750
Loan (W5)	1,000
Canteen meals – not taxable	nil
Less mileage deduction (W4)	(600)
Employment income	10,150

4   *Mileage allowance*

	£
Company pays: 2,500 @ 16p	400
Less: mileage allowance	
2,500 @ 40p	(1,000)
Deduction (expense claim)	600

5   *Loan*

£64,000 × 6.25% × 3/12 = £1,000

6   *Property income*

	£
Income	
Rent	8,600
Less expenses	
letting agent fees	(430)
wear & tear (£8,600 @ 10%)	(860)
	7,310

Note. There is no relief for expenditure on furniture as wear and tear allowance is given.

7   *Rent-a-room relief*

Received: £350 × 9 = £3,150

This is below the limit of £4,250 and therefore this income will be exempt.

8   *Basic rate band*

Extended by gift aid: £780 × 100/78 = £1,000

(b) **Retaining records**

(i)   As Mark has self employment and property income he must retain his records for five years and ten months from the end of the tax year ie until 31 January 2014.

(ii)   He must also retain the records for his other income until this date (even though the usual period would be one year ten months).

(iii) If he does not retain his records for this period of time HMRC can fine him up to £3,000 (although this is usually only collected in serious cases).

7 Clayton Delaney

Text references. Chapters 2, 7, 8 and 9.

Top tips. In this question, you should have dealt with the adjustment of profit for the final period, then the amount assessable on cessation and finally the personal tax computation.

Marking scheme

			Marks
(a)	Net profits	1	
	Telephone	1	
	Repairs – roof	1	
	– bedroom	1	
	Depreciation	½	
	Insurance	½	
	Light and heat	½	
	Car expenses	½	
	Non-trade loan written off	1	
	Council tax	1	
	Wages	1	
	Gifts	1	
	Donation	1	
	Own use goods	1	
	Interest received	½	
	Profit on sale of shop fittings	½	
	Capital allowances	4	
	Taxable profits	1	18
(b)	Salary	1	
	Benefits	1½	
	Trading income	½	
	BSI	1	
	Annuity	1	
	Tax calculations	1	
	Less: Tax at source	1	
			7
			25

BPP
LEARNING MEDIA

(a)   **The adjustment of profit for the year ended 30 June 2007**

	£	£
Net profit per accounts		8,150
Additions		
Telephone £240 × 1/5	48	
Repairs: roof £650 × 2/3	433	
Repairs: bedroom	230	
Depreciation	1,350	
Buildings insurance £600 × 2/3	400	
Lighting and heating £420 × 2/3	280	
Car expenses £1,750 × ½	875	
Irrecoverable debts: non-trade loan written off (impairment loss)	500	
Rates: council tax	650	
Proprietor's wages	11,850	
General expenses: gifts	900	
General expenses: donation to national charity	25	
Goods for own use £600 × 100/(100 − 20)	750	
		18,291
		26,441
Deductions		
Interest received	300	
Profit on sale of shop fittings	20	
Capital allowances	3,440	
		(3,760)
Adjusted profit		22,681

Capital allowances

	Pool £	Proprietor's car (50%) £	Allowances £
Balances b/f	490	5,700	
Disposal		(4,500)	
Balancing allowance		1,200	600
Additions		9,000	
	490	9,000	
Proceeds	(400)	(3,500)	
Balancing allowances	90	5,500	2,840
			3,440

Taxable profits

Year	Basis period	Profits £
2007/08	1.7.06 – 30.6.07	21,481

The final year's profits have been reduced by the overlap profits of £1,200.

(b) **Clayton: income tax computation**

	Non- savings income £	Savings income £	Total income £
Salary £1,500 × 9	13,500		
Car benefit £10,000 × 19% × 9/12	1,425		
Fuel benefit £14,400 × 19% × 9/12	2,052		
Employment income	16,977		
Trading income	21,481		
BI £395 × 100/80		494	
Treasury stock interest £8,000 × 5%		400	
Net income	38,458	894	39,352
Less personal allowance	(5,225)		
Taxable income	33,233	894	34,127

	£
Income tax on non-savings income	
£2,230 × 10%	223
£31,003 × 22%	6,821
Income tax on savings income	
£894 × 20%	179
Tax liability	7,223
Less: tax suffered on BI	(99)
Tax payable (subject to tax paid under PAYE)	7,124

Note. The CO_2 emissions figure of the car is 145g/km rounded down to the nearest 5. This is 5g/km above the baseline figure of 140g/km so the taxable percentage is 16% + 3% (diesel) = 19%.

8 Noel and Liam Wall

Text references. Chapters 2 to 4, 7 to 9 and 12.

Top tips. Using familiar proformas for the adjustment to profits and computation of employment income should ensure that you present your workings in a clear and logical way.

To make sure that you don't miss anything it is a good idea to mark the question in some way, eg tick off items as you deal with them.

Easy marks. The adjustment to profits was fairly straightforward, as was the computation of the income tax liability in both cases. Make sure you allocate your time correctly to enable you to have time to calculate both liabilities.

Marking scheme

			Marks
(a)	Net profit	½	
	Depreciation	½	
	Motor expenses	1	
	Professional fees	1½	
	Repairs and renewals	1	
	Telephone	½	
	Travelling and entertaining	1	
	Other expenses	1½	
	Capital allowances – Motor car	1	
	– Guitar	1	
	Dividends	1	
	Personal allowance	½	
	Income tax	1½	
	Class 2 NIC	1	
	Class 4 NIC	1½	
			15
(b)	Salary	½	
	Car benefit – Relevant percentage	1	
	– Calculation	½	
	Fuel benefit	1	
	Computer	1½	
	Mobile telephone	½	
	Golf club membership	½	
	Professional subscription	½	
	Building society interest	1	
	Personal allowance	½	
	Income tax	1	
	Class 1 NIC	1½	
			10
			25

(a) **Noel Wall – Income tax computation 2007/08**

	Non-savings income £	Dividend income £	Total £
Trading profits (W1)	73,025		
Dividends (£7,560 × 100/90)		8,400	
Net income	73,025	8,400	81,425
Less: PA	(5,225)		(5,225)
Taxable income	67,800	8,400	76,200

Tax	£
£2,230 @ 10%	223
£32,370 @ 22%	7,121
£33,200 @ 40%	13,280
£8,400 @ 32.5 %	2,730
Tax liability	23,354

	£
Class 2 NIC: 52 × £2.20	114
Class 4 NIC: £(34,840 – 5,225) × 8% + (73,025 – 34,840) × 1%	2,751

Workings

1 *Trading profit*

		£
Net profit		70,350
Add: depreciation	1,980	
Motor expenses $(5{,}600 \times \dfrac{8{,}400 - 7{,}560}{8{,}400})$	560	
Personal tax advice fees	510	
New guitar (capital)	1,900	
Private telephone calls	160	
Entertaining clients	370	
Parking fines	120	
Donation to political party	100	
Golf club membership fee	625	6,325
		76,675
B/f		76,675
Less: capital allowances (W2)		(3,650)
Taxable trading profit		73,025

2 *Capital allowances*

	Pool £	Exp Car £	Allowances £
TWDV b/f		32,800	
Addition – guitar	1,900		
WDA – restricted (note 1)		(3,000)	2,700
FYA – 50%	(950)		950
TWDV c/f	950	29,800	
Total allowances			3,650

Note: 90% (7,560/8,400) of the use of the car is for business purposes.

(b) **Liam Wall – Income tax computation 2007/08**

	Non-savings Income £	Savings Income £	Total £
Employment income (W1)	81,542		
BSI (£6,640 × 100/80)		8,300	
Net income	81,542	8,300	89,842
Less: PA	(5,225)		(5,225)
Taxable income	76,317	8,300	84,617

Tax

	£
£2,230 @ 10%	223
£32,370 @ 22%	7,121
£41,717 @ 40%	16,687
£8,300 @ 40%	3,320
Tax liability	27,351
Class 1 NIC: £(34,840 − 5,225) × 11% + £(65,000 − 34,840) × 1%	3,560

Note. Taxable employment benefits are not subject to Class 1 NIC.

Workings

1 *Employment income*

	£
Salary	65,000
Car benefit (W2)	11,016
Fuel benefit (W3)	4,896
Provision of computer (W4)	270
Provision of mobile phone – exempt	–
Golf club membership	580
	81,762
Less: professional subscription	(220)
Employment income	81,542

2 *Car benefit*

Round CO_2 emissions down to nearest 5, ie 220

220 − 140 = 80 gkm

Divided by 5 = 16

Taxable % = 15 + 16 + 3 (diesel powered) – 34%

List price = £32,400

Value of benefit   £32,400 × 34% = £11,016

3 *Fuel benefit*

£14,400 × 34% = £4,896

4 *Provision of computer*

Annual benefit = 20% × £1,800 = £360

The computer is only provided from 6 July 2007, so the benefit is time apportioned.

Assessable benefit = 9/12 × £360 = £270

9 Tony Note

Text references. Chapter 7 for adjustment to profits. Chapter 16 covers CGT reliefs.

Top tips. Work through each item in an adjustment to profits question methodically. You probably won't get every item correct but you can get lots of easy marks if you make sure you don't miss anything out.

Do not confuse income tax and CGT calculations. Keep them separate and remember gains are taxed **after** income.

Marking scheme

			Marks
(a)	Adjustment of profits		
	Net profit	½	
	Depreciation	1	
	Motor expenses	1½	
	Professional fees	1	
	Repairs and renewals	1	
	Travelling and entertaining	1	
	Wages and salaries	1	
	Other expenses	1½	
	Goods for own use	1	
	Use of office	1	
	Telephone	1	
	CAs		
	FYA @ 50%	1	
	WDA @ 25%	1	
	WDA max £3,000	1	
	Private use restriction	½	
	No IBAs	1	
			16
(b)	Income Tax		
	PA	½	
	Tax bands & rates	1	
	CGT		
	Calculation of gain	½	
	Rollover relief	1½	
	Taper relief	½	
	AE	½	
	Remaining basic rate band	½	
	Tax rates	1	
			6
(c)	Time period	1	
	Reason	1	
	Consequences if does not retain	1	
			3
			25

(a)   Tony's adjusted trading profit y/e 5 April 2008

	£	£
Net profit		19,600
Add:		
Depreciation	2,640	
Motor expenses (N1)	2,940	
Professional fees (N2)	3,220	
Repairs and Renewals (N3)	400	
Travelling and entertaining (N4)	480	
Wages and salaries (N5)	4,000	
Other expenses (N6)	770	
Goods for own use (N9)	950	15,400
Less:		
Use of office (N7)	(720)	
Private telephone (N8)	(170)	(890)
Adjusted profits		34,110
Less:		
Capital allowances (N10)		(4,150)
Taxable trading profit		29,960

Notes

1   Motor expenses

Total miles	20,000
Less: personal miles	(2,500)
– vacation	17,500
– private journeys 20% × 17,500	(3,500)
Allowable miles	14,000
(14,000/20,000 = 70% business proportion)	
Total disallowed miles (2,500 + 3,500)	6,000
$\dfrac{6,000}{20,000} \times £9,800$	2,940

2   Professional fees

Legal and professional charges are allowable if connected with the trade and do not relate to capital items. The personal financial planning advice fees are therefore not deductible as they are not connected with the trade. The planning permission fees are not deductible as they relate to capital expenditure.

3   Repairs and renewals

The cost of replacing the hard drive should be allowable so long as it does not significantly improve the computer. The expenditure on the new printer is capital expenditure and therefore is not an allowable deduction. However capital allowances will be available on this expenditure.

4   Travelling and entertaining

Customer/supplier entertaining is never allowable for income tax purposes.

5   Wages and salaries

The salary to Tony's wife is allowable to the extent that it is not excessive. As she is paid more than other staff performing the same job only £12,000 of the £16,000 paid to her will be allowable.

6   Other expenses

As the wedding present to the employee is small, this should be allowable for income tax purposes. Tony's heath club subscription is not allowable as it is not wholly and exclusively for the purpose of the trade. Donations to political parties are never allowed for income tax purposes. The trade subscription is allowable.

7   Use of office

Tony will be allowed a deduction of 1/6 x the running costs in respect of the use of the room in his home for business purposes.

8   Private telephone

The business proportion of home phone calls will be allowable for corporation tax purposes. The cost of the line rental is not allowable. Therefore 25% of the calls will be allowable. It has been assumed that the figure of £680 does not include line rental for these purposes.

9   Goods for own use

Tony cannot simply take goods from his business without making an adjustment to his profit. The market value of the goods taken (i.e. what a customer would pay for them) will need to be added back to the profit.

10   Capital allowances

	FYA £	General Pool £	Exp car £	Allowances £
TWDV b/f		7,400	16,200	
Additions: printer	400			
FYA @ 50%	(200)			200
WDA @ 25%		(1,850)		1,850
WDA max			(3,000) @ 70%	2,100
Transfer to pool	(200)	200		
TWDV c/f	–	5,750	13,200	
Total allowances				4,150

Note that there are no Industrial Buildings Allowances (IBAs) as the premises Tony uses are for retail purposes and therefore do not qualify for IBAs.

Notes 2-9 above are not required unless specifically asked for by the examiner. They are included here for tutorial purposes.

(b)

	£
Income tax:	
Trading profits (from (a))	29,960
Less: personal allowance	(5,225)
Taxable income	24,735

Tax liability
Non savings income

	£
£2,230 @ 10%	223
£22,505 @ 22%	4,951
£24,735	
Total income tax due	£5,174

CGT:	£
Chargeable gain (W1)	27,500
Less: annual exemption	(9,200)
Taxable gain	18,300

CGT liability

		£
£34,600 − £24,735 =	9,865 @ 20%	1,973
18,300 − 9,865 =	8,435 @ 40%	3,374
	18,300	
CGT due		5,347

Workings

1   Chargeable gain

	£
Proceeds	320,000
Less: cost 8.8.03	(188,000)
	132,000
Less: rollover relief	(22,000)
Chargeable gain before taper (W2)	110,000
Gain after taper 4yrs BA: 25%	27,500

2   Rollover relief

Rollover relief is available because one asset used in the trade has been sold and another one purchased within the required time period (one year before the disposal and 3 years after the disposal).

However, as not all of the proceeds are spent, full rollover relief is not available.

Instead, the amount of proceeds not reinvested will remain chargeable, with the remaining gain being deferred until the new building is sold.

	£
Proceeds received	320,000
Less: proceeds spent on new shop	(210,000)
Gain remaining chargeable	110,000

(c)   Retaining records

As Tony is self employed he must retain his records for a period of five years from 31 January after the tax year ie 31 January 2014. This includes any information regarding the chargeable gains.

If he does not keep his records he can be charged up to £3,000 for each year of assessment for which he fails to keep records.

10 Malcolm

> **Text references.** Chapter 10 looks at trading losses.
>
> **Top tips.** You should not be tempted in a question like this merely to list the various loss reliefs. You need to make an attempt at giving your rationale for the use of the losses. Remember that you will probably get marks for your rationale even if you have not used the loss in the most efficient way.

Marking scheme

			Marks
(a)	Trading losses		
	2006/07	2	
	2007/08	2	
	Offset of loss – carry back against general income 2005/06	1	
	– current year general income 2006/07	1	
	Order of claims	1	
	No claims against general income 2007/08	1	
	Why no further claims against general income	2	
	Carry forward against future trade profits	2	
			12
(b)	Time limit – claim against general income	1	
	Time limit – carry forward against trading profits	2	
			3
			15

(a)   Trading losses are:

	£	£
2006/07 (1.8.06 – 5.4.07)		
(£10,000 + 4/12 × £20,000)		(16,667)
2007/08 (1.12.06 – 30.11.07)		
Loss	20,000	
Less used in 2006/07	(6,667)	
		(13,333)
		(30,000)

Each of these losses can be relieved against the general income of the year of the loss and/or the preceding year.

2006/07 loss

	2005/06 £	2006/07 £
Employment income	8,000	5,650
Interest ($£3,040 \times \dfrac{100}{80}$)	3,800	3,800
Total income	11,800	9,450
Loss relief against general income	(11,800)	(4,867)
Net income	0	4,583

A claim against general income in 2005/06 results in a waste of personal allowances. However, the claim is worthwhile as it leads to a repayment of income tax in respect of the year and the alternative is to carry the loss forward.

A claim against general income in 2006/07 to utilise the balance of the 2006/07 loss obtains tax relief for the loss quickly and it only wastes a small amount of personal allowance.

2007/08 loss

A claim against general income in 2007/08 (ie against interest income) would not be worthwhile as it would merely waste the personal allowance. A claim against general income in 2006/07 would also waste the personal allowance but it would allow a further claim to be made to set the loss against the chargeable gain in 2006/07. However, this would waste the CGT annual exemption and would save only £200 (£9,400 − £9,200) × 10% = £20 of CGT.

Alternatively, if a claim against general income was not made for the 2006/07 loss in 2005/06, the 2007/08 loss could be carried back against the general income of the previous three years. £11,800 of the loss would be set off in 2005/06 and the balance in 2006/07 leaving net income in 2006/07 of £7,917. This is clearly less beneficial than the claim against general income for the 2006/07 loss considered above.

A better alternative is to carry the 2007/08 loss forward for relief against trading income of 2008/09:

	2008/09 £
Trading income	15,000
Less carry forward loss relief	(13,333)
	1,667
Building society interest	3,800
	5,467

This leaves enough income in 2008/09 to absorb the personal allowance. Income tax is saved in 2008/09 on the whole of the loss set off.

(b) **The claims against general income for the 2006/07 loss must be made by the 31 January which is nearly two years after the end of the tax year of the loss: thus by 31 January 2009.**

There is no statutory time limit by which a claim to relieve a loss by carry forward must be made. **However, a claim to establish the amount of the loss of 2007/08 to be carried forward must be made by the 31 January which is nearly five years after the end of the year of the loss: thus by 31 January 2013.** Once the loss is established, it will be carried forward and used where possible each year until used up.

11 Li Fung

Text references. Self-employment is covered in Chapters 7 to 9.

Top tips. There are 3 marks for part (a); you should aim to state 3 conditions.

Marking scheme

		Marks
(a)	Notification date	1
	18 month limit	1
	Change within five years	1
		3

(b)	Assessments	– 2003/04	1
		– 2004/05	1½
		– 2005/06	1
		– 2006/07	1½
		– 2007/08	1
	Overlap profits	– 1.10.03-5.4.04	1
		– 1.7.04-30.9.04	1
		– Relieved in 2006/07	1
			9
(c)	Basis periods correspond		1
	Overlap profits		1
	Disadvantages		1
			3
			15

(a) Change of accounting date conditions

(i)   Must notify HMRC by 31 January following the tax year of the change of accounting date.

(ii)   The new accounts must not exceed 18 months in length.

(iii) There must not have been a change of accounting date in the previous 5 years unless there is a commercial reason for this later change.

(b) Trading income assessments

	£	£
2003/04		
Actual basis: 1.10.03 – 5.4.04		
6/9 × £18,600		12,400
2004/05		
<12 months therefore tax first 12 months		
9m to 30.6.04	18,600	
1.7.04 – 30.9.04: 3/12 × £24,900	6,225	
		24,825
2005/06		
CYB: y/e 30.6.05		24,900
2006/07		
Year of change (two periods ending in same tax year)		
Tax both periods and relieve overlap profits		
Y/e 30.6.06	22,200	
9m to 31.3.07	16,800	
21 months worth of profit	39,000	
Less overlap relief (W1) (9 months worth)	(18,625)	
12 months worth of profit		20,375
2007/08		
CYB: y/e 31.3.08		26,400

Working

Overlap profits are any profits that are taxed twice when a business starts (or on a change of accounting date):

		£
1.10.03 – 5.4.04	= 6m	12,400
1.7.04 – 30.9.04	= 3m	6,225
Total	= 9m	18,625

(c) **Advantages and disadvantages of changing accounting date**

Advantages	Disadvantages
All of the overlap profits will be relieved	Tax on the profits of a tax year will be due sooner
The year end will now correspond with the tax year so will make basis periods easier	The profits taxable for a tax year will not be known until after the end of the tax year.
On cessation, only the profits earned in the tax year of cessation will be taxed.	

12 Robert Sax

Text references. The basis period rules are all dealt with in Chapter 9.

Top tips. Be methodical in your approach. Deal with the opening year rules first, then identify the year of change, and apply the CYB to all other years. Apply the cessation rules to the final year.

		Marks
2000/01	– actual basis	1½
2001/02	– Last 12m of period	2
2002/03	– CYB	1
Overlap profits created		2
2003/04	– CYB	
2004/05	– CYB	1½
2005/06	– CYB	
2006/07	– Identify year of change	1
	– 15 m/e 31.12.06	1
	– Deduct overlap profits	2
2007/08	– Identify year of cessation	1
	– Deduct overlap profits	2
		15

2000/01 1.6.00 – 5.4.01

$$\frac{10}{16} \times £30,000$$ £18,750

2001/02 1.10.00 – 30.9.01

$$\frac{12}{16} \times £30,000$$ £22,500

2002/03 Y/e/30.9.02 £40,000

Overlap profits

= 1.10.00 – 5.4.01 (6 months)

= $\frac{6}{16} \times £30,000$ £11,250

2003/04 Y/e 30.9.03 £50,000

2004/05 Y/e 30.9.04 £60,000

2005/06 Y/e 30.9.05 £55,000

2006/07	"Year of change"		
	1.10.05 – 31.12.06 (15m)		£75,000
	less overlap relief		
	$\dfrac{3}{6} \times £11,250$		(5,625)
			£69,375
2007/08	Year of cessation		
	1.1.2007 – 31.3.2008		
	(£40,000 + £12,000)		£52,000
	less overlap relief		
	(£11,250 – £5,625)		(5,625)
			£46,375

13 Vera Old

Text references. Chapter 18.

Top tips. No payments on account are required for capital gains tax – simply one payment due on 31 January following the end of the tax year.

Easy marks. There were some basic administration issues tested in this question relating to payments on account.

Examiner's comments. In part (a) many candidates were unaware that payments on account are not required for capital gains tax, and there was a surprising lack of knowledge regarding due dates. Part (b) was generally badly answered, with few candidates appreciating the fact that payments on account should be reduced to the amount of income and Class 4 NIC payable for the current year. Part (c) was answered reasonably well, as was the first section of part (d). However, few candidates were aware of the circumstances in which a discovery assessment would be made.

Marking scheme

				Marks
(a)		Payments on account	1	
		Balancing repayment	1	
		Due dates	1	
				3
(b)	(i)	**Claim to reduce payments on account**		
		Payments on account	1	
		Revised liabilities	1	
				2
	(ii)	**Incorrect claim**		
		Interest	1	
		Penalty	1	
				2

(c)	Submission date	1	
	Fixed penalty	1	
	Daily penalty	1	
			3

(d)	(i)	**HMRC enquiry**		
		Notification date	1	
		Random basis	1	
		Income/Deductions	1	
				3

	(ii)	**Discovery assessment**		
		Under assessment/excessive relief	1	
		Conduct/no information	1	
				2
				15

(a) **Payment schedule**

Payments on account of 2007/08 will be based on Vera's 2006/07 income tax and Class 4 NIC payable so each payment on account will be £9,090 × 50% = £4,545.

1st payment on account due 31 January 2008 = £4,545
2nd payment on account due 31 July 2008 = £4,545

	£
Total payments on account	9,090
Total tax payable 2007/08	(6,060)
Repayment due	3,030

No set time limit for repayment to be made, but repayment supplement runs on overpaid amount.

(b) (i) **Claim to reduce payments on account**

Vera may claim to reduce her payments on account to reflect the reduction in her tax liability.

Actual tax liability @ 50% = £5,360 × 50% = £2,680

Each POA would therefore be £2,680, payable on 31 January 2008 and 31 July 2008 with a balancing payment for CGT of £700 due on 31 January 2009.

(ii) **Reduction to nil**

If Vera claimed to reduce her payments on account to nil, interest would be due on the underpaid amounts at each of the relevant dates.

Therefore she would be charged interest on the first payment of account of £2,680 from 31 January 2008 until date of payment and on the second payment of £2,680 from 31 July 2008 until date of payment.

In addition, a penalty of up to the amount of the tax due (£5,360) can be imposed if the claim is made fraudulently or negligently.

(c) **Submitting tax returns**

The latest date for submitting a tax return is 31 January following the tax year if the tax return is filed online, or 31 October following the end of the tax year if a paper return is filed. Therefore for 2007/08 the return is due on 31 January 2009 (online) or 31 October 2008 (paper).

If the return is submitted 3 months late, there will be an automatic £100 penalty. This will be reduced to the amount of tax outstanding, if any, at the submission date.

A fixed daily penalty of up to £60 per day can be imposed with approval from the Commissioners.

(d) (i) **Enquiries**

HMRC have up to 12 months from the actual filing date (if filed by the due date) in which to open an enquiry into Vera's return.

HMRC may select tax returns at random for enquiry, although most returns will be selected for a reason.

Possible reasons could include that there is a suspicion that income has been under-declared or because deductions have been incorrectly claimed.

(ii) **Discovery assessments**

HMRC may make a discovery assessment if they discover that income or chargeable gains that ought to have been assessed have not been assessed, or that an assessment to tax is or has become insufficient, or that any relief that has been given is or has become excessive.

A discovery assessment may only be raised if there has been fraudulent or negligent conduct by the taxpayer or his agent or the Officer did not have information to make him aware of the loss of tax.

14 Roger and Brigitte

Text references. Partnerships are covered in Chapter 11.

Top tips. First allocate the profits of each accounting period between the partners.

Marking scheme

	Marks
Apportionment of profits	
– period 30.6.04	1
– y/end 30.6.05	1
– y/end 30.6.06	2
– y/end 30.6.07	1
Assessable profits	
2003/04	1
2004/05	1
2005/06	1
2006/07	2
2007/08	1
	11
Overlap profits	
Roger	1
Brigitte	1
Xavier	2
	4
	15

(a) The profits of each partner are as follows.

	£	Total £	Roger £	Brigitte £	Xavier £
1.10.03 – 30.6.04		30,000	15,000	15,000	
1.7.04 – 30.6.05		45,000	22,500	22,500	
1.7.05 – 30.6.06					
1.7.05 – 30.9.05 (3/12)	12,500		6,250	6,250	
1.10.05 – 30.6.06 (9/12)	37,500		12,500	12,500	12,500
		50,000	18,750	18,750	12,500
1.7.06 – 30.6.07		60,000	20,000	20,000	20,000

The assessable profits for the tax years are, therefore, as follows.

	Roger £	Brigitte £	Xavier £
2003/04			
(1.10.03 – 5.4.04)			
£15,000 × 6/9	10,000	10,000	–
2004/05			
(1.10.03 – 30.9.04)			
£15,000 + (£22,500 × 3/12)	20,625	20,625	–
2005/06			
(1.7.04 – 30.6.05)	22,500	22,500	
(1.10.05 – 5.4.06)			
£12,500 × 6/9			8,333
2006/07			
(1.7.05 – 30.6.06)	18,750	18,750	
(1.10.05 – 30.9.06)			
£12,500 + 3/12 × £20,000			17,500
2007/08			
(1.7.06 – 30.6.07)	20,000	20,000	20,000

(b) The overlap profits for both Roger and Brigitte are:

	Profits £
1.10.03 – 5.4.04	10,000
1.7.04 – 30.9.04	5,625
	15,625

Xavier's overlap profits are:

	£
1.10.05 – 5.4.06	8,333
1.7.06 – 30.9.06	5,000
	13,333

15 Xio, Yana and Zoe

Text references. The adjustment of trading profits is covered in Chapter 7 and capital allowances in Chapter 8. Partnerships are dealt with in Chapter 11. NIC is covered in Chapter 12.

Top tips. Where a partnership changes during a period of account, any salary has to be pro-rated to the periods before and after the change.

Easy marks. The adjustment to trading profits was reasonably standard. If the correct layout for income tax computations was used, the calculation of the tax assessment was straightforward.

Again (as in many, many questions) standard proformas could be used (here capital allowances, adjustments of profits, CGT and income tax computations) to ensure mistakes were minimised and marks gained maximised.

Examiner's comments. Part (a) caused few problems, although a surprising number of candidates did not restrict the balancing allowance to the business proportion. Part (b) was also well answered, although the allocation of a salary to one of the parties for three months caused difficulty. There were a number of perfect answers to part (c).

Marking scheme

				Marks
(a)		Net profit	½	
		Depreciation	½	
		Motor expenses	1	
		Professional fees	1½	
		Repairs	1	
		Other expenses	1½	
		CAs – pool	½	
		X's car	1½	
		Y's car	1½	
		Z's car	1½	
				11
(b)		*Period ended 30 June 2007*		
		Salary	1½	
		Balance	1½	
		Period ended 5 April 2008		
		Allocation	1½	
		Totals	1½	
				6
(c)	(i)	Trading income	½	
		BSI	½	
		PA	½	
		IT liability	1	
		Class 2 NIC	½	
		Class 4 NIC	1	
				4
	(ii)	Trading income	½	
		PA	½	
		IT liability	1	
		Class 2 NIC	½	
		Class 4 NIC	1	
		CGT	2½	
				6

(iii)	Trading income	½
	Dividends	½
	PA	½
	IT liability	1½

$$\frac{3}{30}$$

(a) **Xio, Yana and Zoe – Trading profit y/e 5 April 2008**

	£	£
Net profit		36,000
Add: depreciation	12,600	
private motor expenses (40% × £19,000)	7,600	
professional fees – new lease	2,100	
new wall – capital expense	4,700	
entertaining customers	5,060	
gifts to customers – food	600	32,660
		68,660
Less capital allowances (W)		(8,660)
Trading profit		60,000

Working

	Pool £	X's car £	Y's car £	Z's car £		Allowances £
TWDV b/f	17,000	16,500	7,000	15,000		
Disposal				(12,400)		
Balancing allowance				2,600	× 60%	1,560
WDA @ 25%	(4,250)					4,250
WDA (max)		(3,000)			× 60%	1,800
WDA @ 25%			(1,750)		× 60%	1,050
TWDV c/f	12,750	13,500	5,250			
Total allowances						8,660

(b) **Trading income assessments**

	Total £	X £	Y £	Z £
P/e 30.6.07(3/12)				
Salary 3/12 × £6,000	1,500	1,500	0	0
Profits 50:30:20	13,500	6,750	4,050	2,700
	15,000	8,250	4,050	2,700
P/e 5.4.08 (9/12)				
Profits 50:50	45,000	22,500	22,500	0
Total	60,000	30,750	26,550	2,700

(c) **Income tax, NIC and CGT assessments**

(i)

Xio	Non-savings income	Savings Income	Total
	£	£	£
Trading income	30,750		
BSI £800 × 100/80		1,000	
Net income	30,750	1,000	31,750
Less PA	(5,225)		
Taxable income	25,525	1,000	26,525

	£
Tax on non-savings income	
£2,230 × 10%	223
£(25,525 – 2,230) = £23,295 × 22%	5,125
Tax on savings income	
£1,000 × 20%	200
	5,548

NIC

	£
Class 2	
£2.20 × 52	114
Class 4	
£(30,750 – 5,225) = 25,525 × 8%	2,042
Total due	2,156

(ii) *Yana*

	Non-savings/ Total
	£
Trading income/Net income	26,550
Less PA	(5,225)
Taxable income	21,325

Tax on non-savings income	
	£
£2,230 × 10%	223
£(21,325 – 2,230) = £19,095 × 22%	4,201
	4,424

NIC

	£
Class 2	
£2.20 × 52	114
Class 4	
£(26,550 – 5,225) = 21,325 × 8%	1,706
	1,820

	£
Capital gains	32,800
Less annual exemption	(9,200)
Taxable gain	23,600

CGT

	£
£(34,600 – 21,325) = £13,275 × 20%	2,655
£(23,600 – 13,275) = £10,325 × 40%	4,130
£23,600	6,785

(iii)   *Zoe*

	Non-savings £	*Dividends* £	*Total* £
Trading income	2,700		
Employment income	28,000		
Dividends £10,800 × 100/90		12,000	
Net income	30,700	12,000	42,700
Less PA	(5,225)		
Taxable income	25,475	12,000	37,475

	£
Tax on non-savings income	
£2,230 × 10%	223
£(25,475 − 2,230) = £23,245 × 22%	5,114
Tax on dividend income	
£(34,600 − 25,475) = £9,125 × 10%	913
£(12,000 − 9,125) = £2,875 × 32½%	934
	7,184

16 Wright and Wong

Text references. Chapter 5 on pensions and Chapter 11 on partnerships.

Top Tips. There is no limit on the total amount of contributions that can be made, but there is a limit on the amount qualifying for tax relief. The rules on pensions are new and hence topical for examination purposes.

Easy marks. Explaining the method of obtaining tax relief.

Marking scheme

		Marks	
(a)	Any amount	1	
	Tax relief up to earnings	1	
	Splitting partnership profits	1	
	Maximum contributions	1	
			4
(b)	Basic rate relief	1	
	Higher rate relief	1	
	Sam's liability	1½	
	Geoff's liability	1½	
			5
(c)	No need for earnings	½	
	£3,600	½	1
			10

(a)   **Maximum contributions**

Geoff and Sam can contribute any amount to their personal pension regardless of the level of their earnings. However tax relief will only be given for contributions up to their earnings for the tax year.

The partnership profits of £175,000 split 4:1 gives Geoff £140,000 profit and Sam £35,000. Therefore Geoff should contribute a maximum of £140,000 and Sam £35,000 to ensure that they receive tax relief on their contributions.

(b)   **Tax relief**

Basic rate tax relief is given through the pension holder paying contributions net of 22%. This means that they pay only 78% of the gross payment into the pension. The government pays the extra 22% on their behalf to the pension provider.

Geoff will pay £109,200 (£140,000 × 78%) and Sam will pay £27,300 (£35,000 × 78%).

In addition Geoff will be entitled to higher rate relief. This is given by extending the basic rate band for the year by the amount of the gross contribution.

Tax relief is only available for the year in which the contribution is made.

Sam's tax liability

	£
Trading profit	35,000
Personal allowance	(5,225)
Taxable income	29,775

	£
£2,230 at 10%	223
£27,545 at 22%	6,060
Tax liability	6,283

Geoff's tax liability

	£
Trading profit	140,000
Personal allowance	(5,225)
Taxable income	134,775

	£
£2,230 at 10%	223
£132,545 at 22% (note)	29,160
Tax liability	29,383

Note. Higher rate tax relief will be given by extending Geoff's basic rate tax band for 2007/08 to £174,600 (34,600 + 140,000).

(c)   **No earnings**

There is no need for the individual to have earnings. A contribution of up to £3,600 per tax year may be made into a pension regardless of the level of earnings.

17 Amy Bwalya

Text references. Chapter 9 for sole trader basis period rules. Chapter 11 for partnerships.

Top tips. It is easier to get marks if you set out the rules as well as the dates – that way if you make a silly mistake the examiner can see that you know the rules.

Marking scheme

			Marks
(a)	2005/06	1	
	2006/07	2	
	2007/08	1	
	Overlap profits	1	
			5

(b)　6.4.07 – 31.12.07

Interest	1	
Salary	1	
Split balance	1	
1.1.08 – 5.4.08		
Interest	½	
Salary	½	
Split balance	½	
Totals for each partner	½	
		5

(c)

2005/06	1	
2006/07 year of change		
9m to 30.6.06	½	
Add 3m from prior year	1	
2007/08 year of cessation		
Profits not yet taxed	1½	
Less: overlap from start	½	
Less: overlap from change of accounting date	½	
		5
		15

(a)　Amy's trading profits

	£	£
2005/06		
1 August 2005 – 5 April 2006		
$^8/_{10} \times £38,500$		30,800
2006/07		
<12m so tax 1st 12 months of trade		
1 August 2005 – 31 July 2006		
10m to 31 May 2006	38,500	
$+ ^2/_{12} \times £52,800$	8,800	
		47,300
2007/08		
CYB y/e 31 May 2007		52,800
Overlap profits		
1 August 2005 – 5 April 2006	30,800	
1 June 2006 – 31 July 2006	8,800	
10 months		39,600

(b) Cedric, Eli & Gordon's trading profits

	Total £	C £	E £	G £
6 April 2007 – 31 December 2007				
Interest: $^9/_{12}$ × capital @ 10%	8,250	3,000	5,250	
Salary: $^9/_{12}$ × 6,000	4,500		4,500	
Balance: 60:40	54,750	32,850	21,900	
Total: $^9/_{12}$ × 90,000	67,500	35,850	31,650	
1 January 2008 – 5 April 2008				
Interest: $^3/_{12}$ × capital @ 10%	2,250		1,750	500
Salary: $^3/_{12}$ × 6,000	1,500		1,500	
Balance: 70:30	18,750		13,125	5,625
Total: $^3/_{12}$ × 90,000	22,500		16,375	6,125
Total	90,000	35,850	48,025	6,125

Trading income assessments:

Cedric	£35,850
Eli	£48,025
Gordon	£6,125

(c) Ivan's trading profits

	£	£
2005/06		
CYB y/e 30 September 2005		36,000
2006/07		
Year of change		
9m to 30 June 2006	23,400	
+ 3m from previous yr: 3/12 × 36,000	9,000	
Total 12m		32,400
2007/08		
Year of cessation of trade		
Tax everything not already taxed		
Y/e 30 June 2007	28,800	
6m to 31 December 2007	10,800	
Less: overlap		
(i) From start of business	(4,500)	
(ii) From change of accounting date	(9,000)	
		26,100

18 Preparation question: gains

Computation of taxable gains

	Business assets (25%) £	Non business assets (60%) £
Factory (W1)	75,000	
Painting (W2)		19,350
Less loss relief (W3)	(1,650)	(19,350)
Gains before taper relief	73,350	Nil

Gains after taper relief

	£
£73,350 @ 25%	18,338
Less annual exemption	(9,200)
Taxable gains	9,138

CGT

	£
£8,825 @ 20% (W4)	1,765
£313 @ 40%	125
£9,138	
CGT due	1,890

Workings

1   *Factory*

	£
Proceeds	225,000
Less cost	(150,000)
Gain	75,000

Number of complete years for taper relief (1 July 2003 – 30 June 2007) = 4 years business asset

2   *Painting*

Transfer to Emily on 1 July 2002 on no gain/no loss basis

	£
Cost to Arthur	50,000
Indexation allowance March 1996 to April 1998 (= 0.073) × £50,000	3,650
Base cost for Emily	53,650

Sale by Emily

	£
Proceeds	73,000
Less cost	(53,650)
Gain	19,350

Complete years for taper relief (including ownership by spouse) (6 April 1998 – 5 April 2007 = 9 years plus additional year = 10 years) (NBA)

3   *Vase*

	£
Proceeds	19,000
Less cost	(40,000)
Loss	(21,000)

Indexation cannot increase a loss.

4   *Available basic rate band*

	£
Net income	32,000
Less PA	(5,225)
	26,775
Less basic rate band	
£34,600 + (£780 × 100/78)	(35,600)
20% band remaining	8,825

19 Irene Cutter

> **Text references.** Chargeable gains are covered in Chapters 13, 14, 15, 16 and 17.
>
> **Top tips.** Do a working for each asset and then summarise your findings in the CGT computation. Make sure that you reference in your workings carefully to help the examiner.

		Marks
(a)	**Gains**	
	Building	
	Gain	1
	Gift relief	1
	Vase	
	Gain	1
	Chattels rule	1
	Taper relief	½
	Shares	
	FA85 pool	1
	Indexation	1
	Rights issue	1
	Gain	1
	Taper relief	½
	Land	
	Part disposal	1
	Gain	1
	Taper relief	½
	Car – exempt	1
	Set off loss	1
	Apply taper relief	1
	Annual exemption	1
	CGT rates	1½
	Due date	1
		18
(b)	**Gift relief**	
	Base cost for daughter	1
	Claim deadline	1
		2
		20

(a) **Summary of gains**

	Non-business taper		
	(4 years)	*(6 years)*	*(10 years)*
	£	£	£
Building (W1)	–	–	–
Vase (W2)	500		
Shares (W3)			52,053
Land (W4)		58,393	
Less loss relief	(500)	(13,500)	
Net gains	Nil	44,893	52,053
Gains after taper relief @ 80%		35,914	
@ 60%			31,232

	£
Gains after taper relief £(35,914 + 31,232)	67,146
Less annual exemption	(9,200)
Taxable gains	57,946

	£
Tax due	
£2,230 × 10%	223
£32,370 × 20%	6,474
£23,346 × 40%	9,338
Total tax due by 31 January 2009	16,035

Note. Cars are exempt assets for CGT purposes.

Workings

1   *Building*

	£
Proceeds	90,000
Less cost	(40,940)
Gain before taper relief	49,060
Less deferred by gift relief	(49,060)
Gain chargeable now	Nil

2   *Vase*

	£
Proceeds	6,300
Less cost	(2,800)
Gain before taper relief	3,500
Restricted to: 5/3 × (6,300 − 6,000)	500

Taper relief years (December 2003 − December 2007) = 4 years for a non-business asset

3   *Shares*

	No. of shares	Cost	Indexed cost
		£	£
Acquisition August 1986	6,000	12,000	12,000
Indexed pool @ 4.98			19,947
Rights 1 for 3 @ £5 (9.99)	2,000	10,000	10,000
	8,000	22,000	29,947
Sale September 2007	(8,000)	(22,000)	(29,947)
Carried forward	Nil	Nil	Nil

Gain

	£
Proceeds	82,000
Less cost	(22,000)
Unindexed gain	60,000
Less indexation allowance £(29,947 – 22,000)	(7,947)
Gain before taper relief	52,053

Taper relief years (6 April 1998 – 5 April 2007 = 9 years plus bonus year) = 10 years for non–business assets.

4   *Part disposal of land*

	£
Proceeds	78,000
Less cost: £45,750 × $\dfrac{78,000}{78,000+104,000}$	(19,607)
Gain before taper relief	58,393

Taper relief years (March 2001 – November 2007) = 6 years for non–business assets.

(b)   Irene's daughter's base cost for the building gifted to her is:

	£
Market value	90,000
Less gain deferred	(49,060)
Base cost c/f	40,940

The claim for gift relief must be made by 31 January nearly 6 years after the year the gain was made, ie by 31 January 2014.

20 Stephanie Wood

Text references. Chapters 13 to 17 deal with chargeable gains.

Top tips. There are only a few reliefs that are examinable in the F6 paper: rollover relief, gift relief, PPR relief and the final relief, taper relief. Learn when they apply, for example, which assets the relief applies to, so that you can spot when they are available.

Marking scheme

	Marks
Shares	
Post April 1998 holding	1
Rights issue	1
FA85 pool	1½
Indexation	1
Gains	1
Taper relief	½
House	
Gain	½
Indexation	½
PPR relief	2
Lettings relief	1½
Taper relief	½
Painting	
Chattels rule	1

Land

Part disposal	1
Gain	½
Taper relief	½
Vase	
Chattels rule	1
Set off loss – current year	½
– brought forward	½
Apply taper relief	1½
Annual exemption	1
CGT rates	1½
	20

Summary of gains 2007/08

	Business assets ≥ 2 years £	Non-business assets 10 years £	8 years £
North Seaton Ltd Shares (W1) (a)	6,000		
(b)	6,680		
96 Burnside Close (W2)		7,884	
Land (W4)			17,417
Vase (W5)			4,600
Less current year loss (painting) (W3)			(2,280)
	12,680	7,884	19,737
Less losses b/fwd			(1,833)
Gains before taper relief	12,680	7,884	17,904

Gain after taper relief

	£
Business assets (≥2 years)	
£12,680 @ 25%	3,170
Non-business assets (10 years/8 years)	
£7,884 @ 60%	4,730
£17,904 @ 70%	12,533
Total chargeable gains	20,433
Less: annual exemption	(9,200)
Taxable gains	11,233
CGT @ 40%	4,493

Workings

1   *Shares in North Seaton Ltd*

    (a)   *Match with post April 1998 shares*

	No of shares	Cost £
August 1999	1,000	1,400
Rights issue December 1999 1:2 @ £2	500	1,000
	1,500	2,400

        Gain

	£
Proceeds (1,500/3,000 × £16,800)	8,400
Less cost (above)	(2,400)
Gain before taper relief	6,000

    August 1999 to July 2007 = 7 years of business asset taper relief.

    (b)   *Match with shares in FA 1985 pool*

	No of shares	Indexed cost £	Cost £
January 1992 purchase	2,000	1,200	1,200
Indexed to April 1998			1,439
Rights issue December 1999 1:2 @ £2	1,000	2,000	2,000
	3,000	3,200	3,439
Sale July 2007	(1,500)	(1,600)	(1,720)
Carried forward	1,500	1,600	1,719

        Gain

	£
Proceeds (1,500/ 3,000 × £16,800)	8,400
Less indexed cost	(1,720)
Gain before taper relief	6,680

    April 1998 to July 2007 = 9 years of business asset taper relief.

2   *96 Burnside Close*

	£
Gross Proceeds	150,000
Less agents commission	(1,750)
	148,250
Less cost	(25,000)
	123,250
Less indexation £25,000 × 0.620	(15,500)
Indexed gain	107,750
Less PPR relief (see below)	(60,445)
	47,305
Less lettings relief (see below)	(39,421)
Gain before taper relief	7,884

PPR relief

	Occupation	Absence	Letting
Mar 1987 – Aug 1995	8½		
Sept 1995 – Feb 1997		1½	
Mar 1997 – Aug 2004			7½
Sept 2004 – Aug 2007*	3		
	11½	1½	7½

* Last 3 years of ownership

PPR relief: £107,750 × 11½ /20½ = £60,445

Lettings relief:

Lower of:

(a)   PPR relief = £60,445

(b)   Gain in let period, ie £107,750 × 7½/20½ = £39,421; or

(c)   Maximum = £40,000

April 1998 to August 2007 = 10 years (9 + 1) of non-business asset taper relief.

3   *Painting*

	£
Deemed proceeds	6,000
Less incidental costs of disposal	(280)
	5,720
Less cost	(8,000)
Allowable loss	(2,280)

4   *Part disposal of land*

	£
Proceeds	19,000
Less cost: £12,000 × $\dfrac{19,000}{19,000+125,000}$	(1,583)
Gain before taper relief	17,417

January 2000 to March 2008 = 8 years for non–business assets.

5   *Vase*

	£
Sale proceeds	9,000
Less cost	(4,400)
Gain before taper relief	4,600
Restricted to: 5/3 × (9,000 – 6,000)	5,000

ie take lower gain of £4,600

April 1999 to April 2007 = 8 years for non–business assets.

21 Anita Patel

> **Text references.** Chapters 13-17 cover chargeable gains.
>
> **Top tips**. Where you are asked to calculate both income tax and CGT make sure that you deal with the taxation of the income first, followed by CGT. You can, of course, do your workings in any order. Make sure you reference your workings in carefully.

Marking scheme

	Marks
Painting	
Gain	½
Indexation	½
Chattels rule	1
Taper relief	½
Necklace – compensation	
Gain	½
Defer gain	1
Base cost of replacement	½
Horse – exempt	1
Warehouse	
Gain	½
Rollover relief	½
Gain remaining chargeable	1
Taper relief	½
Land	
Gain	½
Part disposal re cost	1
Indexation	½
Taper relief	½
Thimble collection	
Chattels rule	1
Set off loss – current year	½
– brought forward	½
Apply taper relief	1
Annual exemption	1
Income	½
PA	½
Tax bands	½
Income tax rates	½
Basic rate band remaining	½
CGT rates	1
Due dates	1
No payments on account for 2008/09	1
	20

CGT Summary

	25% Business £	60% Non-business £
Antique Painting (W1)		5,732
Necklace (W2)	–	–
Horse (W3)	–	–
Warehouse (W4)	10,000	
Field (W5)		23,844
Thimble collection (W6)		(2,000)
Less loss b/f		(4,000)
	10,000	23,576
Gain after TR 25%/60%	2,500	14,146
Total gain (2,500 + 14,146)		16,646
Less AE		(9,200)
Taxable gain		7,446

	£
Income £(15,000 + 10,000)	25,000
Less PA	(5,225)
	19,775

	£
£2,230 @ 10%	223
£17,545 @ 22%	3,860
IT payable	4,083
Less PAYE	(3,769)
Income tax due 31 January 2009	314

Payment on account for 2008/09 are not due as > 80% of the tax liability is covered by tax deducted at source.

BR band left £34,600 – 19,775 = £14,825

CGT payable (£7,446 @ 20%) = £1,489 due 31 January 2009

Workings

1   *Antique painting*

	£
Proceeds after selling costs	10,000
Less cost	(4,000)
	6,000
Less IA 0.067 × 4,000	(268)
	5,732

or 5/3 × (10,200 – 6,000) = £7,000

Take smaller gain ie £5,732

TR: April 1998 to August 2007 = 9 years plus additional year = 10 years non-business, ie 60%

2   *Necklace*

	£
Proceeds	12,000
Less cost	(10,000)
Gain	2,000
Less deferred as insurance proceeds fully reinvested	(2,000)
Gain chargeable now	Nil

Note. Gain deferred reduces base cost of replacement necklace:

109

	£
Cost	12,000
Less gain deferred	(2,000)
Base cost of replacement necklace c/f	10,000

3 *Horse is exempt (wasting chattel)*

4 *Warehouse*

	£
Proceeds	246,000
Less cost	(172,000)
Gain	74,000
Less rollover relief (balancing figure)	(64,000)
Gain before taper relief (see below)	10,000

TR: April 1999 to February 2008 = 8 years business, ie 25%

Rollover relief is available as the period for reinvestment is one year before the disposal of the original asset and three years after that disposal.

The gain that remains chargeable is the amount of proceeds received that have not been reinvested in the purchase of the replacement asset, ie (£246,000 – £236,000) = £10,000.

5 *Field*

	£
Proceeds	30,000
Less cost = $10,000 \times \dfrac{30,000}{30,000+20,000}$	(6,000)
	24,000
Less IA 0.026	(156)
	23,844

TR: April 1998 to March 2008 = 9 years plus additional year = 10 years non-business, ie 60%

6 *Thimble collection*

	£
Proceeds (deemed)	6,000
Less cost = probate value	(8,000)
Allowable loss	(2,000)

22 Jack Chan

Text references. Chapters 13 to 17 on CGT.

Top tips. You should set the brought forward loss against the gain that suffers the lowest rate of taper relief. This is the most advantageous way of relieving the loss.

	Marks
Goodwill	
Gift relief	2
Gain chargeable after taper	1
Office	
Gift relief	2
Warehouse	
Gain	1
No gift relief	1
No taper relief	1
Car – exempt	1
Picture	
Gain	½
Indexation	½
NBA taper relief	½
Shares	
Bonus issue	1
NBA taper relief	½
Plot of land	
Part disposal	1
Gain	½
NBA taper relief	½
Set off loss	1
Taper relief	1
Annual exemption	1
CGT	2
Due date	1
	20

Total gains

	BA (25%) £	NBA (100%) £	NBA (60%) £	NBA (85%) £
Goodwill (W1)	50,000			
Office (W2)		–		
Warehouse (W3)		45,000		
Car (W4)		–		
Picture (W5)			19,150	
Shares (W6)				8,000
Land (W7)				26,317
Less loss brought forward		(6,100)		
	50,000	38,900	19,150	34,317
Gain after taper relief 25%/ 60%/ 85%	12,500	38,900	11,490	29,169
Total gains after taper relief				92,059
Less annual exemption				(9,200)
Taxable gains				82,859

CGT

	£
£9,100 (£34,600 – £25,500) × 20%	1,820
£73,759 × 40%	29,504
£82,859	
CGT due on 31 January 2009	31,324

Workings

1   *Goodwill*

	£
Market value	60,000
Less cost	(Nil)
	60,000
Less gift relief	(10,000)
Gain immediately chargeable	50,000

The amount paid for the goodwill exceeds allowable cost by £50,000, so £50,000 is immediately chargeable. The goodwill is a business asset that has been owned for more than 2 years, so 25% of the gain remains chargeable after taper relief.

2   *Office*

	£
Market value	130,000
Less cost	(110,000)
	20,000
Less gift relief	(20,000)
Gain immediately chargeable	–

As the amount paid for the office was less than the allowable cost, gift relief is available to defer the whole gain arising.

3   *Warehouse*

	£
Market value	140,000
Less cost	(95,000)
Gain chargeable	45,000

This is a non-business asset held for two years only, so no taper relief is due. In addition, gift relief is not available to defer a gain on a non-business asset.

4   *Motor car*

The motor car is an exempt asset, so no gain or loss arises.

5   *Picture*

	£
Proceeds	30,000
Less cost	(10,000)
Less indexation 0.085 × £10,000	(850)
Gain chargeable	19,150

TR: April 1998 to May 2007 = 9 years plus additional year = 10 years non-business, ie 60%

6   *Shares*

	Shares	£
Purchase January 2002	10,000	8,000
Bonus issue: 1 for 5	2,000	–
Gain chargeable	12,000	8,000

	£
Proceeds	16,000
Less cost	(8,000)
Gain chargeable	8,000

TR: January 2002 to June 2007 = 5 years non-business, ie 85%

A bonus issue is an issue of free shares in proportion to an existing shareholding. As they are free shares, there is no cost – instead the original cost is allocated to all of the shares held.

7   *Land*

		£
Proceeds		45,600
Less cost £125,000 × $\dfrac{45,600}{45,600+250,000}$		(19,283)
Gain chargeable		26,317

TR: May 2002 to November 2007 = 5 years non-business, ie 85%

Where there is a part disposal of an asset the original cost must be apportioned between the part being sold and the remainder.

23 Chandra Khan

Text references. Chapters 13 to 17 on CGT.

Top tips. With a question in parts like this one, always ensure that you attempt an answer to each part. The best way of maximising marks is usually to allocate your time carefully between the separate parts of the question.

Marking scheme

			Marks
(a)	Deemed proceeds	1	
	Gain immediately chargeable	2	
	Gift relief	1	
	Gain after taper relief	1	
			5
(b)	Gain before taper relief	1	
	Gain qualifying for rollover relief	2	
	Gain immediately chargeable	1	
	Gain after taper relief	1	
			5
(c)	Gain on goodwill	1	
	Allocation	1	
	Incorporation relief	1	
	Gain after taper relief	1	
			4
(d)	Gain before taper relief	1	
	Actual occupation	1	
	Deemed occupation: 3 years for any reason	1	
	Deemed occupation: last 3 years	1	
	Lettings relief	1	
	Gain after taper relief	1	
			6
			20

(a)

	£
Deemed disposal proceeds (MV)	110,000
Less cost	(38,000)
	72,000
Immediately chargeable (£75,000 – £38,000)	(37,000)
Gain held over by gift relief	35,000
Gain chargeable before taper relief	£37,000

The shares are a business asset that has been held for more than 2 years, so after taper relief 25% of the gain is chargeable.

Gain after taper relief (25% × £37,000) = £9,250

Notes

(1)   Deemed disposal proceeds equal the market value of the shares because Chandra's daughter is a connected person.

(2)   The amount immediately chargeable is the amount by which proceeds exceed allowable cost.

(b)

	£
Sale proceeds	146,000
Less indexed cost	(72,000)
Gain before taper relief	74,000

Business proportion (75%) = £55,500

All of the proceeds of the business proportion of the factory (£146,000 × 75% = £109,500) are reinvested in the new factory. This means that all of the £55,500 gain can be rolled over into the base cost of the new factory.

Gain on non-business proportion (25%) = £18,500

This gain cannot be rolled over. However taper relief is due as the factory had been held for 9 years plus the additional year for non-business assets held before 6 April 1998.

Gain after taper relief (60% × £18,500) = £11,100

(c)

	£
Disposal proceeds	100,000
Less: cost	–
Gain on incorporation	100,000

Shares $\dfrac{200,000}{250,000} \times £100,000 = £80,000$

Cash $\dfrac{50,000}{250,000} \times £100,000 = £20,000$

£20,000 of the gain is allocated to the cash consideration and is immediately chargeable.

As the business was owned for one complete year, 50% of this gain was chargeable after taper relief, ie £10,000.

Incorporation relief automatically rolls the gain allocated to the shares into the base cost of the shares for CGT purposes.

(d)

	£
Disposal proceeds	350,000
Less cost	(100,000)
	250,000
Less Indexation 0.369 × £100,000	(36,900)
Gain	213,100
Less PPR relief (note 1) £213,100 × 10/18	(118,389)
	94,711
Less lettings relief (note 2)	(40,000)
Gain before taper relief	54,711

TR: April 1998 to December 2007 = 9 years plus additional year = 10 years for non-business asset

Gain after taper relief (60% × £54,711) = £32,827.

Notes

(1)   *PPR periods*

	Occupation (years)	Non-occupation (years)
1.12.89 – 1.12.92 – actual occupation	3	
1.12.92 – 1.12.97 – 3 years deemed occupation for any reason	3	2
1.12.97 – 1.12.98 – actual occupation	1	
1.12.98 – 1.12.04 – let		6
1.12.04 – 1.12.07 – last 36 months (always deemed occupation)	3	
	10	8

Deemed occupation rules only apply if there is actual occupation both before and after the period of absence. This rule does not apply to the last 36 months rule – this is always a period of deemed occupation.

(2)   *Lettings relief*

Relief available is the lower of:

		£
(i)	PPR relief	118,389
(ii)	Gain in the let period: £213,100 × 6/18	71,033
(iii)	Maximum	40,000

ie £40,000

24 Sophia Tang

Text references. Chapters 13 to 17 on CGT.

Top tips. You can answer the final part of the requirement (about the due date for CGT) first. This will ensure that you do not forget to answer this part and lose an easy mark.

Easy marks. The gains on disposals were not difficult to calculate and you were told that Sophia was a 40% taxpayer making the computation of CGT very easy.

Examiner's comments. Confusion over basics (taper relief, indexation, annual exemption, gift relief given incorrectly).

Marking scheme

	Marks
Shop – MV/cost	1
– gift relief	1½
– taper relief	1
Warehouse – MV/cost	1
– indexation	1
– taper relief	1
Gum plc shares – Match with (i) Sept 2007 shares	1
(ii) Feb 2008 shares (Sept 99)	1
(ii) Feb 2008 shares (FA 85 Pool)	1½
– taper relief	1
House – indexed gain	1
– actual occupation	1
– deemed occupation	1
– lettings relief	1
– taper relief	1
Best use of brought forward loss	1
AE	1
CGT	1
Due date	1
	20

Sophia Tang

	BA (25%) £	NBA (60%) £	NBA (70%) £
Shop (W1)	47,000		
Warehouse (W2)		104,900	
Gum plc shares (W3) – (i)			3,000
– (ii)			4,000
– (iii)		2,097	
House (W4)		151,191	
Total gains	47,000	258,188	7,000
Less loss b/f		(5,350)	(7,000)
GBT	47,000	252,838	Nil
Gain after taper relief @ 25%/ 60%	11,750	151,703	
Total gains after taper relief		163,453	
Less annual exemption		(9,200)	
Taxable gains		154,253	

CGT @ 40% due 31 January 2009 = £61,701

Workings

1   *Shop*

	£
Market value	260,000
Less: cost	(113,000)
Gain	147,000
Excess sale proceeds over cost £(160,000 – 113,000) chargeable	(47,000)
Gain held over under gift relief	100,000

Gain chargeable = £47,000

Taper relief ownership period (1 July 2002 to 31 March 2008) = 2+ years for a business asset, ie 25%

2   *Warehouse*

	£
Market value	225,000
Less cost	(70,000)
Unindexed gain	155,000
Less indexation allowance to April 1998	(50,100)
Indexed gain	104,900

No gift relief is available as the asset is not used in the business.

Taper relief ownership period (6 April 1998 to 5 April 2007) = 9 years plus bonus year = 10 years for a non-business asset, ie 60%

3   *Gum plc shares*

(i)   Match with September 1999

	£
Proceeds (September 2007)	6,000
Less cost (note 1) £6 × 500	(3,000)
Gain before taper relief	3,000

Taper relief ownership period (1 September 1999 to 10 September 2007) = 8 years for a non-business asset, ie 70%

(ii)   Match with September 1999

	£
Proceeds (February 2008) 500/700 × £9,800	7,000
Less cost (note 2) £6 × 500	(3,000)
Gain before taper relief	4,000

Taper relief ownership period (September 1999 to February 2008) = 8 years for a non-business asset, ie 70%

(iii)   Match with FA85 Pool

	£
Proceeds (February 2008) 200/700 × £9,800	2,800
Less cost (notes 2 and 3)	(600)
Unindexed gain	2,200
Less indexation allowance £(703 – 600)	(103)
Gain before taper relief	2,097

Taper relief ownership period (6 April 1998 to 5 April 2007) = 9 years plus bonus year = 10 years for a non-business asset, ie 60%

Notes

1   *Share matching*

	£	£
Shares sold September 2007		500
Match with September 1999 shares	1,000	
Less matched shares (i)	(500)	(500)
Carried forward	500	Nil

2   *Share matching*

	£	£
Shares sold February 2008		700
Match with September 1999 shares (balance)	500	
Less matched shares (ii)	(500)	(500)
	Nil	200
Match with FA85 pool (see note 3)	400	
Less matched shares (iii)	(200)	(200)
Carried forward	200	Nil

3   *FA85 Pool*

	No of shares	Cost	Indexed Cost
		£	£
Purchase July 1992	400	1,200	1,200
Indexed to April 1998			1,405
Disposal February 2008	(200)	(600)	(703)
Carried forward	200	600	702

4   *House*

	£
Disposal proceeds	350,000
Less cost	(35,000)
	315,000
Less: Indexation 0.596 × £35,000	(20,860)
Gain	294,140
Less: PPR relief (note 1) £294,140 × 7/20	(102,949)
	191,191
Less: lettings relief (note 2)	(40,000)
Gain before taper relief	151,191

TR: April 1998 to June 2007 = 9 years plus additional year = 10 years for non-business asset.

Notes

1   *PPR periods*

	Occupation (years)	Non-Occupation (years)
June 1987 – June 1991 – actual occupation	4	
June 1991 – June 2004 – let		13
June 2004 – June 2007 – last 36 months	3	
	7	13

The last 36 months of ownership is always treated as a period of deemed occupation.

2   *Lettings relief*

Relief available is the lower of:

			£
(i)	PPR relief		102,949
(ii)	Gain in the let period: £294,140 × 13/20		191,191
(iii)	Maximum		40,000

ie £40,000

25 Carolyn Kraft

Text references. Chapters 2, 12, and 13 to 17 are required reading for this question.

Top tips. The requirement is already helpfully broken down, so first of all deal with the part you know best to pick up marks early on and boost your confidence. You can really improve your presentation by starting each requirement on a new page. However, do not spend too much time on any one requirement – use the mark allocation as an indication of how much time to spend on each. Finally, do not miss out on the easy marks available for stating payment dates – you could even answer these parts of the relevant requirements first so you don't forget.

Marking scheme

			Marks
(a)	*Income tax – Carolyn*		
	Salary	½	
	Interest	½	
	PA	½	
	Tax bands	1	
	Extension of basic rate band	½	
	Tax rates	½	
	Deduct PAYE	½	
	Deduct tax credit on interest	½	
	Due date	½	
	Income tax – Mike		
	Profits less CAs	½	
	Dividends	½	
	PA	½	
	Tax bands	1	
	Extension of basic rate band	½	
	Tax rates	½	
	Deduct tax credit on dividends	½	
	Due date	½	
	POAs – amounts	½	
	– dates	1	
			11
(b)	*NIC – Carolyn*		
	Class 1	1½	
	NIC – Mike		
	Class 2	1	
	Class 4	1½	
			4

(c) *CGT – Carolyn*

Proceeds less cost	1
Enhancement expenditure	1
No taper relief	1
AE	½
Tax rate	½
Due date	½

CGT – Mike

Proceeds less cost	1
Taper relief	1
AE	½
Tax rate	½
Due date	½

8

(d)		
	Rollover relief	½
	Time period	½
	Reinvestment of proceeds	½
	Taper earned to date is lost	½

2
25

(a) **Income tax calculations**

Carolyn

	Non-savings income £	Savings income £
Salary	32,600	
Bank interest (£8,000 × 100/80)		10,000
Net income	32,600	10,000
Less PA	(5,225)	
Taxable income	27,375	10,000

Tax

	£
£2,230 × 10%	223
£25,145 × 22%	5,532
£7,225 × 20%	1,445
£1,000 × 20% (W1)	200
£1,775 × 40%	710
Total tax liability	8,110
Less tax credits	
(i) PAYE	(5,366)
(ii) Interest: £10,000 @ 20%	(2,000)
Tax due by 31 January 2009	744

Mike

	Non-savings income £	Dividend income £
Trade profit (W2)	51,800	
Dividends £9,000 × 100/90		10,000
Net income	51,800	10,000
Less PA	(5,225)	
Taxable income	46,575	10,000

Tax

	£
£2,230 × 10%	223
£32,370 × 22%	7,121
£4,000 × 22% (W3)	880
£7,975 × 40%	3,190
£10,000 × 32.5%	3,250
Total tax liability	14,664
Less: tax credit on dividends: £10,000 @ 10%	(1,000)
Tax due 31 January 2009	13,664

Mike also needs to make payments on account as more than 20% of his tax is **not** collected at source:

	£
1ˢᵗ POA: 50% × £13,664	6,832
Total due 31 January 2009	20,496
2ⁿᵈ POA: due 31 July 2009	6,832

Workings

1   *Carolyn's basic rate band*

Extend by gross donation: £780 × 100/78 = £1,000

2   *Mike's taxable trading profits*

	£
Adjusted profit	53,400
Less capital allowances	(1,600)
Taxable trade profits	51,800

3   *Mike's basic rate band*

Extend by gross pension contribution: (£260 × 12) × 100/78 = £4,000

(b)   **National Insurance contributions 2007/08**

(i)   *Carolyn*

Class 1 primary contributions
First   £5,225 @ 0%

£27,375 @ 11%	£3,011
£32,600 (below UEL)	

(ii)   *Mike*

	£
Class 2	
£2.20 × 52	114
Class 4	
£(34,840 − 5,225) = £29,615 @ 8%	2,369
£(51,800 − 34,840) = £16,960 @ 1%	170
	2,539

121

(c) **Capital gains tax**

    (i) *Carolyn*

	£
Proceeds	250,000
Less: cost	(180,000)
Renovation (enhancement expenditure)	(30,000)
Gain	40,000
No taper relief – not owned three years (non business asset)	
Less annual exemption	(9,200)
	30,800
CGT @ 40% due 31 January 2009	12,320

    (ii) *Mike*

	£
Proceeds	85,000
Less cost	(53,300)
Gain before taper relief	31,700

	£
Gain after taper relief	
10 April 2006 – 9 April 2007 = 1 year for business asset (50% × £31,700)	15,850
Less AE	(9,200)
	6,650

    CGT @ 40% due 31 January 2009 = £2,660

(d) **Available relief**

    (i) Mike can claim 'rollover' relief for reinvestment into replacement business assets.

    (ii) He must invest in the new shop within three years of the disposal of the original shop.

    (iii) If any proceeds are not reinvested they will be chargeable immediately and only the balance of the gain can be deferred.

    (iv) Any taper relief earned on the original shop is lost.

26 Peter Shaw

Text references. Chapters 13 to 17 on CGT.

Top tips. Where you are asked to calculate both income tax and CGT make sure that you deal with the taxation of the income first, followed by CGT. You can, of course, do your workings in any order. Make sure you reference your workings in carefully.

Marking scheme

	Marks
Building	
Gain	½
Taper relief	½
Takeover	
Gain on cash received	1½
No gain on shares	1
Taper relief	½
Shares	
FA85 pool	2
Gain	½
Taper relief	½
Vase	
Gain	½
Chattels rule	1
Taper relief	½
Cartoon	
Chattels rule	1
Plant	
Chattels rule	1
Taper relief	½
Set off loss – current year	1
– brought forward	1
Apply taper relief	1
Annual exemption	1
PAA	1½
Tax bands	1
Basic rate band remaining	1
CGT rates	1
	20

Summary of gains:

	Business assets (25%) £	(65%) £	Non business assets (60%) £	(80%) £
Building (W1)	400,000			
Forum Follies plc (W2)		5,000		
Dassau plc (W3)			5,836	
Vase (W4(a))				3,333
Plant (W4(c))	3,200			
	403,200	5,000	5,836	3,333
Less loss on cartoon (W4(b))				(1,200)
Less losses b/f		(4,267)		(2,133)
Gains before taper relief	403,200	733	5,836	Nil
Gains after taper relief	100,800	476	3,502	

	£
Total gains after taper relief	104,778
Less annual exemption	(9,200)
Taxable gain	95,578

BPP LEARNING MEDIA

	£
CGT	
£22,650 @ 20% (W7)	4,530
£72,928 @ 40%	29,171
CGT due 31 January 2009	33,701

Workings

1   *Building*

	£
Proceeds	600,000
Less cost	(200,000)
Gain before taper relief	400,000

January 2001 to April 2007 = 6 years for business asset, ie 25% chargeable

Any asset let to an unquoted trading company qualifies as a business asset.

2   *The takeover of Forum Follies plc*

The elements in the takeover consideration have the following values:

	£
Ordinary shares (30,000 × £3.00)	90,000
Cash	10,000
Total consideration received	100,000

A gain only arises on the date of the takeover in respect of the cash element of the takeover consideration. The gain in respect of the shares received is deferred until those shares are sold.

	£
Cash received (above)	10,000
Cost £50,000 × 10,000/100,000	(5,000)
Gain before taper	5,000

June 1998 to March 2008 = 9 years for non-business asset, ie 65% chargeable

3   *Dassau plc shares*

(i)   The 1985 pool

	Shares	Indexed cost	Cost
		£	£
December 1984	1,000	2,000	2,000
Indexed to April 1988			3,580
Rights issue April 2000 1:2 @ £2	500	1,000	1,000
	1,500	3,000	4,580
Disposal November 2007	(1,200)	(2,400)	(3,664)
	300	600	916

		£
(ii)	Proceeds	9,500
	Less cost	(2,400)
	Indexation allowance £(3,664 – 2,400)	(1,264)
	Indexed gain	5,836

6 April 1998 to November 2007 = 9 years plus additional year for non- business asset, ie 60% chargeable

4   (a)   *Ming vase*

	£
Proceeds	8,000
Allowable cost	(2,000)
Gain before taper relief	6,000

Gain cannot exceed 5/3 × (8,000 − 6,000) = <u>3,333</u>, ie £3,333

September 2000 to August 2007 = 6 years for non- business asset, ie 80% chargeable

     (b)   *Leonardo cartoon*

	£
Proceeds (deemed)	6,000
Allowable cost	(7,200)
Allowable loss	(1,200)

Indexation cannot increase a loss

     (c)   *Plant*

As the plant is sold at a gain, any capital allowances that may have been given will be clawed back by way of a balancing charge. Any profit is charged as a capital gain:

	£
Proceeds	8,500
Allowable cost	(5,300)
Gain before taper relief	3,200

Restrict to 5/3 × £(8,500 − 6,000) = <u>£4,167</u>

Restriction does not apply.

March 2000 to August 2007 = 7 years for business asset, ie 25% chargeable

5   *Basic rate band*

	£
Interest (× 100/80)	7,500
Dividends (× 100/90)	12,000
Net income	19,500
Less PAA > 65 (no restriction as Net income < £20,900)	(7,550)
Taxable income	11,950
Less basic rate band	(34,600)
20% band remaining	22,650

27 Paul Opus

Text references. Chapters 13 to 17 for CGT.

Top tips. There is no reason why you cannot do the workings first and then feed the results into a summary table. Make sure that when you put your answer together that the summary is on top – followed by the workings.

Marking scheme

			Marks
Symphony Ltd	– Proceeds		½
	– Cost		1
	– Taper relief		1½
Concerto plc	– Proceeds		2
	– Cost		½
	– Indexation		1
	– Taper relief		1½
Motor car			½
Antique vase			2
House	– Proceeds		½
	– Cost		½
	– Exemption		2
	– Taper relief		1
Land	– Proceeds		½
	– Cost		2
Holiday cottage			1
Annual exemption			½
Capital gains tax			1
Due date			½
			20

Paul Opus – 2007/08 CGT Liability

Summary

	NBA 100% £	NBA 80% £	NBA 60% £	BA 50% £
Symphony Ltd shares (W1)				9,800
Concerto Plc shares (W2)			34,720	
Car – exempt				
Vase (W4)	4,000			
House (W5)		7,800		
Land (W6)	117,800			
Cottage (W7)	23,400			
Gains before taper relief	145,200	7,800	34,720	9,800
Gains after taper relief	145,200	6,240	20,832	4,900
Total gains before taper relief	177,172			
Less AE	(9,200)			
Taxable gains	167,972			

	£
£(34,600 – 15,800) = 18,800 @ 20%	3,760
£(167,972 – 18,800) = 149,172 @ 40%	59,669
CGT due 31.1.09	63,429

Workings

1   *Symphony Ltd shares*

	£
Proceeds	23,600
Less cost £110,400 × 5,000/40,000	(13,800)
Gain before taper relief	9,800

Business asset with 1 complete year of ownership: 50%

2   *Concerto Plc shares*

	£
Proceeds (W3) £5.11 × 10,000	51,100
Less: cost	(14,000)
Less: IA 0.170 × 14,000	(2,380)
Gain before taper relief	34,720

Non business asset with 9 complete years of ownership plus the bonus year: 60%

Note. Although strictly the shares are in the FA 1985 pool, as there was only one acquisition you can treat this as a single asset.

3   *Market value of Concerto Plc shares*

As this is a gift, the market value is used as the proceeds.

For quoted shares this is the lower of the:

(i)   Quarter up:

        [¼ × £(5.18 − 5.10)] + 5.10 = 5.12

(ii)   Average:

        £(5.00 + 5.22) / 2 = 5.11, ie £5.11 per share

4   *Vase*

This is a non-wasting chattel and a restriction therefore applies:

	£
Proceeds	8,400
Less cost	(4,150)
Gain before taper relief	4,250

Restricted to:

5/3 × £(8,400 − 6,000) = 4,000, ie £4,000

Non-business asset with < 3 complete years of ownership therefore no taper relief available

5   *House*

Total ownership period: 1.4.01 − 31.12.07 = 81 months

PPR period:

Actual occupation 1 April 2001 to 30 June 2004 = 39 months

Last 36 months   = 36 months

                               = 75 months

	£
Proceeds	220,000
Less cost	(114,700)
	105,300
Less PPR relief	
75/81 × £105,300	(97,500)
Gain before taper relief	7,800

Non-business asset with 6 complete years of ownership: 80%

6   *Part disposal of land*

	£
Proceeds	285,000
Less cost £220,000 × $\dfrac{285,000}{285,000 + 90,000}$	(167,200)
Gain before taper relief	117,800

Non-business asset with < 3 complete years of ownership therefore no taper relief available

7   *Cottage*

Spouse transfer takes place at no gain, no loss therefore Paul takes on his wife's original base cost.

	£
Proceeds	125,000
Less cost	(101,600)
Gain before taper relief	23,400

Non-business asset with < 3 complete years of ownership therefore no taper relief available

28 Cube Ltd

Text references. Chapter 19 deals with the calculation of chargeable gains for shares and securities for a company. Chapter 16 deals with capital gains tax reliefs.

Top tips. Ensure your layout is clear and easy to read. This will maximise your marks.

Use workings for each of your gain/ loss calculations and reference them in carefully and clearly to assist the examiner in awarding you as many marks as possible.

Marking scheme

	Marks
Parallel plc	
Proceeds less cost	1½
Indexation	1½
Rectangle plc	
Takeover calculation	2
Loss calculation	1
Racehorse – exempt	1
Square plc	
FA85 pool	1½
Bonus issue	1
Loss calculation	½
Office	
Gain	1½
Rollover relief	2½
Triangle plc	
Matching rules	2
Rights issue	2
CT calculation	2
	20

CT liability y/e 31 March 2008

	£
UK trading profit	90,000
Gains (W1)	28,155
PCTCT	118,155
CT @ 20% (W8)	23,631

Workings

1   Chargeable gains

	£
Parallel plc shares (W2)	24,305
Triangle plc (W7)	17,000
	41,305
Less: loss on Rectangle plc (W3)	(10,000)
Less: loss on Square plc (W5)	(3,150)
Net chargeable gain	28,155

The racehorse is exempt from CGT (W4)
The gain on the disposal of the office can be rolled over into the base cost of the replacement office (W6)

2   Parallel plc

FA85 pool

Event	No.of shares	Cost £	Indexed cost £
Purchase 1.11.01	22,000	101,200	101,200

Index to May 2007

$$\frac{209.4 - 173.6}{173.6} \times 101,200$$

			20,870
			122,070
Sale	(4,000)	(18,400)	(22,195)
C/f	18,000	82,800	99,875

Gain	£
Proceeds	46,500
Less: cost	(18,400)
Less: indexation (22,195 – 18,400)	(3,795)
Chargeable gain	24,305

3   Rectangle plc

Original Quadrangle plc FA85 pool

Event	No. of shares	Cost £	Indexed cost £
Pool at 15.7.07	15,000	96,000	96,000

Takeover 15.7.07

Share type:	No of shares	MV £	Cost £	Indexed cost £
Ordinary	15,000	67,500	72,000	72,000
Preference	15,000	22,500	24,000	24,000
	30,000	90,000	96,000	96,000

Note. The cost is allocated to the new shares received in proportion to their market value immediately after the takeover

Gain	£
Proceeds	38,000
Less: cost $\frac{10,000}{15,000} \times 72,000$	(48,000)
Allowable loss	(10,000)

Note. Indexation is not available as the transactions took place in the same month. In any case indexation cannot increase a loss.

4   Racehorse – exempt wasting chattel

5   Square plc

      FA85 pool

Event	No. of shares	Cost £	Indexed cost £
Purchase 1.10.07	12,000	60,000	60,000
No indexation as no expenditure			
Bonus issue 16.10.07 1:3	4,000	–	–
	16,000	60,000	60,000
Sale 31.10.07	(8,000)	(30,000)	(30,000)
C/f	8,000	30,000	30,000

Gain	£
Proceeds	26,850
Less: cost	(30,000)
Allowable loss	(3,150)

Note. Indexation is not available as the transactions took place in the same month. In any case indexation cannot increase a loss.

6   Office

Gain	£
Proceeds	335,760
Less: cost	(126,000)
Unindexed gain	209,760
Less: IA	
Index to January 2008	
$\dfrac{210.8 - 170.1}{170.1} = 0.239 \times 126,000$	(30,114)
Indexed gain	179,646
Less: rollover relief (full)	(179,646)
Chargeable gain	Nil

Full rollover relief is available as all of the proceeds received were spent on buying a replacement office within the required time period (12 months before and 3 years after the disposal).

7   Triangle plc

      FA85 pool

Event	No. of shares	Cost £	Indexed Cost £
Purchase 1.3.08	8,000	28,800	28,800
No indexation as in same month			
Rights issue 15.3.08 1:1 @ £3.20	8,000	25,600	25,600
	16,000	54,400	54,400
Sale 31.3.08	(12,000)	(40,800)	(40,800)
C/f	4,000	13,600	13,600

Gain	£
Proceeds	57,800
Less: cost	(40,800)
Chargeable gain	17,000

Note. Indexation is not available as the transactions took place in the same month.

8   CT limits (no associated companies)

Lower limit   £300,000
Upper limit   £1,500,000

Therefore Cube Ltd is a small company paying tax at 20%

29 Forward Ltd

Text references. Chapters 13 to 17 deal with chargeable gains and reliefs and Chapter 19 covers the rules for companies.

Top tips. Remember that rollover relief is not available for shares. However, it will be partially available for the gain on the freehold building to the extent that the proceeds of sale are reinvested in the new asset.

Easy marks. The due date for payment of corporation tax was an easy mark, as was the calculation of the tax due.

Examiner's comments. This question was generally quite well answered. Few candidates had any problems when calculating the capital gain on the disposal of the freehold building or in identifying the amount of available rollover relief. The calculation of the gain on the disposal of the quoted shares was also dealt with quite well, although the answers of a number of candidates were quite hard to follow.

Marking scheme

		Marks	
(a)	**CT**		
	Trading income	1	
	Gains	1	
	CT rate	1	
	Due date	1	
	Freehold office		
	Gain	1	
	Rollover relief	1	
	Gain remaining chargeable	1	
	Shares		
	Matching rules	1	
	Same day acquisition	1	
	FA85 pool	1	
	Gain	1	
	Indexation	1	
	Painting – compensation		
	Gain	1	
	Indexation	1	
	Deferral relief	1	
	Gain remaining chargeable	1	
			16
(b)	**Rollover relief**		
	Frozen not rolled over	1	
	Gain crystallises – no longer used	1	
	– sale	1	
	– 10 years	1	
			4
			20

(a) **CT liability 31 March 2008**

	£
Trading income	75,000
Capital gains (W1, W2, W3)	79,512
PCTCT	154,512

CT × 20% = 30,902

Due date: 1 January 2009

Workings

1   *Freehold office building*

	£
Proceeds	290,000
Less cost	(148,000)
Unindexed gain	142,000
Less indexation allowance	
$\dfrac{205.2 - 140.7}{140.7}$ (0.458) × 148,000	(67,784)
Gain	74,216
Less rollover relief £(74,216 − 40,000)	(34,216)
Gain left in charge	40,000

Note. Since £40,000 of the sale proceeds are not reinvested ie £(290,000 − 250,000), this amount of gain remains in charge.

2   *Shares in Backward plc*

Same day acquisition

	£
Proceeds 500/5,000 × £62,500	6,250
Less cost	(6,500)
Loss	(250)

FA 1985 pool

	No. of shares	Cost £	Indexed cost £
20 April 1989 acquisition	9,000	18,000	18,000
30 November 2007 indexed rise			
$\dfrac{209.4 - 114.3}{114.3}$ × £18,000			14,976
			32,976
Disposal	(4,500)	(9,000)	(16,488)
	4,500	9,000	16,488

Gain

	£
Proceeds 4,500/5,000 × £62,500	56,250
Less cost	(9,000)
Unindexed gain	47,250
Less indexation £(16,488 − 9,000)	(7,488)
Indexed gain	39,762

Net gain on shares £(39,762 − 250) = 39,512

Note. There is no rollover relief on the disposal of shares.

3   *Painting*

		£
Proceeds		155,000
Less cost		(100,000)
Unindexed gain		55,000
Less indexation allowance		
$\dfrac{211.5 - 165.5}{165.5}$ (=0.278) × 100,000		(27,800)
Gain		27,200
Less deferral – full amount		(27,200)
Gain left in charge		Nil

Note. The date of disposal is the date the insurance money is received and not the date the accident occurred. Since all of the insurance proceeds have been reinvested in the replacement painting, no gain remains in charge.

(b)   As the whole of the proceeds of the sale of the office building of £290,000 will be reinvested in the new building, the whole of the gain is subject to relief.

However, as the new asset is a depreciating asset (useful life of 60 years or less) the gain will be 'frozen' instead of being rolled over into the base cost of the new asset.

The gain will come back into charge on the earliest of:

(1)   ceasing to be used in the trade
(2)   ceasing to be owned by the company
(3)   10 years after the acquisition

30 Preparation question: corporation tax computation

Corporation tax computation for the accounting period

	£	£
Trading income	245,000	
Trading losses brought forward	(20,000)	
		225,000
Property business income		115,000
Interest income		4,000
Capital gains (£35,000 + £7,000)	42,000	
Less capital losses brought forward	(40,000)	
		2,000
		346,000
Less gift aid donation		(7,000)
Profits chargeable to corporation tax		339,000

'Profits' = PCTCT as there is no FII

	£
Corporation tax £339,000 × 30%	101,700
Less marginal relief £(1,500,000 – 339,000) × 1/40	(29,025)
Corporation tax payable	72,675

31 Unforeseen Ultrasonics Ltd

Text references. Chapters 19 and 20 cover the calculation of PCTCT and Corporation Tax. Chapter 13 covers chargeable gains.

Top tips. You had to spot that the managing director's old car was cheap enough to have been pooled, even though his new car had to be kept out of that pool because it cost over £12,000.

The way to approach this question is to do some workings first ie calculate the IBAs and capital allowances on plant. Also calculate the gain. Only then can you start to calculate PCTCT.

Marking scheme

	Marks
Trading profit	1
Capital allowances – industrial building working	3
– plant and machinery working	4
Trade loss b/f	2
Interest income	2
Gains – calculation	3
– offset of loss	1
– loss c/f	1
Gift aid payment	1
PCTCT	1
Corporation tax liability	3
Instalments of CT – amount due	1
Dates	2
	25

Unforeseen Ultrasonics Limited
Corporation tax computation y/e 31 December 2007

	£
Trading profit	2,300,000
Less capital allowances (W1)	(101,713)
Trading income	2,198,287
Less loss brought forward (no balance to c/f)	(600,000)
	1,598,287
Interest income £(1,500 + 80,000)	81,500
Chargeable gains (W2)	0
	1,679,787
Less Gift Aid payment	(5,000)
Profits chargeable to corporation tax	1,674,787

Corporation tax

The full rate remains unchanged for FY 2006 and FY 2007 – thus £1,674,787 × 30% = £502,436

As Unforeseen Ultrasonics Ltd pays corporation tax at the full rate, its corporation tax liability for the year to 31 December 2007 was due for payment by quarterly instalments as follows:

	Amount due £
Due date	
14 July 2007	125,609
14 October 2007	125,609
14 January 2008	125,609
14 April 2008	125,609
	502,436

There are capital losses of £2,111 (W2) remaining to be carried forward at 31 December 2007.

Workings

1   *Capital allowances*

(a)   *The industrial building*

The total for the original building, excluding land, is £430,000, and the office part (£70,000) is less than 25% of this, so all £430,000 initially qualifies.

The new extension (£60,000) puts the total cost of the office part up to £130,000, which is over 25% of the new total expenditure of £490,000: this means none of the expenditure on the offices will now qualify.

IBAs are £360,000 × 4% = £14,400.

(b)   *Plant and machinery*

	FYA £	Pool £	Expensive car £	Short-life asset £	Total £
WDV b/f		190,000		4,000	
Transfer		4,000		(4,000)	
		194,000			
Additions			18,000		
Disposals					
£(10,000 + 8,000)		(18,000)			
		176,000	18,000		
WDA @ 25%		(44,000)	(3,000)		47,000
Additions					
(£56,251 + £24,375)	80,626				
FYA @ 50%	(40,313)				40,313
		40,313			
WDV c/f		172,313	15,000		87,313

(c)   Total allowances are £(14,400 + 87,313) = £101,713.

2   *Capital gains*

	£
Proceeds	69,874
Less cost	(27,000)
Unindexed gain	42,874
Less indexation allowance	
0.555 × £27,000	(14,985)
Indexed gain	27,889
Less loss b/f	(27,889)
Chargeable gain	Nil

Loss c/f £(30,000 − 27,889) = £2,111

32 Arable Ltd

Text references. Chapters 19 and 20 for calculation of PCTCT and CT. Property income is also covered in Chapter 19. Chapter 13 looks at gains. Chapter 24 covers the administration of Corporation Tax.

Top tips. Be especially careful when dealing with a short accounting period such as in this question.

For short accounting periods and capital allowances WDAs are pro-rated but FYAs are not. Similarly CT limits must also be pro-rated. In addition take care with the associated companies as this affects the Upper and Lower CT limits.

The pre-trading expenditure is treated as incurred on the first day of trading.

Easy marks. The capital allowances (IBAs and Plant and machinery) should have yielded good marks.

If you learn a proforma to calculate capital allowances you will find it easy to obtain marks for such computations. The 3 marks at the end for basic CT admin should have been very simple to achieve.

Examiner's comments. This question was generally very well answered although the lease premium aspect caused problems. The calculation of the capital gain also confused many candidates, since they applied the matching rules applying to individuals. A worrying number of candidates were unaware of the relevant dates in part (b) and very few candidates were aware of the possibility of an error or mistake claim.

Marking scheme

			Marks
(a)	Trading income	½	
	IBA – Land	½	
	– Showroom	1½	
	– Eligible expenditure	1½	
	– Allowance	1½	
	PM – Pool	1½	
	– Car	1½	
	– 40% FYA	2½	
	– 100% FYA	1	
	Lease premium – assessable	1½	
	– deduction	1½	
	Property business income – Premium	1½	
	– Relief	1	
	– Rent	1	
	Interest income	1	
	Capital gain – Purchases	½	
	– Indexation	2	
	– Disposal	½	
	– Gain	1	
	FII	1	
	CT	2½	
			27
(b)	Due date	1	
	Amendment	1	
	Error or mistake	1	
			3
			30

(a) **Arable Ltd – corporation tax**

	£	£
Trading income		284,600
Less IBA (W1)	6,180	
CAs (W2)	39,850	
Deduction for lease premium (W3)	2,700	(48,730)
Taxable trading income		235,870
Property business income (W4)		31,700
Interest income (accruals basis)		9,000
Capital gain (W5)		25,173
PCTCT		301,743
FII £18,000 × 100/90		20,000
'Profits'		321,743

Small companies' limits

Arable Ltd has two associated companies.

Lower limit

$$\frac{300,000}{3} \times \frac{9}{12} = £75,000$$

Upper limit

$$\frac{1,500,000}{3} \times \frac{9}{12} = £375,000$$

Corporation tax

	£
PCTCT × 30%	90,523
Less small companies' marginal relief	
$£(375,000 - 321,743) \times \dfrac{301,743}{321,743} \times \dfrac{1}{40}$	(1,249)
Corporation tax due	89,274

Workings

1   *Industrial buildings allowance*

Allowable expenditure:

	£
Site preparation	14,000
Professional fees	6,000
Drawing office	40,000
Factory	146,000
	206,000

Note. Showroom does not qualify as cost exceeds 25% of £280,000 (206,000 + 74,000). Land never qualifies for IBAs.

WDA (9 month period) 9/12 × 4% × £206,000 = £6,180

2   *Capital allowances on plant and machinery*

	FYA £	Pool £	Car £	Allowances £
Additions not qualifying for FYAs				
12 June 2007 Car		11,200		
14 June 2007 Car			14,600	
WDA @ (25%/£3,000) × 9/12		(2,100)	(2,250)	4,350
Additions qualifying for FYAs				
15 February 2007 Machine (N)	29,150			
18 February 2007 Alterations (N)	3,700			
20 April 2007 Lorry	19,000			
29 October 2007 Computer	4,400			
	56,250			
FYA @ 40%	(22,500)			22,500
		33,750		
17 June 2007 Low emission car	13,000			
FYA @ 100%	(13,000)	0		13,000
TWDV c/f /Allowances		42,850	12,350	39,850

3   *Deduction for lease premium*

Available in relation to property number 1 as used for business purposes.

Rent treated as received by landlord:

	£
Premium	75,000
Less £75,000 × 2% × (15-1)	(21,000)
	54,000

÷ 15 (number of years of lease) = £3,600

Deductible for 9 month period £3,600 × 9/12 = £2,700

4   *Property business income*

	£
Premium received for Property No. 2	50,000
Less £50,000 × 2% × (5 − 1)	(4,000)
	46,000
Less relief for premium on head lease £54,000 (W3) × 5/15	(18,000)
	28,000
Add rent receivable to 31 December 2007 £14,800 × 3/12	3,700
Property business income	31,700

5   *Capital gains*

	No.	Cost £	Indexed cost £
10 June 2006 Acquisition	15,000	12,000	12,000
20 August 2006 Indexed rise			
$\dfrac{199.2 - 198.5}{198.5} \times £12,000$			42
Acquisition	5,000	11,250	11,250
	20,000	23,250	23,292
5 December 2007 Indexed rise			
$\dfrac{210.1 - 199.2}{199.2} \times £23,292$			1,275
			24,567
Disposal	(10,000)	(11,625)	(12,284)
Carried forward	10,000	11,625	12,283

Gain

	£
Proceeds	37,457
Less cost	(11,625)
Unindexed gain	25,832
Less indexation £(12,284– 11,625)	(659)
Indexed gain	25,173

(b)   Arable Ltd must submit its corporation tax return by 31 December 2008 (12 months from the end of the accounting period).

Arable Ltd may amend its return at any time before 31 December 2009 (12 months from the filing date).

If Arable Ltd believed it has paid excessive tax because of an error in the return, an error or mistake claim may be made before 31 December 2013 (six years from the end of the accounting period).

33 Scuba Ltd

Text references. Calculation of taxable profits, PCTCT and CT in Chapters 19 and 20. Chapter 8 for IBAs and capital allowances. Administration in Chapter 24. VAT in Chapter 26.

Top tips. When dealing with an adjustment to profits, make a brief note to the examiner about why you have treated an item in a particular way. Ensure that you comment on every item in the question to obtain maximum marks.

Most of the calculations are fairly straightforward with perhaps the lease premium being the most challenging and only possible if you have studied this topic.

The most likely trap is not reading the question carefully and missing some information. It is good to mark the question in some way when you have dealt with each item (eg tick off or highlight each item dealt with).

With plant and machinery be careful with dates of purchase and which rate of FYA applies.

Easy marks. The adjustment to profit was straightforward, as was the calculation of corporation tax.

Once again using a proforma for

- adjustments of profit
- capital allowances
- calculation of PCTCT

would have helped gain marks. You can slot the appropriate item into the proformas as you read through the question in many cases.

Marking scheme

		Marks
(a)	Trading profit	
	Operating profit	½
	Depreciation	½
	Entertaining	1
	Gifts to customers	1
	Lease premium – Assessable amount	1½
	– Deduction	1½
	IBA – Land	½
	– General offices	1
	– Eligible expenditure	1
	– Allowance	1
	P & M – Pool	2
	– Motor car	1
	– 50% FYA	2½
		15
	Corporation tax computation	
	Trading profit	½
	Property business profit – Rent receivable	1
	– Expenses	1
	Interest	½
	Corporation tax	1
		4
(b)	Default surcharge	
	Quarter ended 30 June 2005	1
	Quarter ended 30 September 2005	1
	Quarter ended 31 March 2006	2
	Quarter ended 30 June 2006	1
	Extension of surcharge period	1
	Four consecutive VAT returns on time	1
	Quarter ended 30 September 2007	1
		8
	Errors on VAT return	
	Net errors of less than £2,000	1
	Net errors of more than £2,000	1
	Default interest	1
		3
		30

(a) (i) **Scuba Ltd – tax adjusted trading profit year ended 31 December 2007**

	£	£
Profit before tax		170,400
Add depreciation	45,200	
customer entertaining (N1)	7,050	
gifts to customers (N2)	1,600	
		53,850
Less lease premium (W1)		(1,860)
Adjusted profits		222,390
Less IBAs (W2)		(6,880)
Capital allowances (W3)		(27,510)
Taxable trading profit		188,000

Notes

(1) Customer entertaining is never an allowable expense. Staff entertaining is allowable.

(2) Expenditure on gifts to customers is only allowable if the gift (i) costs less than £50 per item, (ii) is not food, tobacco, alcohol or vouchers, and (iii) clearly advertises the business's name.

(ii) **CT liability year ended 31 December 2007**

	£
Taxable trading profit (above)	188,000
Property income (W4)	11,570
Interest (W5)	430
PCTCT	200,000

Small company (profits < £300,000)

		£
FY 2006	3/12 × £200,000 × 19%	9,500
FY 2007	9/12 × £200,000 × 20%	30,000
Total CT liability		39,500

Workings

1   *Lease premium*

	£
Premium (P)	80,000
Less 2% × (n − 1) × P	
2% × (20 − 1) × 80,000	(30,400)
Taxable as Landlord's income	49,600

This amount is deductible for the company over the life of the lease:

$$\frac{£49,600}{20} = £2,480$$

Allowable on an accruals basis ie 1 April 2007 to 31 December 2007 = 9/12 × £2,480 = £1,860

2   *IBAs*

	£
Allowable cost	
Expenditure	240,000
Less land	(68,000)
Total cost	172,000

Expenditure on offices only allowable if represents < 25% × total cost:

$$\frac{40,000}{172,000} = 23\% \text{ therefore allowable}$$

IBA: 4% × £172,000 = £6,880

3   *Capital Allowances*

		FYA	Pool	Exp. car	Allowances
		£	£	£	£
	TWDVs b/f		47,200	22,400	
	Additions not qualifying				
	for FYAs				
	4 May 2007		10,400		
			57,600		
	Disposal				
	15 November 2007		(12,400)		
			45,200		
	WDA @ 25%		(11,300)		11,300
			33,900		
	WDA (restricted)			(3,000)	3,000
	Additions qualifying				
	For FYAs				
	3 January 2007	18,020			
	29 February 2007	1,100			
	18 August 2007	7,300			
		26,420			
	FYA @ 50%	(13,210)	13,210		13,210
	TWDVs c/f		47,110	19,400	
	Allowances				27,510

4   *Property income*

1 May 2007 to 31 December 2007 = 8m

	£
£7,200 × 4 = £28,800 × 8/12 =	19,200
Less expenses:	
decorating	(6,200)
advertising	(1,430)
Property income	11,570

5   *Interest*

Non-trading loan relationship therefore £430 is taxable as non-trading interest receivable.

(b)   (i)   **Default surcharge**

	Quarter ended	Circumstance	Default surcharge consequence
1	30 June 2005	Late return and payment	Surcharge liability notice (SLN) issued, ending 30 June 2006. As this is the first default there is no surcharge.
2	30 September 2005	Late return and payment	SLN extended to 30 September 2006 Surcharge @ 2% = £644
3	31 December 2005	On time	SLN remains in place until 30 September 2006
4	31 March 2006	Late return and payment	SLN extended to 31 March 2007 Surcharge @ 5% = £170 Not collected as < £400
5	30 June 2006	Late return but no VAT due	SLN extended to 30 June 2007 No surcharge as no VAT due
6	30 September 2006 to 30 June 2007	On time	As returns and payments have been on time until the end of the SLN period, the SLN record is wiped clean
7	30 September 2007	Late return and payment	New SLN issued to 30 September 2008 As this is the first default there is no surcharge.
8	31 December 2007	On time	SLN remains in place until 30 September 2008

(ii)   **Voluntary disclosure of errors**

- Voluntary disclosure can be made of errors whether they are more or less than £2,000.

- If the error is <£2,000 it can be reported on the next VAT return ie for the quarter ended 31 March 2008 and no interest will be collected.

- If the error is >£2,000 it must be disclosed separately to HMRC and default interest may be charged.

34 Unforgettable Units Limited

Text references. Chapters 19 and 20 for calculation of profits and PCTCT.

Top tips. It is very important that you learn to deal with industrial buildings allowances. They are tested in nearly every exam.

Adjustment of profit yielded many marks in this question. It is a popular topic in the exam.

As fines are not incurred wholly and exclusively for the purpose of the trade they are not deductible in computing trading income profits.

Easy marks. A proforma for the adjustment of profits would be very helpful. You can virtually copy items from the question straight into your proforma in many instances gaining very easy marks.

Similarly a proforma for calculating capital allowances on the plant is also very useful. In addition such proformas are liked by the examiner since they improve the layout of an answer and make marking an answer much easier.

Answer plan

1   Adjustment of Profit

   + gift aid
   + fine
   – Debenture interest   PCTCT (see 3)
   – bank interest   PCTCT (see 3)
   – dividend

   then deduct capital allowances (see 2)

2   Calculate   Capital allowances

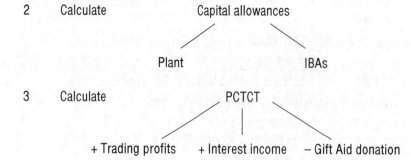

                  Plant   IBAs

3   Calculate   PCTCT

        + Trading profits   + Interest income   – Gift Aid donation

4   Calculate CT

Marking scheme

	Marks
Interest income	1
Less: Gift Aid payment	1
Adjustment to profit (W1)	
Gift Aid	1
Fine	1
Debenture interest	1
Bank interest	1
Dividend	1
Capital allowances – plant and machinery (W2)	
Addition	1
Disposal	1
WDAs	2
FYA at 40%	1
Capital allowances – industrial buildings (W3)	
Allowances on residue of expenditure	3
Remaining tax life	2
Allowance given	2
Corporation tax	
Calculation of 'P'	2
Computation of liability	4
	25

Corporation tax computation y/e 31 August 2007

	£
Trading income (W1)	754,217
Interest income (£64,000 + £5,000)	69,000
Less Gift Aid donation	(58,000)
Profits chargeable to corporation tax	765,217

Corporation tax (W4)

	£	£
FY 2006		
£446,377 × 30%		133,913
Less 11/400 (875,000 − 453,668) × $\frac{446,377}{453,668}$		(11,400)
		122,513
FY 2007		
£318,840 × 30%	95,652	
Less 1/40 (625,000 − 324,049) × $\frac{318,840}{324,049}$	(7,403)	
		88,249
Corporation tax payable		210,762

Workings

1   *Trading income*

		£
Profit per accounts		817,875
Add	gift aid donations	58,000
	fine	10,000
Less	debenture interest	(64,000)
	bank interest	(5,000)
	dividend	(11,250)
	capital allowances (W2)	(41,500)
	industrial buildings allowance (W3)	(9,908)
Trading income		754,217

2   *Capital allowances*

	FYA £	Pool £	Expensive car £	Allowances £
TWDV b/f		100,000		
Addition			13,000	
Disposal		(2,000)		
		98,000	13,000	
WDA @ 25%/restricted		(24,500)	(3,000)	27,500
Additions (January 2007)	35,000			
FYA @ 40%	(14,000)			14,000
		21,000		41,500
		94,500	10,000	

3   *Industrial buildings allowance*

IBAs are due on the residue of expenditure before sale ie original cost	£250,000
Less allowances given to original owner	
4% × 250,000 × 7	(70,000)
Residue of expenditure	180,000

Tax life ends on 1 August 2025

Date of purchase is 1 June 2007

Unexpired life is therefore 18 years 2 months

Allowances due to Unforgettable Units Ltd

$$\frac{\text{Residue of expenditure}}{\text{Remaining tax life}} = \frac{180,000}{18\,^2/_{12}} = £9,908$$

4   *'Profits'*

		£
Profits chargeable to corporation tax		765,217
FII (£11,250 × 100/90)		12,500
'Profits'		777,717

	FY 2006 *7 months to 31.3.07*	*FY 2007* *5 months to 31.8.07*
PCTCT (7:5)	446,377	318,840
'Profits' (7:5)	453,668	324,049
Lower limit		
£300,000 × $\frac{7}{12}$ / $\frac{5}{12}$	175,000	125,000
Upper limit		
£1,500,000 × $\frac{7}{12}$ / $\frac{5}{12}$	875,000	625,000
Marginal relief applies in both FYs		

35 Thai Curry Ltd

Text references. Chapters 19 and 20 for calculation of profits and PCTCT. Chapter 8 covers capital allowances and IBAs. Chapter 24 for CT administration.

Top tips. It is essential to set out your capital allowances proforma in the correct layout to achieve maximum marks. Ensure that you state all of your assumptions so that you do not miss out on any method marks.

You cannot avoid administration questions in the exam so make sure you know due dates for returns and tax payments.

Marking scheme

			Marks
(a)	Capital allowances		
	TWDV b/f	½	
	Disposals	1	
	Balancing charge/allowance	1½	
	Additions	1	
	Exclude non-qualifying expenditure	½	
	WDA max £3,000	½	
	FYA @ 100%	1	
	FYA @ 50%	2	
	IBAs		
	Residue of expenditure	3	
	Remaining tax life	1	
	Trading loss	½	
	Deduct allowances	½	
			13

ANSWERS

(b)	Trading profit nil			½	
	Property income				
		Property 1	– rent	1	
			– expense	½	
			– bad debt	1	
		Property 2	– rent	½	
			– lease premium	1½	
	Interest			1	
	Chargeable gain			½	
	Deduct CY loss			1	
	FII			½	
	CT limits			1	
	CT @ 30%			½	
	Marginal relief			1½	
					11
(c)	(i)	Return deadline		1	
		Fixed penalty		1	
		Tax geared penalty		1	
					3
	(ii)	9 months 1 day		1	
		Late payment interest		1	
		Interest calculation		1	
					3
					30

(a)   Thai Curry's adjusted trading loss y/e 30 September 2007

	£
Trading loss	(32,800)
Less: Capital allowances (W1)	(34,355)
Less: IBAs (W2)	(13,800)
Allowable trading loss	(80,955)

Workings

1   *Capital allowances*

	FYA £	General Pool £	Exp car £	SLA £	Allowances £
TWDV b/f		10,600	16,400	2,900	
Disposals:					
1.11.06		(12,800)			
15.12.06				(800)	
14.1.07			(9,700)		
Balancing (charge/) allowance		(2,200)	6,700	2,100	6,600
Additions:					
26.2.07			15,800		
WDA max			(3,000)		3,000
19.5.07	9,700				
FYA @ 100%	(9,700)				9,700
8.1.07	7,360				
20.9.07	22,750				
	30,110				
FYA @ 50%	(15,055)				15,055
Transfer to pool	(15,055)	15,055			
TWDV c/f		15,055	12,800		
Total allowances					34,355

Note. It has been assumed that the SLA has had fewer than 5 WDAs claimed on it up to this date and that therefore a balancing allowance arises.

Note. When a balancing charge arises in the general pool it must be charged as trading profit (ie it has reduced the allowances claimed here.) If instead the result had been a balancing allowance the pool would have continued.

Note. Most of the items included within the cost of the office building purchased on 20 September 2007 will qualify for plant and machinery capital allowances. The remainder of the cost (£10,700 for the electrical and lighting systems) is not eligible for these allowances or for Industrial Buildings Allowances as it is not used for industrial purposes.

2   *IBAs*

		£
Residue of expenditure		
Original cost		345,000
Less: allowances given		
4% × £345,000 × 5		(69,000)
		276,000

Remaining tax life   = 25 yrs – 5 yrs
                         = 20 yrs

Thus IBA available is $\dfrac{276,000}{20}$ = £13,800

(b)   Corporation tax liability y/e 30 September 2007

	£
Trading profit	Nil
Property income (W1)	72,800
Interest (W3)	11,500
Chargeable gain	152,300
PCTCT	236,600
Less: current year loss relief	(80,955)
Revised PCTCT	155,645
Add: gross dividends: £36,000 × 100/90	40,000
'Profits'	195,645

CT liability	£	£
FY 2006: £77,822 × 30%		23,347
Less 11/400 (187,500 – 97,822) × $\dfrac{77,822}{97,822}$		(1,962)
		21,385
FY 2007: £77,823 × 30%	23,347	
Less 1/40 (187,500 – 97,823) × $\dfrac{77,823}{97,823}$	(1,784)	
		21,563
Total CT liability		42,948

Workings

1   Property income

    Property 1

	£	£
8m × £2,200	17,600	
Less: redecoration costs	(8,800)	
Less: rent not recoverable: 2m × £2,200	(4,400)	
Property income		4,400

    Property 2

	£	£
8/12 × £18,000	12,000	
Premium taxable as income (W2)	56,400	
Property income		68,400
Total property income		72,800

2   Lease premium

	£
Premium (P)	60,000
Less: 2% × (n-1) × P	
2% × (4-1) × 60,000	(3,600)
Taxable as income	56,400

3   Loan interest

Received at 30.6.07	8,000
Accrued at 30.9.07	3,500
Total amount (accruals basis)	11,500

4

	FY 2006 *6 months to 31.3.07*	FY 2007 *6 months to 30.9.07*
PCTCT (6:6)	77,822	77,823
'Profits' (6:6)	97,822	97,823
Lower limit		
£300,000/4 (6:6)	37,500	37,500
Upper limit		
£1,500,000/4 (6:6)	187,500	187,500

Therefore marginal relief applies in both FYs.

(c)   (i)   Date for return submission and penalties

The CT return must be submitted one year after the end of the period of account i.e. by 30 September 2008.

If the return is not submitted until 31 May 2009 it will be 8 months late. If the return is up to 3 months late there is a fixed penalty of £100. If it more than 3 months late, as it is here, the fixed penalty increases to £200.

As the return is more than 6 months late there is also a tax geared penalty of 10% × unpaid tax, ie 10% × £42,948 = £4,295.

(ii)   Date for CT payment & interest

As the company is not large it must pay its corporation tax by 9 months and 1 day after the accounting period, ie by 1 July 2008.

If the tax is not paid until 31 May 2009 it will be 11 months late and interest will be charged from the due date (in practice interest is calculated on a daily basis.)

The rate of interest on unpaid tax is 7.5% and therefore the amount that will be charged is:

7.5% × 11/12 × £42,948 = £2,953.

36 Spacious Ltd

Text references. Chapter 19 and 20 for PCTCT and CT calculations. Chapters 13 and 16 for chargeable gains. CT loss relief covered in Chapter 21.

Top tips. Use a loss proforma when apportioning losses to accounting periods.

Use a proforma when calculating capital allowances.

Proformas improve the layout of an answer and are liked by the examiner as they help with marking an answer.

Make sure you follow closely the question requirements. Part (b) asks you to consider a loss claim against total profits (and no other loss relief). Don't waste time and effort doing anything extra or different.

Part (c) then allows you to discuss carrying the loss forward. Only discuss that option in this section.

Easy marks. The adjustment of the loss was fairly straightforward. Adjustment of a profit/loss is something that you should expect to see in nearly every exam.

Calculating capital allowances is another topic which appears regularly in the exam and provides easy marks for the knowledgeable student.

Examiner's comments. A number of candidates achieved maximum marks. In part (b) some candidates carried back all of the loss to the previous period. Part (c) was reasonably well answered if candidates appreciated that the main benefit of carrying the loss forward was that relief was obtained at a higher rate.

Marking scheme

		Marks
(a)	Loss before tax	½
	Depreciation	½
	Patent	½
	Professional fees	2
	Repairs/renewals	1
	Other expenses	1½
	Office building	½
	Bank interest receivable	½
	Interest payable	½
	IBA – Land	½
	– General offices	2
	– Eligible expenditure	1
	– Allowance	½
	Long life asset	1
	P&M – pool	2
	– car sold	1½
	– car acquired	1
	– FYA	2
		19

(b)

Trading income	1
Interest income	1
Gain	2
Capital loss	1
Loss relief	2
Gift aid	1
	8

(c)

Year ended 31 March 2008	1
Period ended 31 March 2007	1
Carry forward	1
	3
	30

(a) **Trading loss**

	£	£
Loss before taxation		(124,200)
Depreciation	54,690	
Patent royalties (N1)	–	
Legal fees – share capital (N2)	8,800	
Legal fees – court action (N2)	900	
New wall (N3)	9,700	
Entertaining	1,800	
Gift aid	1,000	76,890
		(47,310)
Office building profit		(54,400)
Bank interest		(7,000)
Interest payable (N4)		–
Capital allowances – IBAs (W1)	6,540	
– P&M (W2)	28,150	
– Long life (W3)	6,600	
Trading loss		(41,290)
		(150,000)

Notes

1 No adjustment needed for patent royalties as treated as part of trading expenses.

2 Costs relating to share capital need to be added back as they relate to a capital expense. Legal fees in relation to fine are not deductible as the fine is a payment contrary to public policy.

3 The cost of the new wall has been added back as a capital expense but the cost of the roof is allowable as it is a repair and therefore a revenue expense.

4 No adjustment is needed for the interest because it relates to a trade purpose loan.

Workings

1   *IBAs*

	£
Drawing office	54,000
Factory £(360,000 – 135,000 – 61,500 – 54,000)	109,500
Allowable cost	163,500

WDA @ 4% = <u>6,540</u>

Note. General offices cost more than 25% of £(360,000 – 135,000) = £225,000. This means that the expenditure on the general office is not eligible for IBAs.

2   *Plant and machinery*

	FYA £	Pool £	Car (1) £	Car (2) £	Allowances £
TWDV b/f		28,400	14,800		
Additions not qualifying for FYAs					
5 February 2008 car				13,600	
31 March 2008 car		9,400			
		37,800			
Disposals					
5 February 2008			(9,800)		
20 March 2008		(17,600)			
Balancing allowance			5,000		5,000
		20,200			
WDA @ 25%/restricted		(5,050)		(3,000)	8,050
		15,150			
Addition qualifying for FYA					
10 April 2007	30,200				
Less FYA @ 50%	(15,100)	15,100			15,100
TWDVs c/f		30,250		10,600	
Allowances					28,150

Note. The private use of the car by the employee is not relevant for capital allowance purposes. No adjustment is ever made to a company's capital allowances to reflect the private use of an asset.

3   *Long life asset*

WDA £110,000 × 6% = £6,600

(b)

	Period ended 31 March 2007 £	Year ended 31 March 2008 £
Trading income	183,200	0
Interest income	5,200	7,000
Capital gain (W)	0	15,100
	188,400	22,100
Less: carry back/current year loss relief	(127,900)	(22,100)
	60,500	0
Less: Gift Aid payment	(800)	0
PCTCT	59,700	0

Working

Gain on building

	£
Proceeds	380,000
Less indexed cost	(345,400)
Indexed gain	34,600
Less rollover relief £34,600 – (380,000 – 360,000)	(14,600)
	20,000
Less loss b/f	(4,900)
Capital gain	15,100

(c) Using the loss in the year to 31 March 2008, Spacious Ltd has saved tax as follows:

£22,100 @ 20% = £4,420

Using the rest of the loss in the period to 31 March 2007, Spacious Ltd has saved 19% × £127,900 = £24,301.

Total tax saved is therefore £28,721.

However, if the loss of £150,000 had been carried forward to year ended 31 March 2009, it would have saved tax of £150,000 × 32.5% = £48,750.

37 Loser Ltd

Text references. Chapter 21 deals with loss relief for companies.

Top tips. In a loss relief question, set out your proforma then copy in the numbers from the question – remember the trading profits figure is 'nil' when there is a loss in a period. You can then apply the loss relief rules.

Remember that a company **must** make a current year claim if it wishes to then carry back losses to an earlier period (individuals may choose which claim, if any, to make first.)

Marking scheme

			Marks
(a)	Rate of corporation tax	1	
	Timing of relief	1	
	Gift aid donations	1	
			3
(b)	Trading profit	½	
	Property business profit	½	
	Loss relief against total profits	2	
	Gift aid	1	
	Unrelieved trading loss	1	
			5
(c)	Extension of relief	1	
	Year ended 30 June 2005	1	
			2
			10

(a) **Choice of loss relief factors**

(i) The marginal rate of tax – losses will be better used in years where the tax rate is higher.

(ii) Timing – it will be preferable to obtain relief in earlier years as this will result in a repayment of tax already paid.

(iii) Gift aid – loss relief may lead to gift aid donations becoming wasted (as they cannot be carried forward – only group relieved in the current period) in which case it may be better to use the loss in a year where they will not be wasted.

(b) **Losses**

	y/e 30.6.05 £	9m to 31.3.06 £	y/e 31.3.07 £	y/e 31.3.08 £
Trading profit	86,600	Nil	27,300	Nil
Property income	–	4,500	8,100	5,600
Total profits	86,600	4,500	35,400	5,600
Less CY loss	–	(4,500)(i)	–	(5,600)(iii)
Less loss carried back	(21,200)(ii)	–	(35,400)(iv)	–
Revised profits	65,400	Nil	Nil	Nil
Less Gift aid donations	(1,400)	–	–	–
PCTCT	64,000	–	–	–

Loss memo

	£
Loss of 9m to 31.3.06	25,700
(i) CY	(4,500)
(ii) CB	(21,200)
c/f	Nil
Loss of y/e 31.3.08	78,300
(iii) CY	(5,600)
(iv) CB	(35,400)
c/f	37,300

(c) **Difference if company ceased trading 31 March 2008**

(i) If the year to 31 March 2008 had been the company's final period it would have been able to carry back the losses of the year to 31 March 2008 against the profits of the previous 36 months, compared to the normal 12 month carry back period.

(ii) It would be therefore be able to reach back to the trading profits of the year ended 30 June 2005.

(iii) It would have been able to set off the lower of the profits and the unrelieved loss ie £37,300.

38 Unforeseen Upsets Limited

Text references. Chapters 8, 13, 19, 20 and 24 are required reading for this question.

Top tips. Break a long question like this down into manageable parts in order to gain the easy marks. It is essential that you are aware that a long period of account is split into two accounting periods and that the first period is always twelve months in length. If you do not make this split correctly you cannot hope to pass the question.

				Marks
(a)	Trading profits (12:3)	1		
	Trading losses brought forward	1		
	Bank interest	1		
	Debenture interest	1½		
	Chargeable gains (W3)	1½		
	Gift Aid donations	1		
	Capital allowances (W1)			
	Year to 31 December 2007			
	Additions and disposals	1		
	WDA	1		
	FYA 50%	1		
	Period to 31 March 2008			
	WDA	1		
	FYA	1		
	Year to 31 December 2007			
	Small companies rate	1		
	Tax calculation	2		
	Period to 31 March 2008			
	Calculation of 'P'	1		
	Calculation of reduced limits	1		
	Marginal relief	1		
	Calculation of liability	2		
				20
(b)	Due dates for payment	2		
	Due dates for returns	2		
	Penalties	5		
				9
(c)	Capital losses c/fwd			1
				30

(a) **Corporation tax computations**

	Year to 31 December 2007 £	3 months to 31 March 2008 £
Trading profits 12:3	900,000	225,000
Less capital allowances (W1)	(83,750)	(11,279)
	816,250	213,721
Less losses b/f	(600,000)	–
	216,250	213,721
Interest income (W2)	32,000	5,500
Chargeable gains (W3)	–	–
	248,250	219,221
Less Gift Aid donations	(11,000)	(9,000)
PCTCT	237,250	210,221
Dividends plus tax credits £6,300 × 100/90	–	7,000
'Profits' for small companies' rate purposes	237,250	217,221

Corporation tax (W4)

	£	£
FY 2006: £59,312 × 19%	11,269	
FY 2007: £177,938 × 20%	35,588	
FY 2007		
£210,221 × 30%		63,066
Less Small companies' marginal relief		
$1/40 \; (£375,000 - £217,221) \times \dfrac{210,221}{217,221}$		(3,817)
	46,857	59,249

(b) £46,857 in respect of the 12 months to 31 December 2007 must be paid by 1 October 2008.

£59,249 in respect of the 3 months to 31 March 2008 must be paid by 1 January 2009.

A return for the 12 months to 31 December 2007 and a return for the 3 months to 31 March 2008 must be filed by 31 March 2009.

If a return is filed late there is an initial penalty of £100. This rises to £200 if the return is more than 3 months late. These penalties rise to £500 and £1,000 respectively for the third consecutive late filing of a return.

There is in addition a tax geared penalty, if the return is more than six months late. The penalty is 10% of the tax unpaid six months after the return was due if the total delay is up to 12 months, but it increases to 20% of that tax if the return is over 12 months late.

(c)   At 31 March 2008 there are capital losses to carry forward of £20,000 (W3).

Workings

1   *Capital allowances*

	FYA £	Pool £	Expensive Car £	Allowances £
Year to 31 December 2007				
TWDV b/f		142,000		
Additions		24,000	14,000	
Disposals		(27,000)		
		139,000	14,000	
WDA @ 25%/(restricted)		(34,750)	(3,000)	37,750
Additions (30.11.07)	92,000			
FYA @ 50%	(46,000)			46,000
		46,000		83,750
TWDV c/f		150,250	11,000	
3 months to 31 March 2008				
WDA @ 25%				
(restricted) × 3/12		(9,391)	(688)	10,079
Additions (28.2.08)	2,400			
FYA @ 50%	(1,200)			1,200
		1,200		11,279
		142,059	10,312	

2   *Interest income*

The interest is taxable on an accruals basis:

	Year to 31 December 2007 £	3 months to 31 March 2008 £
Bank interest	20,000	–
Debenture interest	12,000	5,500
	32,000	5,500

3   *Chargeable gains*

	Year to 31 December 2007 £
Gain	30,000
Loss/b/f	(30,000)
Net gain	–

The loss c/f on 1 April 2008 is £20,000 (£50,000 – £30,000).

4   *Corporation tax*

Year to 31 December 2007

The year to 31 December 2007 straddles FY 2006 and FY 2007. The lower limit for both years is £300,000, so the small companies' rate applies:

	FY 2006 *3 months to 31.3.07*	FY 2007 *9 months to 31.12.07*
PCTCT (3:9)	59,312	177,938
'Profits' (3:9)	59,312	177,938
Lower limit		
£300,000 × $\frac{3}{12}$ / $\frac{9}{12}$	75,000	225,000

Small companies rate applies in both FYs

3 months to 31 March 2008

	FY 2007 (3/12) £
Profits	210,221
PCTCT	217,221
Lower limit	75,000
Upper limit	375,000

Marginal relief applies.

39 B and W Ltd

Text references. Chapter 20 for CT computation. Chapter 23 for overseas aspects of CT.

Top tips. The set off of DTR must be made on a source by source basis.

Easy marks. Using a proforma for the DTR calculation not only improves your layout but reduces the risk of making mistakes and losing marks.

Marking scheme

		Marks
B Ltd –	Trading income	½
	Capital gains	½
	Overseas income	1
	Interest income	½
	Gift Aid payment	1
	FII	1
W Ltd –	Trading income/PCTCT	½
B Ltd –	Tax calculation	3
DTR –	UK profits	1
	Overseas income	1
	Average rate of CT	1
	DTR set off	1
W Ltd –	CT	3
		15

Corporation tax

	B Ltd	W Ltd
	£	£
Trading income	296,000	6,000
Capital gains	30,000	0
Overseas income ($\times$ 100/80)	2,000	0
Interest income	8,000	0
Less Gift Aid donation	(18,000)	0
PCTCT	318,000	6,000
FII	32,000	0
'Profits'	350,000	6,000

B Ltd

FY 2007

Lower limit = £150,000
Upper limit = £750,000

Note. There are two associated companies so the upper and lower limits must be divided by two.

Marginal relief applies.

	£
£318,000 $\times$ 30%	95,400
Less 1/40 (750,000 − 350,000) $\times \dfrac{318,000}{350,000}$	(9,086)
	86,314
Less DTR (W1)	(400)
Mainstream corporation tax	85,914

W Ltd

CT

FY2007

£6,000 $\times$ 20% = £1,200

Working: Double tax relief

	UK profits	Overseas income	Total
	£	£	£
Profits	334,000	2,000	336,000
Less Gift Aid	(18,000)	–	(18,000)
	316,000	2,000	318,000
CT $\dfrac{86,314}{318,000}$ = 27.14276%			
	85,771	543	86,314
Less DTR lower of:			
(i) UK tax (£543)			
(ii) Overseas tax (£400)		(400)	(400)
	85,771	143	85,914

40 Sirius Ltd

Text references. Chapter 20 for corporation tax calculation. Chapter 8 for capital allowances and IBAs. Chapter 21 for CT losses and Chapter 23 for overseas aspects of CT.

Top tips. You need to deal with underlying tax and withholding tax for DTR on a subsidiary.

Easy marks. You should have been able to get a couple of the points in part (b) and calculate the tax on the permanent establishment for easy marks.

Examiner's comments. This question was quite well answered by many of the candidates. Part (a) caused few problems, and many candidates achieved full marks. When dealing with the permanent establishment in part (b), the main problem was only including the profits remitted. As regards the 100% subsidiary, many candidates had difficulty in calculating the underlying tax relief.

Marking scheme

				Marks
(a)	(i)	Depreciation	½	
		Loss on disposals	½	
		Gift Aid	½	
		Dividends paid/ received	½	
		Capital allowances	3	
		IBAs – no BA/BC	1	
		Chargeable gain	1½	
		Capital loss	½	
		Use of trading loss	1	
		CT rate	1	
				10
	(ii)	Tax due dates	1	
		Return submission date	1	
				2
	(iii)	Prior year	1	
		Carry forward	1	
		Best use	1	
				3
(b)		CT incidence	1	
		Losses	1	
		Capital allowances	1	
		Associated companies	1	
				4
(c)		**Permanent establishment**		
		Trading income	½	
		Overseas income	1	
		CT	1½	
		DTR	1	
		Subsidiary		
		Trading income	½	
		Overseas income	1	
		Underlying tax	2	
		CT	½	
		Associated company	1	
		Total overseas tax	1	
		DTR	1	
				11
				30

(a)   (i)   Corporation tax computation – year ended 31 March 2008

	£
Taxable trading profit (W1)	Nil
Net chargeable gain (W4)	1,601,750
	1,601,750
Less current year loss relief (W1)	(43,180)
	1,558,570
Less Gift Aid donation	(25,000)
PCTCT	1,533,570
Add: FII (£18,000 × 90/100)	20,000
'Profits'	1,553,570

Corporation tax payable (W5)

£1,533,570 × 30% = £460,071

Workings

1   *Taxable trading profits*

	£	£
Loss per accounts		(125,000)
Add depreciation	42,750	
loss on disposal of computer equipment	5,260	
loss on sale of factory	39,500	
gift aid donation paid	25,000	
dividends paid	21,000	
		133,510
Less dividends received		(18,000)
		(9,490)
Less capital allowances (W2)		(33,690)
Adjusted trading loss		(43,180)
Taxable trading profits		Nil

If loss relief is claimed as early as possible, the loss will be set off against other profits of the current period of the year ended 31 March 2008.

2   *Capital allowances – year ended 31 March 2008*

	FYA £	Pool £	Expensive Car £	SLA £	CAs £
TWDV b/f		42,000	13,000	3,600	
Additions eligible for FYAs:					
Computer (note 1)	12,000				
Van	21,680				
	33,680				
Disposal (note 2)				(250)	
BA				3,350	3,350
FYA @ 50%	(16,840)				16,840
WDA @ 25%/ max (note 3)		(10,500)	(3,000)		13,500
Transfer to pool	(16,840)	16,840			
TWDV c/f	Nil	48,340	10,000		
Total allowances					33,690

Notes

(1)   The computer system is eligible for 50% FYA in the year of purchase. As for the original computer system It will usually be beneficial to elect for the new system to be treated as a short life asset (SLA) particularly if it is envisaged that it will be disposed of within five years. If this is done, a balancing allowance will crystallise on its disposal, whereas if it remains in the general pool no balancing allowance can arise. If an SLA election is made, a separate column will need to be used for the new computer. In any case, the amount of the allowances will be the same in this particular accounting period (ie FYAs will be given as normal).

(2)   The lower of original cost and disposal proceeds is used in the capital allowances computation.

(3)   The private use of the car by the director does not affect the company's allowances, which are given in full. Instead the director will be taxable on the benefit of using the car.

3   *Factory sale*

No balancing adjustment arises on the sale of an industrial building after 21 March 2007.

4   *Disposal of factory – Net chargeable gain*

	£
Proceeds	1,750,000
Less: Cost	(85,000)
Unindexed gain	1,665,000
Less Indexation allowance	
$\dfrac{206.6 - 164.4}{164.4} = 0.257 \times £85,000$	(21,845)
Chargeable gain	1,643,155
Capital loss b/f	(41,405)
Net chargeable gain	1,601,750

5   *Corporation tax rate*

FY 2007 Upper limit = £1,500,000

Profits > £1,500,000, therefore Sirius Ltd is a large company for corporation tax purposes

(ii)   **Due dates**

CT payment

The Corporation tax must be paid in four equal instalments of £115,018 (25%) due on the following dates:

- 14 October 2007
- 14 January 2008
- 14 April 2008 and
- 14 July 2008

Tax return

The return must be submitted by 31 March 2009.

(iii)   **Use of trading loss**

Sirius Ltd has two options available for its trading loss:

(1)   Carry forward to set off against the first available future trade profits only; and
(2)   Set off against profits of the current accounting period (as above).

Sirius Ltd cannot carry back the loss to the previous period as there is not enough loss to carry back. A carry back claim can only be made if the current year's PCTCT has been fully relieved first.

The anticipated profits for the next year are below the corporation tax limit of £300,000 ignoring the possible foreign subsidiary (or £150,000 if a foreign subsidiary is set up). Sirius Ltd would therefore only save tax at 20%, and the relief would be obtained at a later date.

The best solution is therefore a current year claim as above, which saves tax at 30%.

(b) A non-UK subsidiary will only be assessed to UK corporation tax to the extent it remits dividends to the UK. In contrast, the income of the profits of the permanent establishment will be subject to UK corporation tax on an arising basis.

If the overseas operation trades at a loss, UK tax relief will only be available if it is a permanent establishment, not a subsidiary.

Capital allowances will only be available to a permanent establishment, not to a subsidiary.

In the case of a subsidiary, it will be an associated company and so will reduce the corporation tax limits.

(c) (i) *Permanent establishment*

	£
Trading income	105,000
Overseas income	200,000
PCTCT	305,000
CT @ 30%	91,500
Less marginal relief	
£(1,500,000 − 305,000) × 1/40	(29,875)
	61,625

Less DTR lower of:

(1) $\dfrac{200,000}{305,000} \times £61,625 = £40,410$

(2) £40,000, ie	(40,000)
CT liability	21,625

(ii) *100% subsidiary*

	£
Trading income	105,000
Overseas income (W1)	100,000
PCTCT	205,000
CT @ 30% (W2)	61,500
Less marginal relief	
£(750,000 − 205,000) × 1/40	(13,625)
	47,875
Less DTR (W3)	(23,354)
CT liability	24,521

Workings

1 *Overseas income*

	£
Gross dividend	80,000
Add underlying tax	
$£80,000 \times \dfrac{40,000}{(200,000 - 40,000)}$	20,000
Total overseas income	100,000

2   *CT limits (two associated companies)*

Lower limit $\dfrac{300,000}{2}$ = £150,000

Upper limit $\dfrac{1,500,000}{2}$ = £750,000

Therefore marginal relief applies.

3   *DTR*

Lower of:

UK tax $\dfrac{100,000}{205,000}$ × £47,875 = £23,354

Overseas tax:

		£
– withholding tax £80,000 × 15%		12,000
– underlying tax		20,000
		32,000

therefore the lower amount of UK tax of £23,354 is allowable.

41 Preparation question: group relief

Text references. Chapter 22 for group relief.

Top tips. You are asked to use group relief in the most efficient manner. This means giving it first to companies with marginal relief, then to companies paying tax at the full rate. You must recognise that T Ltd is an associated company, being under common control with the P Ltd group.

(a)   There are six associated companies, so the lower and upper limits are £50,000 and £250,000 respectively.

S Ltd and T Ltd are outside the P Ltd group for group relief purposes. P Ltd's loss should be surrendered first to Q Ltd, to bring its taxable profits down to £50,000, then to R Ltd to bring its taxable profits down to £50,000 and finally to M Ltd, or used by P Ltd as these latter two companies both pay tax at 20%.

	M Ltd £	P Ltd £	Q Ltd £	R Ltd £	S Ltd £	T Ltd £
Trading income	10,000	0	64,000	260,000	0	70,000
Property business income	0	6,000	4,000	0	0	0
	10,000	6,000	68,000	260,000	0	70,000
Less Gift Aid	(4,000)	(4,500)	(2,000)	(5,000)	0	0
	6,000	1,500	66,000	255,000	0	70,000
Less group relief	(2,000)	0	(16,000)	(205,000)	0	0
PCTCT	4,000	1,500	50,000	50,000	0	70,000
Corporation tax:						
at 20%	800	300	10,000	10,000	0	
at 30%						21,000
Less marginal relief						
1/40 (£250,000 – 70,000)						(4,500)
CT payable	800	300	10,000	10,000	0	16,500

(b)   If P Ltd were to acquire another 8% of the share capital of S Ltd, bringing the total holding to 75%, S Ltd's losses could be surrendered to P Ltd, Q Ltd, R Ltd or M Ltd.

42 A Ltd

Text references. Chapters 19, 20, 22 and 24 required reading for this question.

Top tips. B Ltd's loss could be set only against the available profits of the corresponding accounting period.

	Marks
Trading income	½
Property business income	½
Interest income	2
Gift aid	1
Group relief	5
FII	1
CT calculation	3
Due dates	2
	15

Corporation Tax computation 9 m/e 31 December 2007

	£	£
Trading income		342,000
Property business income		13,000
Interest income		
Bank interest accrued	5,000	
Loan interest accrued	8,000	
		13,000
		368,000
Less: Gift Aid donation		(17,000)
		351,000
Less: group relief (W1)		(34,000)
PCTCT		317,000
Add: Franked Investment Income		1,000
'Profits'		318,000

	£
Corporation tax	
FY 2007	
£317,000 × 30%	95,100
Less marginal relief	
$1/40 (£562,500 - 318,000) \times \dfrac{317,000}{318,000}$	(6,093)
Mainstream corporation tax	89,007

£89,007 must be paid by 1 October 2008.

The corporation tax return for the period must be filed by 31 December 2008.

Note. It is assumed that the loan interest and the bank interest arose on non-trading loans and is therefore taxable as interest income.

Workings

1   B Ltd joined the group with A Ltd on 1 July 2007 so for A Ltd's profit making accounting period to 31 December 2007 there are 6 months in common with B Ltd's loss making period.

   Thus

   A Ltd   6/9 × £351,000 = £234,000
   B Ltd   6/12 × (£68,000) = £34,000

   Maximum group relief available is lower of two, ie £34,000.

2   The 9 months to 31 December 2007 falls into FY 2007.

   'Profits' are between the upper and lower limits of £1,500,000 × 9/12 ÷ 2 = £562,500 and £300,000 × 9/12 ÷ 2 = £112,500, so marginal relief applies.

43 Gold Ltd

Text references. Chapters 19 and 20 for corporation tax computation and Chapter 8 for capital allowances. Group relief is dealt with in Chapter 22.

Top tips. You may want to draw a simple diagram showing the accounting periods of each company and how they overlap.

Easy marks. Part (c) required a list of the allocation of group relief which did not need to be related to the facts of the question and therefore should have been answerable even if the figure work in the other parts of the question was not correct.

Drawing a diagram matching profits of the corresponding periods is a good way to ensure you answer the question correctly and gain all the marks. Such a drawing is a perfectly acceptable part of your workings and should be handed in as part of your answer to the examiner.

Examiner's comments. In part (b) many candidates had problems in calculating the group relief for non-coterminous periods. Part (c) was well answered by most candidates. In part (d), the majority of candidates did not appreciate that group relief should be restricted to bring the holding company's profits down to the SCR lower limit.

			Marks
(a)	Depreciation	½	
	Dividends	½	
	Deduct CAs/ IBAs	1	
	P&M – Pool	3	
	– Car sold	2	
	– SLA	1½	
	– Car acquired	1	
	– FYA	1	
	IBA – residue of expenditure	2	
	– offices	1	
	– balance of tax life	1	
	– WDA	½	
			15
(b)	Trading income	½	
	Property business income/capital gain	½	
	Gift aid donation	1	
	Group relief – year ended 31 December 2006	1½	
	– year ended 31 December 2007	1½	
	Associated company	1	
	Corporation tax	2	
			8
(c)	Marginal rate	1	
	Full rate	½	
	Small companies rate	½	
	Loss of Gift Aid relief	1	
	Other considerations	1	
			4
(d)	Year ended 31 December 2006 (Gold Ltd)	1	
	Year ended 31 December 2007 (Gold Ltd)	1	
	Year ended 30 June 2007 (Silver Ltd)	1	
			3
			30

(a) **Trade loss year ended 30 June 2007**

	£	£
Loss before taxation		(50,950)
Add depreciation		37,560
		(13,390)
Less dividend income	116,514	
capital allowances (W1)	3,869	
IBAs (W2)	6,227	
		(126,610)
Trade loss		(140,000)

Workings

1   *Capital allowances*

	FYA £	Pool £	Car (1) £	SLA £	Car (2) £	Allowances £
TWDV b/f		18,225	11,750	2,700		
Additions						
1 July 2006 equipment	3,360					
31 August 2006 car (2)					23,250	
12 November 2006 car (3)		9,500				
		27,725				
Disposals						
5 July 2006 car			(18,700)			
7 October 2006 van (restrict to cost)		(11,750)				
16 April 2007 SLA				(555)		
		15,975				
BC			(6,950)			(6,950)
BA				2,145		2,145
FYA @ 50%	(1,680)					1,680
WDA @ 25%/£3,000		(3,994)			(3,000)	6,994
Transfer to general pool	(1,680)	1,680				
TWDV c/f/ Allowances		13,661			20,250	3,869

2   *Industrial buildings allowance*

Second-hand factory

WDA based on residue of expenditure before sale

Original cost £(215,000 – 55,000) (general offices allowable as <25% of £160,000)	£160,000
Less allowances given: 4% × 160,000 × 7	(44,800)
Residue of expenditure	115,200

Remaining life of factory at purchase (1 June 2007 to 30 November 2025) = 18½ years

$$WDA = \frac{115,200}{18\frac{1}{2}} = £6,227$$

(b)   **Gold Ltd – Corporation tax computation**

	Year ended 31 December	
	2006 £	2007 £
Trading income	177,000	90,000
Property business income	5,000	–
Capital gain	–	12,000
	182,000	102,000
Less gift aid donation	(2,000)	(2,000)
	180,000	100,000
Less group relief (W1)	(70,000)	(50,000)
PCTCT	110,000	50,000
CT (W1)	20,900	
£110,000 × 19%		2,375
£12,500 × 19%		7,500
£37,500 × 20%		9,875

Working

Gold Ltd

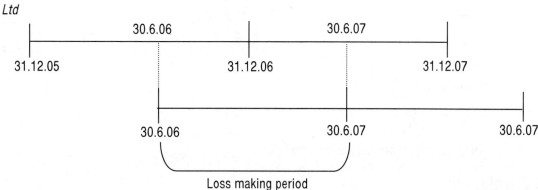

For year ended 31 December 2006 profits of the corresponding period (1 July 2006 to 31 December 2006) are £180,000 × 6/12 = £90,000 and the corresponding loss is £140,000 × 6/12 = £70,000.

Therefore maximum group relief is £70,000.

For year ended 31 December 2007, profits of the corresponding period (1 January 2007 to 30 June 2007) are £100,000 × 6/12 = £50,000 and the corresponding loss is £70,000.

Therefore maximum group relief is £50,000.

(c) Group relief should be allocated in the following order:

   (1) To companies in the small companies' marginal relief band paying 32.5% tax (or 32.75 in FY 2006 and FY 2005) to bring them down to the small companies' rate limit.

   (2) To companies paying the full rate of 30%.

   (3) To companies paying the small companies' rate of 19%/20%.

   Consideration should also be given to the loss of Gift Aid relief.

   Subject to the above considerations, loss relief should be claimed as early as possible.

(d) The group relief claim should be restricted to £30,000 for the year ended 31 December 2006 to bring the PCTCT to the lower limit of £150,000. No claim should be made for year ended 31 December 2007 since the PCTCT is already below £150,000. Instead the remainder of the loss £(140,000 − 30,000) = £110,000 should be carried back against Silver Ltd's own profit for year ended 30 June 2006 which is mostly taxable at 32.75%.

Workings

1 CT rate

   Year ended 31 December 2006

   The accounting period straddles FY 2005 and FY 2006. The company will pay tax at small companies rate, which is 19% in both years.

Year ended 31 December 2007

The accounting period straddles FY 2006 and FY 2007.

	FY 2006 3 months to 31 March 2007	FY 2007 9 months to 31 December 2007
PCTCT (3:9)	12,500	37,500
Lower limit		
£300,000 × $\frac{3}{12}\Big/\frac{9}{12}$	75,000	225,000

Small companies rate applies for both FYs.

44 Apple Ltd

> **Text references.** Corporation tax computations are covered in Chapter 20. Chargeable gains are dealt with in Chapters 13 and 16. Group relief is covered in Chapter 22.
>
> **Top tips.** When using losses, consider the marginal rates of tax of each company.

Marking scheme

				Marks
(a)	(i)	*Surrender of trading losses*		
		Rate of corporation tax	1	
		Order of set off	1	
		Minority interests	1	
	(ii)	*Chargeable assets*		
		Capital losses cannot be group relieved	1	
		Optimum use of capital losses	1	
		Available	5	
		Maximum		4
(b)	(i)	*Profits chargeable to corporation tax*		
		Apple – Trading profits	1	
		– Capital gains	1	
		Bramley Ltd's Loss	1	
		Cox Ltd's loss	1	
		Delicious Ltd's loss	1	
				5
	(ii)	*Corporation tax saving*		
		Delicious Ltd – Transfer leasehold to Apple Ltd	1	
		Capital loss – use in Apple Ltd	2	
		Rollover relief	1	
		Proceeds not reinvested still chargeable	1	
		Corporation tax saving	1	
		Bramley Ltd's loss	2	
		Cox Ltd's loss	2	
		Delicious Ltd's loss	1	
		Corporation tax savings	3	
		Available	14	
		Maximum		11
		Maximum		20

(a) (i) The most important factor that should be taken into account when deciding which group companies the trading losses should be surrendered to is the rate of corporation tax applicable to those companies. Surrender should be made initially to companies subject to corporation tax at the marginal rate of 32.5% (or 32.75% in FY 2006 and FY 2005). The amount surrendered should be sufficient to bring the claimant company's profits down to the corporation tax lower limit. Surrender should then be to those companies subject to the full rate of corporation tax of 30%, then to companies subject to corporation tax at the small company rate of 20% (or 19% in FY 2006 and FY 2005). The ability of companies with minority interests to compensate for group relief surrenders will be another factor.

(ii) *Chargeable assets*

It would probably be beneficial for all the eligible subsidiary companies to elect to deem the transfer of chargeable assets to Apple Ltd prior to their disposal outside of the group, because capital losses cannot be group relieved. Such deemed transfers would therefore allow chargeable gains and allowable losses to arise in the same company. These losses can then either be offset against chargeable gains of the same period, or carried forward against future chargeable gains. Such elections must be made within 2 years of the end of the accounting period in which the disposal is made.

(b) (i) *Apple Ltd*

	Years ended 31 March		
	2007	2008	2009
	£	£	£
Trading profits	620,000	250,000	585,000
Capital gain	–	120,000	80,000
PCTCT	620,000	370,000	665,000

Bramley Ltd

	Years ended 31 March		
	2007	2008	2009
	£	£	£
Trading profits	–	52,000	70,000
Less: carry forward loss relief	–	(52,000)	(12,000)
PCTCT	–	–	58,000

Cox Ltd

	Years ended 31 March		
	2007	2008	2009
	£	£	£
Trading profits	83,000	–	40,000
Less: carry back loss relief	(58,000)	–	–
PCTCT	25,000	–	40,000

Delicious Ltd

	Years ended 31 March		
	2007	2008	2009
	£	£	£
Trading profits	–	90,000	–
Less: carry back loss relief	–	(15,000)	–
PCTCT	–	75,000	–

(ii)   *Apple Ltd*

	Years ended 31 March		
	2007	*2008*	*2009*
	£	£	£
Trading profits	620,000	250,000	585,000
Chargeable gain	–	20,000	36,000
Less group relief	(64,000)	(58,000)	–
PCTCT	556,000	212,000	621,000

In the year to 31 March 2007 group relief has been claimed for Bramley Ltd's loss. This saves Apple Ltd corporation tax of £19,200 (£64,000 × 30%). If the loss had been carried forward as shown above it would have saved Bramley Ltd tax of £12,800 (20% × £64,000). The overall tax saving to the group arising as a result of the group relief claim is £6,400.

Rollover relief has been claimed to defer £100,000 of the chargeable gain arising in the year to 31 March 2008. The £20,000 gain remaining chargeable is equal to the amount of proceeds not reinvested by Cox Ltd in the freehold factory. The lower limit for the year to 31 March 2008 is £75,000 so the rollover relief saves Apple Ltd corporation tax of £32,500 (£100,000 × 32.5%).

It is assumed that Delicious Ltd and Apple Ltd will make an election to deem the transfer of the leasehold factory between them immediately before sale. If this occurs, the loss on the sale of the factory will arise on Apple Ltd in the year to 31 March 2009. Apple Ltd will be able to relieve the £44,000 loss by setting it against its chargeable gain for the year, saving tax of £13,200 (£44,000 × 30%)

In the year to 31 March 2008 group relief has been claimed for Cox Ltd's loss. This saves corporation tax of £18,850 (£58,000 × 32.5%). If the loss had been carried back as shown above, it would have saved Cox Ltd corporation tax of £11,600 (£58,000 × 20%). The overall tax saving to the group of a group relief claim is therefore £7,250 (£18,850 – £11,600).

Delicious Ltd could surrender its loss of £15,000 in the year to 31 March 2009 to Cox Ltd. This would not be beneficial as the tax saving would be at 20% whereas the tax saving will be at 32.5% if the carry back relief claim shown in (b) (i) above is made.

45 Tock-Tick Ltd

Text references. Calculation of taxable profits PCTCT and CT in Chapters 19 and 20. Capital allowances covered in Chapter 8. Group relief is covered in Chapter 22. Rollover relief in Chapter 16.

Top tips. Make sure you know the tax consequences of a company being in different type of group and can apply the rules accordingly. In addition ensure you understand the differences between a small, medium and large company for capital allowance FYAs.

Easy marks. Part (a) was an adjustment of profits with many standard items to adjust for easy marks. Always show workings and state why you are/are not adjusting profits for items in the question to gain all possible marks (see examiner's comments below). Follow question requirements carefully, for example calculation of CT was **not** required. Don't waste your time and effort doing things the examiner doesn't ask for – no marks for doing this.

Examiner's comments. This question was generally very well answered, with many candidates achieving maximum marks. Parts (a) and (b) caused few problems. However, some candidates lost marks by not showing their workings for disallowed items when calculating the trading profit. Many candidates wasted time by calculating the corporation tax liability when this was not required. It was pleasing to see that part (c) was also generally well answered, given that the areas covered were not so straightforward as those in parts (a) and (b).

Marking scheme

			Marks
(a)	Depreciation	½	
	Impairment losses	2	
	Gifts	1	
	Long service award	½	
	Donations	1½	
	Professional fees	3	
	Repairs and renewals	1	
	Other expenses	1½	
	Disposal of office building	½	
	Loan interest received	½	
	Interest payable	½	
	Capital allowances – Pool	1	
	– Expensive motor car	2	
	– Short-life asset sold	1½	
	– FYA	2	19
(b)	Trading income	½	
	Interest income	1	
	Capital gain	2	
	Gift aid donation	1½	5
(c)	**Large-sized company**		
	First-year allowances	1½	
	PCTCT effect	½	
	Group relief		
	Group relief claim	1½	
	PCTCT effect	½	
	Rollover relief		
	Rollover relief claim	1½	
	PCTCT effect	½	6
			30

(a) **Tock-Tick Ltd – trading income**

		£	£
Profit before tax			184,220
Add	depreciation	99,890	
	impairment loss – non-trade	6,200	
	gifts to customers (N1)	720	
	gift aid donation (N3)	600	
	donation to national charity	250	
	legal fees – Share capital issue	2,900	
	legal fees – Court action	900	
	repairs and renewals – extension (N5)	53,300	
	other expenses – customer entertaining	2,160	
			166,920
			351,140
Less:	profit on disposal of office building	78,100	
	loan interest	12,330	
	CAs (W)	10,640	
			(101,070)
Trading income			250,070

Notes

(1)	The gifts of pens are allowable as they cost less than £50 per recipient in the tax year and carry a conspicuous advertisement for the company making the gift. The hampers are not allowed as they are food gifts.

(2)	Long service awards are allowable as a trading expense.

(3)	If a donation has been made under the gift aid scheme this is deductible from total income.

(4)	Costs of renewing a short lease (50 years or less) and costs of registering the company's trademark are specifically allowed by statute.

(5)	The cost of the extension is capital expenditure and therefore is not allowable. The replacement of the roof should be fully allowable so long as it can be shown that the company could not carry on its business at the premises without the repair.

(6)	The counselling services and costs of seconding an employee to charity are allowable.

(7)	The interest payable on a loan taken out for a trading purpose is an allowable deduction in computing trading income

Working: Capital allowances

	FYA £	Pool £	Exp car £	SLA £	Allowances £
TWDV b/f		12,200	20,800	3,100	
Disposals					
Proceeds (restricted to cost)			(33,600)	(460)	
Balancing charge			(12,800)		(12,800)
Balancing allowance				2,640	2,640
WDA @ 25%		(3,050)			3,050
Additions qualifying for FYAs					
Equipment (N2)	6,700				
FYA @ 50%	(3,350)				3,350
				3,350	
Low emission car (N1)	14,400				
FYA @ 100%	(14,400)	0			14,400
TWDV c/f		9,150		3,350	
Allowances					10,640

Notes

(1)	The 'low emission' car (ie g/km < 120g/km) attracts 100% FYAs (for all size companies).

(2)	Tock-Tick Ltd is a small company (stated in the question) and will therefore receive FYAs on plant and machinery at a rate of 50% in the period 1 April 2007 to 31 March 2008.

(b)	**PCTCT**

	£
Trading income	250,070
Interest income *(N)*	12,330
Chargeable gain *(W)*	38,200
	300,600
Less gift aid donation	(600)
PCTCT	300,000

Note. Interest received is taxed as interest income on accruals basis.

Working

	£
Chargeable gain	
Proceeds	276,000
Less: cost	(197,900)
Unindexed gain	78,100
Less: IA to date of disposal	(39,900)
Indexed gain	38,200

(c) (i) **Effect if large sized company**

If Tock-Tick Ltd had been a large company rather than a small company there would be no FYAs available except in respect of the low emission car.

The capital allowances figure deducted from adjusted profits would have been smaller resulting in an increase in PCTCT of £1,675 (£3,350 – £1,675).

(ii) **Group relief**

Only 9 months of the two companies' accounting periods overlap (1 April 2007 to 31 December 2007) and therefore the maximum group relief available would be the lower of:

(a) 9/12 × Tock-Tick's PCTCT of £300,000 ie £225,000; and

(b) 9/12 × subsidiary's loss of £62,400 ie £46,800.

Therefore Tock-Tick Ltd's total profits before gift aid of £300,600 would be reduced by £46,800 to £253,800. Its PCTCT would therefore be reduced to £253,200.

(iii) **Rollover relief**

The sale proceeds of the disposal of the freehold office building (£276,000) are partially reinvested in the new office building (£260,000).

To the extent that they are not reinvested, £(276,000 – 260,000) = £16,000, the gain remains in charge.

The balance of the gain (£38,200 – 16,000) = £22,200 can be rolled over and thus reduce the company's PCTCT by that amount.

46 Lithograph Ltd

Text references. Chapters 25 and 26 deal with VAT.

Top tips. Read the question carefully to determine whether the figures you have been given include the VAT or not.

Marking scheme

		Marks
(a)	Monthly payments	½
	Based on prior year	½
	10%	½
	Months 4 to 12	½
	Calculation	1
		3

(b)	(i)		
		Sales @ 17½%	½
		Office equipment sale @ 17½%	½
		Fuel scale charge @ 7/47	1
		Purchases	½
		Expenses	½
		Machinery	½
		Bad debt	1
		Output VAT less input VAT @ 17½%	½
			5
	(ii)	Balancing payment	1
		Due date	1
			2
			10

(a)   Monthly payments on account

As Lithograph Ltd uses the annual accounting scheme it will be paying monthly payments on account based on its previous year's liability.

It will make payments in months 4 to 12 of its VAT accounting period, each payment being 10% of the previous year's liability.

Lithograph Ltd will therefore have made payments of 10% x £10,200 = £1,020 from April 2007 to December 2007.

(b)   (i)   **VAT for y/e 31 December 2007**

	£		£
Output VAT			
Sales	160,000	@ 17.5%	28,000
Office equipment sale	8,000	@ 17.5%	1,400
Fuel scale charge (N1)	1,385	@ $^7/_{47}$	206
			29,606
Less: Input VAT			
Purchases	38,000		
Expenses			
28,000 – 3,600 (N2)	24,400		
Machinery purchase	24,000		
Bad debt (N3)	4,800		
	91,200	@ 17.5%	(15,960)
VAT due			13,646

Notes

1   Fuel scale charge

As the whole of the fuel VAT expense, including private fuel, has been deducted (included in the expenses) we need to restrict by using the fuel scale charge.

As this is a VAT inclusive figure we need to adjust by multiplying by $^7/_{47}$

2   Expenses

Customer entertaining is never allowable for VAT purposes.

3   Bad debt

As the debt is over 6 months old and has been written off in the company's books, it is possible to claim bad debt relief.

(ii) **Balancing payment and due date**

The balancing payment due would be:

	£
VAT due	13,646
Less: paid on account (9 payments)	(9,180)
Due by 28 February 2008	4,466

47 Tardy Ltd

Text references. VAT is covered in Chapters 25 and 26.

Top tips. Do not ignore the administrative side of VAT as most exam questions will test both numerical and written aspects of the tax.

Easy marks. Bad debts are often examined and the conditions and how to deal with the debts should have been easy marks. The examiner frequently mentions that students are weak at applying their knowledge to the given facts in a question. Part (a) dealt with default surcharge. You need to outline which returns were in default but **also** discuss the impact of the default. There were 7 marks for doing this – easy marks for the knowledgeable student.

Examiner's comments. Part (a) caused problems for a number of candidates. The main problem was that candidates explained the default surcharge rules, without applying them to the information given. Many candidates did not appreciate that the submission of four consecutive VAT returns on time resulted in a clean default surcharge record.

Marking scheme

			Marks
(a)	Quarter ended 30 September 2005	1	
	Quarter ended 31 December 2005	1	
	Quarter ended 30 June 2006	1½	
	Quarter ended 30 September 2006	1	
	Extension of surcharge period	½	
	Four consecutive VAT returns on time	1	
	Quarter ended 31 December 2007	1	
			7
(b)	Net errors of less than £2,000	1	
	Net errors of more than £2,000	1	
	Default interest	1	
			3
			10

(a) **Surcharge Liability Notices**

Following the first default for the quarter ended 30 September 2005, a Surcharge Liability Notice (SLN) will have been issued for a period of 12 months ie to 30 September 2006. There is no penalty at this stage.

When Tardy Ltd defaulted for the quarter ended 31 December 2005, which fell within the SLN period, there will have been a surcharge of 2% of the outstanding tax, ie £644 (£32,200 × 2%). The SLN period would have been extended until 31 December 2006.

T Ltd is late again for the quarter ended 30 June 2006. The SLN period will now extend until 30 June 2007. The surcharge would strictly be 5% of the unpaid VAT, £170 (as it is the second default within the period to

31 December 2006. However, as this is would be less than the de minimis limit of £400, no surcharge assessment would have been issued.

The next return for the quarter ended 30 September 2006 is also late, so the SLN period would be extended to 30 September 2007. However there would be no surcharge as there is a repayment due and only late payment incurs a surcharge.

The next four returns for the period to 30 September 2007 are submitted on time and therefore the SLN period expires on 30 September 2007.

The return for the quarter ended 31 December 2007 is late. The company has had a clean record for one whole 12 months period and therefore the SLN period starts again, running to 31 December 2008, and there will be no surcharge for this default.

(b)   **Errors < £2,000**

Net VAT errors of £2,000 or less discovered may be included in the VAT return for the quarter ending 30 June 2008.

No interest will be charged on net VAT errors of £2,000 or less.

Errors > £2,000

Net VAT errors over £2,000 can be voluntarily disclosed but they must be notified separately to HMRC, not just by putting them on the next VAT return.

Default interest will be charged.

48 Ram-Rom Ltd

Text references. VAT is dealt with in Chapters 25 and 26.

Top tips. In part (a) you are given the input VAT recoverable so you must make sure that your answer reconciles with this figure. For part (b), make a rough list of the contents of the VAT invoice and then see which items are missing from the sample invoice given.

Easy marks. There were plenty of easy marks in this question. You should have been able to work out the items for part (a) since the examiner gave the amount of input tax recovered. Discounts are often examined, so you should ensure that you are very familiar with them.

Examiner's comments. Candidates often failed to show their workings of how they calculated pre-registration input VAT.

Marking scheme

			Marks
(a)	Goods – explanation	1	
	– stock	½	
	– fixed assets	1½	
	Services – explanation	½	
	– calculation	1½	5
(b)	Registration number	½	
	Invoice number	½	
	Rate of VAT	½	
	VAT exclusive amount	½	
	Total VAT exclusive price	½	
	Total VAT	½	3

(c) Charge to VAT   1

     No change if not taken up   <u>1</u>   <u>2</u>

     <u>10</u>

(a) Input VAT recovery – pre registration inputs

Input VAT is recoverable on goods if they are:

- Acquired within 3 years prior to registration
- For business purposes
- Not supplied onwards or consumed prior to registration

	£
Fixed assets – July 2007 acquisition £42,000 × 17.5%	7,350
– February 2008 acquisition £66,600 × 17.5%	11,655
Stock still held £92,000 × 17.5%	<u>16,100</u>
Input VAT on goods recoverable	<u>35,105</u>

Input VAT is recoverable on services if they are:

- Supplied within six months prior to registration
- For purposes of business

	£
September 2007	7,400
October 2007	6,300
November 2007	8,500
December 2007	9,000
January 2008	9,200
February 2008	<u>8,200</u>
	48,600

× 17.5% = £8,505

Total VAT recoverable £(35,105 + 8,505) = £43,610

(b) Alterations to invoice – must include

- Registration number
- Invoice number
- Rate of VAT for each supply of goods
- VAT exclusive amount for each supply of goods
- Total invoice price excluding VAT
- The total amount of VAT

(c) Where a discount is offered for prompt payment, VAT is chargeable on the net amount, regardless of whether the discount is taken up.

49 Sandy Brick

> **Text references.** Chapters 25 and 26 for VAT.
>
> **Top tips.** As with any question which requires a calculation, setting out the figures in a proforma will help both you and the examiner marking your paper.
>
> **Easy marks.** The tax point and invoice issuing rules were easy marks.
>
> **Examiner's comments.** Well answered but some candidates were penalised for not clearly showing which of their calculations were output VAT and which were input VAT.

Marking scheme

	Marks
Sales – VAT registered customers	1½
– Non-VAT registered customers	1½
Advance payment	1
Materials	1
Office equipment	2
Telephone	1
Motor repairs	1
Equipment	1
	10

VAT return

	£	£
Output VAT		
Sales to VAT registered customers		
£(44,000 × 95%) = £41,800 × 17.5%		7,315
Sales to non-VAT registered customers		
£(16,920 – 5,170) = £11,750 × 7/47		1,750
Payment on account		
£5,000 × 7/47		745
Total output VAT		9,810
Less: Input VAT		
Materials £(11,200 – 800) = £10,400 × 17.5%	1,820	
Office equipment £(120 × 9) = £1,080 × 17.5% (N1)	189	
Telephone £(400 × 70%) = 280 × 17.5%	49	
Motor repairs £920 × 17.5%	161	
Equipment £6,000 × 17.5%	1,050	(3,269)
Net VAT payable		6,541

Notes

(1) **Pre-registration VAT can be recovered on services for six months before the registration date.** Therefore 9 months of input tax can be recovered.

(2) **If a car is used for business purposes, then any VAT charged on repairs and maintenance costs can be treated as input tax. No apportionment has to be made for private use.**

50 Carolyn Kraft

Text references. Chapters 2, 12, and 13 to 17 are required reading for this question.

Top tips. The requirement is already helpfully broken down, so first of all deal with the part you know best to pick up marks early on and boost your confidence. You can really improve your presentation by starting each requirement on a new page. However, do not spend too much time on any one requirement – use the mark allocation as an indication of how much time to spend on each. Finally, do not miss out on the easy marks available for stating payment dates – you could even answer these parts of the relevant requirements first so you don't forget.

Marking scheme

			Marks
(a)	*Income tax – Carolyn*		
	Salary	½	
	Interest	½	
	PA	½	
	Tax bands	1	
	Extension of basic rate band	½	
	Tax rates	½	
	Deduct PAYE	½	
	Deduct tax credit on interest	½	
	Due date	½	
	Income tax – Mike		
	Profits less CAs	½	
	Dividends	½	
	PA	½	
	Tax bands	1	
	Extension of basic rate band	½	
	Tax rates	½	
	Deduct tax credit on dividends	½	
	Due date	½	
	POAs – amounts	½	
	– dates	1	11
(b)	*NIC – Carolyn*		
	Class 1	1½	
	NIC – Mike		
	Class 2	1	
	Class 4	1½	4

ANSWERS

(c) *CGT – Carolyn*

Proceeds less cost	1
Enhancement expenditure	1
No taper relief	1
AE	½
Tax rate	½
Due date	½

CGT – Mike

Proceeds less cost	1	
Taper relief	1	
AE	½	
Tax rate	½	
Due date	½	8

(d)

Rollover relief	½	
Time period	½	
Reinvestment of proceeds	½	
Taper earned to date is lost	½	2
		25

(a) **Income tax calculations**

Carolyn

	Non-savings income £	Savings income £
Salary	32,600	
Bank interest £8,000 × **100/80**		10,000
Net income	32,600	10,000
Less PA	(5,225)	
Taxable income	27,375	10,000

> Don't forget to gross up net income

	£
Tax	
£2,230 × 10%	223
£25,145 × 22%	5,532
£7,225 × 20%	1,445
£1,000 × 20% (W1)	200
£1,775 × 40%	710
Total tax liability	8,110
Less tax credits	
(i) PAYE	(5,366)
(ii) Interest: £10,000 @ 20%	(2,000)
Tax **due by 31 January 2009**	744

> Do a working to show the extension of the basic rate band

> Always state the due dates – it's a good habit to get into

Mike

	Non-savings income	Dividend income
	£	£
Trade profit (W2)	51,800	
Dividends £9,000 × 100/90		10,000
Net income	51,800	10,000
Less PA	(5,225)	
Taxable income	46,575	10,000

	£
Tax	
£2,230 × 10%	223
£32,370 × 22%	7,121
£4,000 × 22% (W3)	880
£7,975 × 40%	3,190
£10,000 × 32.5%	3,250
Total tax liability	14,664
Less tax credit on dividends: £10,000 @ 10%	(1,000)
Tax due 31 January 2009	13,664

Consider POAs for anyone whose tax is not all collected at source

Mike also needs to make **payments on account** as more than 20% of his tax is **not** collected at source:

1st POA: 50% × £13,664 = 6,832

Total due 31. January 2009: 20,496

2nd POA: due 31 July 2009: 6,832

Make sure you reference your workings clearly

Workings

1   *Carolyn's basic rate band*

Extend by gross donation: £780 × 100/78 = £1,000

2   *Mike's taxable trading profits*

	£
Adjusted profit	53,400
Less capital allowances	(1,600)
Taxable trade profits	51,800

3   *Mike's basic rate band*

Extend by gross pension contribution: (£260 × 12) × 100/78 = £4,000

(b)   **National Insurance contributions 2007/08**

(i)   *Carolyn*

Class 1 primary contributions

First   £5,225 @ 0%
         £27,375 @ 11% = £3,011
         £32,600 (below UEL)

(ii) *Mike*

Class 2

£2.20 × 52 = 114

Class 4

	£
£(34,840 − 5,225) = £29,615 @ 8%	2,369
£(51,800 − 34,840) = £16,960 @ 1%	170
	2,539

(c) **Capital gains tax**

(i) *Carolyn*

	£
Proceeds	250,000
Less cost	(180,000)
Renovation (enhancement expenditure)	(30,000)
Gain	40,000
No taper relief – not owned three years (non business asset)	
Less annual exemption	(9,200)
	30,800

> Don't forget to get the easy marks!

CGT @ 40% due 31 January 2009: £12,320

(ii) *Mike*

> State the dates so if you make a mistake with the rate the examiner can see you know the rules

	£
Proceeds	85,000
Less cost	(53,300)
Gain before taper relief	31,700
Gain after taper relief	
10 April 2006 – 9 April 2007 = 1 year for business asset	
50% × £31,700	15,850
Less AE	(9,200)
	6,650

CGT @ 40% due 31 January 2009: £2,660

(d) **Available relief**

> Be brief. Make your sentences snappy. Use bullet points for clarity.

(i) Mike can **claim 'rollover' relief** for reinvestment into replacement business assets.

(ii) He must invest in the new shop within three years of the disposal of the original shop.

(iii) If any proceeds are not reinvested they will be chargeable immediately and only the balance of the gain can be deferred.

(iv) Any taper relief earned on the original shop is lost.

51 Unforeseen Upsets Limited

Text references. Chapters 8, 13, 19, 20 and 24 are required reading for this question.

Top tips. Break a long question like this down into manageable parts in order to gain the easy marks. It is essential that you are aware that a long period of account is split into two accounting periods and that the first period is always twelve months in length. If you do not make this split correctly you cannot hope to pass the question.

Marking scheme

			Marks
(a)	Trading profits (12:3)	1	
	Trading losses brought forward	1	
	Bank interest	1	
	Debenture interest	1½	
	Chargeable gains (W3)	1½	
	Gift Aid Donations	1	
	Capital allowances (W1)		
	Year to 31 December 2007		
	Additions and disposals	1	
	WDA	1	
	FYA 50%	1	
	Period to 31 March 2008		
	WDA	1	
	FYA	1	
	Year to 31 December 2007		
	Small companies rate	1	
	Tax calculation	2	
	Period to 31 March 2008		
	Calculation of 'P'	1	
	Calculation of reduced limits	1	
	Marginal relief	1	
	Calculation of liability	2	
			20
(b)	Due dates for payment	2	
	Due dates for returns	2	
	Penalties	5	
			9
(c)	Capital losses c/fwd		1
			30

(a) **Corporation tax computations**

	Year to 31 December 2007 £	3 months 31 March 2008 £
Trading profits 12:3	900,000	225,000
Less: capital allowances (W1)	(83,750)	(11,279)
	816,250	213,721
Less: **losses b/f**	(600,000)	–
	216,250	213,721
Interest income (W2)	32,000	5,500
Chargeable gains (W3)	–	–
	248,250	219,221
Less: Gift Aid donations	(11,000)	(9,000)
PCTCT	237,250	210,221
Dividends plus tax credits £6,300 × 100/90	–	7,000
'Profits' for small companies' rate purposes	237,250	217,221

Corporation tax (W4)	£	£
FY 2006: £59,312 × 19%	11,269	
FY 2007: £177,938 × 20%	35,588	
FY 2007: £210,221 × 30%		63,066
Less: Small companies' marginal relief		
1/40 (£375,000 – £217,221) × $\frac{210,221}{217,221}$		(3,817)
	46,857	59,249

Boxes (left annotations):
- Split on time basis → Trading profits
- Set against trading income → Less: losses b/f
- Deduct in period paid → Interest income (W2) / Chargeable gains (W3)
- FII → Dividends plus tax credits
- Profits below small companies rate limits → Corporation tax (W4)

(b) £46,857 in respect of the 12 months to 31 December 2007 must be paid by 1 October 2008.

£59,249 in respect of the 3 months to 31 March 2008 must be paid by 1 January 2009.

A return for the 12 months to 31 December 2007 and a return for the 3 months to 31 March 2008 must be filed by **31 March 2009.**

Box (left annotation): Same date for both.

If a return is filed late there is an initial penalty of £100. This rises to £200 if the return is more than 3 months late. These penalties rise to £500 and £1,000 respectively for the third consecutive late filing of a return.

There is in addition a tax geared penalty, if the return is more than six months late. The penalty is 10% of the tax unpaid six months after the return was due if the total delay is up to 12 months, but it increases to 20% of that tax if the return is over 12 months late.

(c)   At 31 March 2008 there are capital losses to carry forward of £20,000 (W3).

Workings

1   *Capital allowances*

	FYA £	Pool £	Expensive Car £	Allowances £
Year to 31.12.07				
TWDV b/f		142,000		
Additions		24,000	14,000	
Disposals		(27,000)		
		139,000	14,000	
WDA @ 25%/(restricted)		(34,750)	(3,000)	37,750
Additions (30.11.07)	92,000			
FYA @ 50%	(46,000)			46,000
		46,000		83,750
TWDV c/f		150,250	11,000	
3 months to 31.3.08				
WDA @ 25%/(restricted)				
× 3/12		(9,391)	(688)	10,079
Additions (28.2.08)	2,400			
FYA @ 50%	(1,200)			1,200
		1,200		11,279
		142,059	10,312	

FYA between 1.4.06 and 31.3.08 @ 50% not 40%

Restricted for short accounting period.

Not restricted in short period

FYA between 1.4.06 and 31.3.08 @ 50% not 40%

2   *Interest income*

The interest is taxable on an accruals basis:

	Year to 31 December 2007 £	3 months 31 March 2008 £
Bank interest	20,000	–
Debenture interest	12,000	5,500
	32,000	5,500

3   *Chargeable gains*

	Year to 31 December 2007 £
Gain	30,000
Loss/b/f	(30,000)
Net gain	–

1 easy mark

The loss c/f on 1 April 2008 is £20,000 (£50,000 – £30,000).

4   *Corporation tax*

Year to 31 December 2007

The year to 31 December 2007 straddles FY 2006 and FY 2007.

	FY 2006 *3 months to* *31.3.07*	*FY 2007* *9 months to* *31.12.07*
PCTCT (3:9)	59,312	177,938
'Profits' (3:9)	59,312	177,938
Lower limit		
£300,000 × $\frac{3}{12}$ $\Big/$ $\frac{9}{12}$	75,000	225,00

Small companies rate applies in both FYs.

3 months to 31 March 2008

	FY 2007 (3/12) £
Profits	210,221
PCTCT	217,221
Lower limit	75,000
Upper limit	375,000

Marginal relief applies.

52 A Ltd

Text references. Chapters 19, 20, 22 and 24 required reading for this question.

Top tips. B Ltd's loss could be set only against the available profits of the corresponding accounting period.

	Marks
Trading income	½
Property business income	½
Interest income	2
Gift aid	1
Group relief	5
FII	1
CT calculation	3
Due dates	2
	15

Corporation Tax computation 9 m/e 31 December 2007

	£	£
Trading income		342,000
Property business income		13,000
Interest income		
Bank interest accrued	5,000	
Loan interest accrued	8,000	
		13,000
		368,000
Less: Gift Aid donation		(17,000)
		351,000
Less: **group relief** (W1)		(34,000)
PCTCT		317,000
Add: franked Investment Income		1,000
'Profits'		318,000

Non-trading → (pointing to Interest income)

	£
Corporation tax	
FY 2007	
£317,000 × 30%	95,100
Less: marginal relief	
$1/40 \ (£562,500 - 318,000) \times \dfrac{317,000}{318,000}$	(6,093)
Mainstream corporation tax	89,007

Work out limits first

£89,007 must be paid by **1 October 2008.**

The corporation tax return for the period must be filed by **31 December 2008**.

These are easy marks.

Note. It is **assumed** that the loan interest and the bank interest arose on non-trading loans and is therefore taxable as interest income.

State any assumptions made

Workings

1   B Ltd joined the group with A Ltd on 1 July 2007 so for A Ltd's profit making accounting period to 31 December 2007 there are 6 months in common with B Ltd's loss making period.

   Thus

   A Ltd   6/9 × £351,000 = £234,000
   B Ltd   6/12 × (£68,000) = £34,000

   Maximum group relief available is **lower of two**, ie £34,000.

Be careful here

2   The 9 months to 31 December 2007 falls into FY 2007.

   'Profits' are between the upper and lower limits of £1,500,000 × 9/12 ÷ 2 = £562,500 and £300,000 × 9/12 ÷ 2 = £112,500, so marginal relief applies.

Mock Exams

ACCA

Paper F6

Taxation (United Kingdom)

Mock Examination 1

Question Paper	
Time allowed	
Reading and Planning	**15 minutes**
Writing	**3 hours**
ALL FIVE questions are compulsory and MUST be attempted.	

During reading and planning time only the question paper may be annotated.

DO NOT OPEN THIS PAPER UNTIL YOU ARE READY TO START UNDER EXAMINATION CONDITIONS

ALL FIVE questions are compulsory and MUST be attempted

53 William Wong (BTX 12/05)

William Wong is the finance director of Glossy Ltd. The company runs a publishing business. The following information is available for the tax year 2007/08:

(1)   William is paid director's remuneration of £2,400 per month by Glossy Ltd.

(2)   In addition to his director's remuneration, William received two bonus payments from Glossy Ltd during the tax year 2007/08. The first bonus of £22,000 was paid on 30 June 2007 and was in respect of the year ended 31 December 2006. William became entitled to this bonus on 15 March 2007. The second bonus of £37,000 was paid on 31 March 2008 and was in respect of the year ended 31 December 2007. William became entitled to this second bonus on 15 March 2008.

(3)   From 6 April 2007 until 31 December 2007 William used his private motor car for business purposes. During this period William drove 12,000 miles in the performance of his duties for Glossy Ltd, for which the company paid an allowance of 30 pence per mile. The relevant statutory mileage rates to be used as a basis of an expense claim are 40 pence per mile for the first 10,000 miles, and 25 pence per mile thereafter.

(4)   From 1 January 2008 to 5 April 2008 Glossy Ltd provided William with a diesel powered company motor car with a list price of £46,000. The motor car cost Glossy Ltd £44,500, and it has an official CO_2 emission rate of 239 grams per kilometre. Glossy Ltd also provided William with fuel for his private journeys.

(5)   William was unable to drive his motor car for two weeks during February 2008 because of an accident, so Glossy Ltd provided him with a chauffeur at a total cost of £1,800.

(6)   Throughout the tax year 2007/08 Glossy Ltd provided William with a television for his personal use that had originally cost £3,825.

(7)   Glossy Ltd has provided William with living accommodation since 1 January 2006. The property was purchased in 1993 for £90,000, and was valued at £210,000 on 1 January 2006. It has an annual value of £10,400.

(8)   Glossy Ltd pays an annual insurance premium of £680 to cover William against any liabilities that might arise in relation to his directorship.

(9)   During May 2007 William spent ten nights overseas on company business. Glossy Ltd paid him a daily allowance of £10 to cover the cost of personal expenses such as telephone calls to William's family.

(10)   William pays an annual professional subscription of £450 to the Institute of Finance Directors, an approved professional body, and a membership fee of £800 to a golf club. He uses the golf club to entertain clients of Glossy Ltd.

Required

(a)   State the rules that determine when a bonus paid to a director is treated as being received for tax purposes.

(3 marks)

(b)   Calculate William's taxable income for the tax year 2007/08.   **(15 marks)**

(c)   Calculate the total amount of both Class 1 and Class 1A national insurance contributions that will have been paid by William and Glossy Ltd in respect of William's earnings and benefits for the tax year 2007/08.

(5 marks)

(d)   Advise William of the forms that Glossy Ltd must provide to him following the end of the tax year 2007/08 in respect of his earnings and benefits for that year, and state the dates by which these forms have to be provided to him.   **(2 marks)**

(Total = 25 marks)

54 Hipster Ltd

(a)   Hipster Ltd commenced trading on 1 January 2007 as a clothing manufacturer, preparing its first accounts for the six-month period ended 30 June 2007. The following information is available:

Trading profit

The tax adjusted trading profit is £334,500. This figure is before making any tax adjustments required for:

(1)   Capital allowances.

(2)   The premium paid in respect of the leasehold property.

(3)   Advertising expenditure of £4,600. This expenditure was incurred during December 2006 and was deducted in arriving at the accounting profit for the period ended 30 June 2007.

Plant and machinery

The following purchases and disposals of plant and machinery took place in respect of the six-month period ended 30 June 2007:

		Cost/proceeds £
10 November 2006	Purchased equipment	8,900
12 January 2007	Purchased machinery	22,140
29 March 2007	Purchased motor car (1)	11,600
18 April 2007	Purchased motor car (2)	14,800
7 May 2007	Purchased equipment	7,700
28 June 2007	Sold motor car (2)	(11,300)
28 June 2007	Purchased motor car (3)	18,500

Hipster Ltd is a small company as defined by the Companies Acts.

Industrial building

Hipster Ltd purchased a new factory from a builder on 1 January 2007 for £460,000, and this was immediately brought into use. The cost was made up as follows:

	£
Land	112,000
Factory	220,000
Canteen for employees	38,000
Showroom	90,000
	460,000

Leasehold property

On 1 January 2007 Hipster Ltd acquired a leasehold office building, paying a premium of £80,000 for the grant of a twenty-year lease. The office building was used for business purposes by Hipster Ltd throughout the six-month period ended 30 June 2007.

Loan interest received

Loan interest of £1,650 was received on 30 June 2007. The loan was made for non-trading purposes.

Profit on disposal of shares

On 28 June 2007 Hipster Ltd sold 5,000 £1 ordinary shares in Bellbottom plc for £23,600. Hipster Ltd had originally purchased 8,000 shares in Bellbottom plc on 8 February 2007 for £3,000. On 21 February 2007 Bellbottom plc made a 1 for 4 bonus issue. The indexation factor from February 2007 to June 2007 is 0·020.

Dividends received

During the period ended 30 June 2007 Hipster Ltd received dividends of £21,600 from Drainpipe plc, an unconnected UK company. This figure was the actual cash amount received.

Other information

Hipster Ltd has no associated companies.

Required:

Calculate Hipster Ltd's corporation tax liability for the six-month period ended 30 June 2007.   **(20 marks)**

(b)   Victor Ltd has been in business as a hairdresser since 1 June 2005. Its sales from the date of commencement of the business to 30 September 2007 were £5,300 per month. On 1 October 2007 Victor Ltd increased the prices that it charged customers, and from that date its sales have been £5,550 per month. Victor Ltd's sales are all standard rated.

As a result of the price increase, Victor Ltd was required to register for value added tax (VAT) from 1 January 2008. Because all of its customers are members of the general public, it was not possible to increase prices any further as a result of registering for VAT.

Victor Ltd's standard rated expenses are £400 per month.

Where applicable, the above figures are inclusive of VAT.

Required

(i)   Explain why Victor Ltd was required to compulsorily register for VAT from 1 January 2008, and state what action it then had to take as regards notifying HM Revenue and Customs of the registration.

(4 marks)

(ii)   Calculate the total amount of VAT payable by Victor Ltd during the year ended 31 December 2008. You should ignore pre-registration input VAT.   **(3 marks)**

(iii)   Advise Victor Ltd why it would have been beneficial to have used the VAT flat rate scheme from 1 January 2008. Your answer should include a calculation of the amount of VAT that Victor Ltd would have saved for the year ended 31 December 2008 by joining the scheme. The flat rate scheme percentage for hairdressing is 12%.

(3 marks)

(Total = 30 marks)

55 Michael Chin (BTX 06/05)

Michael Chin made the following gifts of assets to his daughter, Mika, during 2007/08:

(1)   On 30 June 2007 Michael gave Mika a business that he had run as a sole trader since 1 January 2002. The market value of the business on 30 June 2007 was £250,000, made up as follows:

	£
Goodwill	60,000
Freehold property	150,000
Net current assets	40,000
	250,000

The goodwill has been built up since 1 January 2002, and had a nil cost. The freehold property had cost £86,000 on 20 September 2006. Michael used 75% of this property for business purposes, but the other 25% has never been used for business purposes.

(2)   On 8 December 2007 Michael gave Mika his entire holding of 50,000 50p ordinary shares (a 60% holding) in Minnow Ltd, an unquoted trading company. The market value of the shares on that date was £180,000. Michael had originally purchased the shares on 5 January 2007 for £87,500. On 8 December 2007 the market value of Minnow Ltd's chargeable assets was £250,000, of which £200,000 was in respect of chargeable business assets.

(3)   On 15 February 2008 Michael gave Mika 18,000 £1 ordinary shares in Whale plc, a quoted trading company. On that date the shares were quoted at £6·36 – £6·52. Michael had originally purchased 15,000 shares in Whale plc on 7 December 2006 for £63,000, and he purchased a further 12,000 shares on 21 August 2007 for £26,400. The total shareholding was less than 1% of Whale plc's issued share capital.

Where possible, Michael and Mika have elected to hold over any gains arising. Taper relief is not available in respect of any of the above disposals, and so can be ignored.

Michael also made the following unconnected disposals during the year.

(4)   On 18 July 2007 he sold his BMW car to a neighbour for £16,500. He had purchased the car on 13 December 2005 for £23,500.

(5)   On 2 April 2008 he sold an antique teapot for £8,600 at auction. He had purchased the teapot on 16 May 2003 for £4,500. He incurred auctioneer's fees of 10% of the proceeds.

Michael incurred a capital loss of £17,300 during 2005/06, and made a capital gain of £11,200 during 2006/07. His net income for 2007/08 is £6,305.

Required

Calculate Michael's capital gains tax liability for 2007/08, clearly showing the amount of any gains that can be held over. You should assume that the rate of annual exemption for 2007/08 applies throughout.

(20 marks)

56 Richard Desk (BTX 12/04)

Richard Desk has been a self-employed manufacturer of office furniture since 1994. He has the following income, capital gains and capital losses for 2005/06, 2006/07 and 2007/08:

	2005/06	2006/07	2007/08
	£	£	£
Trading profit/(loss)	8,800	(26,500)	8,600
Property business profit/(loss)	(600)	3,000	2,800
Building society interest (gross)	600	400	500
Capital gains	16,100	7,800	14,900
Capital losses	(2,000)	(9,000)	(4,000)

The capital gains are stated after taking account of indexation, but before taking account of loss relief and the annual exemption. No taper relief is available.

Required

(a)   Calculate Richard's taxable income and chargeable gains for 2005/06, 2006/07 and 2007/08 on the basis that he relieves the trading loss of £26,500 for 2006/07 against his general income for 2005/06 (ie carry back loss relief) and then against the capital gains of the same year. You should assume that the tax allowances for 2007/08 apply throughout.   **(12 marks)**

(b)   Explain why the claim in (a) above is probably Richard's most beneficial trading loss relief claim. No further calculations are required.   **(3 marks)**

(Total = 15 marks)

57 Oscar Thomson

Oscar owns three freehold properties as follows:

A   27 Alwyn Crescent
B   18 Byrd Avenue
C   5 Copland Road

All are let out unfurnished.

A   Let out until 5 June 2007 at an annual rent of £12,000 payable monthly in advance on the 6th of each month. On 6 October 2007 the property was let out to a new tenant on a 10 year lease agreement at an annual rental of £8,000 payable on the 6th of each month. The new tenant also paid a premium of £5,000.

B   Let out throughout 2007/08. The annual rental was £18,000 payable monthly in advance on the 6th of each month. However, the rental due on 6 February 2008 was not received until 10 April 2008 and the rental due on 6 March 2008 was never received and the tenant could not be traced.

C   Acquired on 6 July 2007 and let out from that date at an annual rental of £6,000 payable monthly in advance on the 6th of each month. No premium was payable. The property was damaged in a flood in December 2007.

Expenditure in connection with the properties was as follows:

	A £	B £	C £
Agent's commission	750	800	600
Advertising for new tenants	100	–	–
Legal fees: lease agreement	–	–	150
Repairs: flood damage	–	–	1,500
new kitchen units	1,000	–	–
Loan interest	–	–	2,500

Oscar also rented out a furnished room in his main residence. The rental payable in 2007/08 was £4,000. He has expenses of £800 in connection with the letting.

Required

Compute Oscar's property business income for 2007/08.   **(10 marks)**

Answers

DO NOT TURN THIS PAGE UNTIL YOU HAVE
COMPLETED THE MOCK EXAM

A plan of attack

What's the worst thing you could be doing right now if this was the actual exam paper? Sharpening your pencil? Wondering how to celebrate the end of the exam in about 3 hours time? Panicking, flapping and generally getting in a right old state?

Well, they're all pretty bad, so turn back to the paper and let's sort out a **plan of attack**!

First things first

You have fifteen minutes of reading time. Spend this looking carefully through the questions and deciding the order in which you will attempt them. As a general rule you should attempt the questions that you find easiest first and leave the hardest until last. Depending on how confident you are we recommend that you follow one of the following two options:

Option 1 (if you're thinking 'Help!')

If you're a bit worried about the paper, do the questions in the order of how well you think you can answer them. You may find the shorter questions less daunting than the longer questions. Alternatively, you may feel better prepared for questions 53 and 54 and wish to start there.

- The requirements of question 53 are broken down into parts which should help you allocate your time and see where the marks are. If you could answer part (d) there is no reason why you should not start with this part. Ensure you use the correct proforma in part (b) even if you don't fill every number in.

- Question 54 is also helpfully broken down into parts. Make sure you make a good attempt at both the corporation tax and VAT aspects.

- Approach question 55 by breaking it down into parts; calculating each gain; dealing with losses; dealing with reliefs; calculating tax.

- Question 56 is an income tax losses question. Students traditionally find these questions hard and, if this is the case for you, you should leave this question until last.

- Question 57 is a question on property income. Make sure you follow the proforma computation when tackling such a question.

Lastly, what you mustn't forget is that you have to **answer all of the questions in the paper. They are all compulsory**. Do not miss out any questions or you will seriously affect your chance of passing the exam.

Option 2 (if you're thinking 'It's a doddle')

It never pays to be over confident but if you're reasonably confident about the exam then it is best to work through the questions sequentially starting with question 53.

No matter how many times we remind you....

Always, always **allocate your time** according to the marks for the question in total and then according to the parts of the question. And **always, always follow the requirements** exactly. Question 53 part (d), for example, asks you to advise William of the forms he will receive from Glossy Ltd. Two easy marks that you could have obtained even before you attempted the rest of the question. Make sure you get them.

You've got spare time at the end of the exam.....?

If you have allocated your time properly then you **shouldn't have time on your hands** at the end of the exam. But if you find yourself with five or ten minutes to spare, check over your work to make sure that there are no silly arithmetical errors.

Forget about it!

And don't worry if you found the paper difficult. More than likely other candidates did too. If this were the real thing you would need to **forget** the exam the minute you leave the exam hall and **think about the next one**. Or, if it's the last one, **celebrate**!

53 William Wong

Marking scheme

		Marks	
(a)	Payment made	½	
	Entitlement	½	
	Credited in accounts	½	
	End of a/c period	1	
	Determined	½	
			3
(b)	Salary	1	
	Bonus	1	
	Car – %	1	
	– calculation	1	
	Chauffer	1	
	Fuel	1½	
	TV	1	
	Living accommodation – annual	1	
	– additional	2	
	Insurance	½	
	Overseas allowance	½	
	Mileage allowance	2	
	Professional subscription	½	
	Golf club membership	½	
	PA	½	
			15
(c)	Annual earnings period	1	
	Employee Class 1 NICs	1½	
	Employer Class 1 NICs	1½	
	Employer Class 1A NICs	1	
			5
(d)	Form P60	1	
	Form P11D	1	
			2
			25

(a)   If an employee is a director of a company, earnings (eg a bonus) are treated as received on the earliest of:

- the time payment is made
- the time when a person becomes entitled to payment of the earnings
- the time when the amount is credited in the company's accounting records
- the end of the company's period of account (if the account was determined by then)
- the time the amount is determined (if after the end of the company's period of account)

(b)   **Taxable income**

	£
Salary (£2,400 × 12)	28,800
Bonus 15 March 2008	37,000
Car (W1)	4,025
Chauffeur	1,800
Fuel (W2)	1,260
TV (W3)	765
Living accommodation (W4)	18,838
	92,488
Less mileage allowance (W5)	(900)
professional subscription	(450)
Employment income/Net income	91,138
Less personal allowance	(5,225)
Taxable income	85,913

Notes

(1)   Liability insurance is not a taxable benefit.

(2)   Overseas allowance is not above the £10 per night exempt limit, so there is no taxable benefit.

(3)   Golf club membership is not allowable expense as it is not 'necessary' (*Brown v Bullock 1961*).

Workings

1   *Car benefit*

Round down CO_2 emissions to nearest 5 = 235g/km

Exceeds base limit 235g/km – 140g/km = 95g/km

Divide by 5 = 19

Taxable % is 15 + 19 + 3 (diesel) = 37% limited to maximum = 35%

Benefit is 35% × £46,000 (list price) × 3/12 = £4,025

The benefit needs to be prorated as the car was only available for three months of the year.

2   *Fuel benefit*

£14,400 × 35% × 3/12 = £1,260

3   *TV*

Use of asset

£3,825 × 20% = £765

4   *Living accommodation*

	£
Annual value	10,400
Additional benefit	
Use MV at provision since acquired more than 6 years before	
£(210,000 – 75,000) × 6.25%	8,438
Accommodation benefit	18,838

5   *Mileage allowance*

	£
Allowance paid 12,000 @ 30p	3,600
Less first 10,000 miles @ 40p	(4,000)
next 2,000 miles @ 25p	(500)
Allowable expense	(900)

(c)   **Employee Class 1 NICs**

Annual earnings period for directors

£(28,800 + 37,000) = £65,800 earnings for NIC purposes

	£
£(34,840 – 5,225) = £29,615 × 11%	3,258
£(65,800 – 34,840) = £30,960 × 1%	310
	3,568

Employer Class 1 NICs

No upper limit

£(65,800 – 5,225) = £60,575 × 12.8% = £7,754

Employer Class 1A NICs

Taxable benefits £(4,025 + 1,800 + 1,260 + 765 + 18,838) = £26,688

£26,688 × 12.8% = £3,416

(d)   Form P60 – total taxable earnings, tax deducted, code number, NI number and the employer's name and address. Must be provided by 31 May 2008.

Form P11D – taxable benefits – must be provided by 6 July 2008.

54 Hipster Ltd

Text references. Calculation of PCTCT and CT in Chapters 19 and 20. Chapter 8 for IBAs and capital allowances. VAT in Chapters 25 and 26.

Top tips. It is important that you learn how to deal with industrial buildings allowances as they are regularly tested. The change in the small companies rate for FY 2007 means that in many cases the results for an accounting period straddling FY 2006 and FY 2007 will have to be apportioned. Make sure you include supporting workings. Ensure you make a good attempt at both parts of the question.

Easy marks. It is useful to learn the proforma for calculating plant and machinery allowances as this will improve the layout of your answer. The registration aspects of VAT are easy marks.

Marking scheme

			Marks
(a)	Trading profit		½
	Pre-trading expenditure		1
	P&M	– Pool	1½
		– Exp car 1	1½
		– Exp car 2	1½
		– 50% FYA	1
	IBA	– Land	½
		– Showroom	1
		– Allowable expenditure	1
		– IBA	1
	Lease premium	– Assessable amount	1½
		– Deduction	1½
	Loan interest		½
	Capital gain	– Purchase	½
		– Bonus issue	½
		– Indexation	½
		– Disposal	1
		– Chargeable gain	1
	Franked investment income		1
	Corporation tax		1½
			20
(b)	(i)	Registration limit	1
		30 November 2007	1
		Date of registration	1
		Notification	1
			4
	(ii)	Output VAT	1
		Input VAT	1
		VAT payable	1
			3
	(iii)	Simplified administration	1
		VAT payable	1
		VAT saving	1
			3
			30

(a) **Hipster Ltd – Corporation tax liability – 6 month ended 30 June 2007**

	£	£
Trading profit (W1)		302,280
Loan interest		1,650
Capital gains (W5)		22,070
PCTCT		326,000

Corporation tax (W6)
FY 2006:

	£
£163,000 × 30%	48,900
Less: 11/400 (375,000 – 175,000) × $\dfrac{163,000}{175,000}$	(5,123)
	43,777

FY 2007:

	£	£
£163,000 × 30%	48,900	
Less: 1/40 (375,000 – 175,000) × $\dfrac{163,000}{175,000}$	(4,657)	44,243

CT liability		88,020

Workings

1   *Trading profit*

	£
Adjusted profit	334,500
Less: capital allowances (W2)	(25,820)
IBAs (W3)	(5,160)
lease premium (W4)	(1,240)
	302,280

Note. The advertising expenditure incurred in December 2006 is pre-trading, and is treated as incurred on 1 January 2007. No adjustment is required.

2   *Plant and machinery*

	FYA 50% £	General Pool £	Exp Car (1) £	Exp Car (2) £	Allowances £
Additions					
10 November 2006 (Note)	8,900				
12 January 2007	22,140				
29 March 2007		11,600			
18 April 2007			14,800		
7 May 2007	7,700				
28 June 2007				18,500	
Disposals			(11,300)		
Balancing allowance			(3,500)		3,500
	38,740	11,600		18,500	
FYA – 50%	(19,370)				19,370
WDA – 25% × 6/12		(1,450)			1,450
– £3,000 (max) × 6/12				(1,500)	1,500
Transfer to pool	(19,370)	19,370			
TWDV c/f	–	29,520		17,000	
Total allowances					25,820

Note. The equipment purchased on 10 November 2006 is pre-trading, and is treated as incurred on 1 January 2007.

3   *IBAs*

	£
Allowable cost	
Expenditure	460,000
Less land	(112,000)
Total cost	348,000

Expenditure on showroom is not allowed as it exceeds 25% × total cost.

IBA: 4% × (£348,000 − £90,000) × 6/12 = £5,160

The IBA is restricted to 6/12 because the accounting period is 6 months long.

4   *Lease premium*

Premium (P)	80,000
Less: 2% × (n − 1) × P	
2% × (20 − 1) × 80,000	(30,400)
Taxable as landlords income	49,600

This amount is deductible for the company over the life of the lease:

$$\frac{£49,600}{20} = £2,480$$

Allowable on an accruals basis, ie 1 January 2007 to 30 June 2007 = 6/12 × £2,480 = £1,240

5   *Chargeable gain*

	Number	Cost £	Indexed cost £
Purchase February 2007	8,000	3,000	3,000
Bonus issue (8,000 x ¼)	2,000		
Indexation to June 2007			
£3,000 × 0.020			60
	10,000	3,000	3,060
Disposal June 2007			
Cost × 5,000/10/000	5,000	1,500	1,530
Balance carried forward	5,000	1,500	1,530

	£
Disposal proceeds	23,600
Cost	(1,500)
	22,100
Indexation (1,530 − 1,500)	(30)
Chargeable gain	22,070

6   *'Profits'*

Profits chargeable to corporation tax	326,000
FII (£21,600 × 100/90)	24,000
'Profits'	350,000

	FY 2006 3 months to '31 March 2007'	FY 2007 3 months to '30 June 2007'
PCTCT (3:3)	163,000	163,000
'Profits' (3:3)	175,000	175,000
Lower limit		
£300,000 × 3/12	75,000	75,000
Upper limit		
£1,500,000 × 3/12	375,000	375,000

Marginal relief applies in both FYs.

(b) (i) A trader becomes liable to register for VAT if the value of taxable supplies in any period up to 12 months exceeds £64,000.

This happened on 30 November 2007 when taxable supplies amounted to:

	£
December 2006 – September 2007 (10 × £5,300)	53,000
October – November 2007 (2 × £5,550)	11,100
Total taxable supplies	64,100

Victor Ltd was required to notify HMRC within 30 days of the end of the month in which the £64,000 was exceeded, that is by 30 December 2007.

It was then registered with effect from the end of the month following the month in which the £64,000 limit was exceeded, that is, from 1 January 2008.

(ii)

	£
Output VAT £5,550 × 12 = £66,600 × 7/47	9,919
Less input VAT £400 × 12 = £4,800 × 7/47	(715)
Total VAT payable	9,204

(iii) Using the flat rate scheme will simplify Victor Ltd's administration. It will not have to issue VAT invoices since none of its customers are registered for VAT.

Since Victor Ltd first registers for VAT on 1 January 2008 it is entitled to a 1% reduction in the flat rate scheme percentage for its first year of registration. Thus 11% (12 – 1)% is used.

Under the flat rate scheme, VAT payable would have been 11% × £66,600 = £7,326 to 31 December 2008.

The saving would therefore have been £(9,204 – 7,326) = £1,878 for the year.

55 Michael Chin

Text references. Chapters 13 to 17 on CGT.

Top tips. Learn your CGT reliefs as they are often examined. You must be able to perform the calculations and explain the conditions.

Easy marks. The gain calculations were not particularly difficult and you were given a useful hint that there was no taper relief to take into account which simplified the calculation of total gains.

The actual taxation of the total gains utilising what was left of the lower income tax bands was another simple task and easy marks could be obtained here.

Examiner's comments. This was a popular question, and there were many first rate answers. Some candidates caused difficulty for themselves by treating the business as a single asset, rather than dealing with goodwill, freehold property and net current assets separately. Despite the question quite clearly stating that taper relief should be ignored, a number of candidates insisted on calculating this relief. Only a few candidates appreciated that the taxpayer could utilise all of the basic rate tax band and some of the 10% band.

Marking scheme

	Marks
Goodwill – Deemed proceeds/Cost	1
– Gift relief	1
Freehold property – Deemed proceeds/Cost	1
– Gift relief	1½
Net current assets	1
Minnow Ltd – Deemed proceeds/Cost	1
– Gift relief	1½
Whale plc – Deemed proceeds	1
– Cost	2
BMW	1
Teapot – Auctioneer's fees	1
– Chattels rules	2
Capital loss brought forward	2
Annual exemption	1
Capital gains tax	2
	20

Michael Chin – CGT liability

	(100%) £	NBA (90%) £
Total gains on gifts (W1, 2 and 3)	98,100	
Car (W4) – exempt		
Teapot (W5)		3,240
Less loss b/f (W5)	(15,300)	
Net gains	82,800	3,240
Chargeable gains after taper relief @ 100%/ 90%	82,800	2,916
Total chargeable gains		85,716
Less annual exemption		(9,200)
Taxable gains		76,516

Tax	£
£1,150 (W8) @ 10%	115
£32,370 @ 20%	6,474
£42,996 @ 40%	17,198
CGT due 31 January 2009	23,787

Workings

1   *Business*

    (i)   *Goodwill*

	£
Proceeds (MV)	60,000
Less cost	(NIL)
Gain	60,000
Less gift relief	(60,000)
Gain before taper relief	NIL

(ii)   *Freehold property*

	£
Proceeds (MV)	150,000
Less cost	(86,000)
Gain	64,000
Less gift relief – 75% business use	(48,000)
Gain before taper relief	16,000

Note that the net current assets are not chargeable assets and therefore do not give rise to a gain when the business is gifted.

2   *Minnow Ltd shares*

Any number of unquoted trading company shares qualify as business assets for gift relief purposes.

	£
Proceeds (MV)	180,000
Less cost	(87,500)
Gain	92,500
Less gift relief $\left(\dfrac{\text{CBA}}{\text{CA}}\right)\dfrac{200,000}{250,000} \times £92,500$	(74,000)
Gain before taper relief	18,500

3   *Whale plc – 18,000 shares*

No gift relief applies since, for quoted company shares to qualify as business assets for the purpose of this relief, the donor must own at least 5% of the shares (ie it must be his 'personal company').

(i)   *21 August 2007 acquisition – 12,000 shares*

	£
Proceeds (W4) £115,200 $\times \dfrac{12,000}{18,000}$	76,800
Less: cost	(26,400)
Gain before taper relief	50,400

(ii)   *7 December 2006 acquisition – 6,000 shares*

	£
Proceeds (W4) £115,200 $\times \dfrac{6,000}{18,000}$	38,400
Less cost £63,000 $\times \dfrac{6,000}{15,000}$	(25,200)
Gain before taper relief	13,200

4   *Whale plc – proceeds*

Use quarter-up rule $\dfrac{6.52 - 6.36}{4} = 0.04 + 6.36 = 6.40 \times 18,000 = £115,200$

5   *BMW car*

The motor car is an exempt asset, so no gain or loss arises.

6   *Teapot*

	£
Gross proceeds	8,600
Less fees (10% × £8,600)	(860)
	7,740
Less cost	(4,500)
Gain before taper relief	3,240
Restricted to: 5/3 × (8,600 – 6,000)	4,333

Take lower gain ie £3,240

May 2003 to April 2008 = 4 years non business asset, ie 90%.

The chattels rules apply as the teapot is a tangible movable asset that cost less than £6,000. The 5/3rds rule applies to the gross proceeds figure, ie before the fees are deducted.

7   *Loss b/f*

	£
2005/06 loss	17,300
Less: used 2006/07 (to bring down to level of AE) (11,200 – 9,200)	(2,000)
C/f to 2007/08	15,300

8   *Tax bands*

	£
Net income	6,305
Less personal allowance	(5,225)
Taxable income	1,080

	£
Starting rate band	2,230
Less used by taxable income	(1,080)
Remaining for gains	1,150

56 Richard Desk

Text references. Chapter 10 deals with trading losses.

Top tips. Layout is vital in loss relief questions. Set out your proforma and then fill in the figures.

Easy marks. Stating the amounts of income and gains correctly would give easy marks, as would setting off the Personal Allowance and Annual Exemption.

Once again using a proforma for loss relief over several years not only improves the look of your answer (it's neat and clear) but also helps you to avoid making mistakes and failing to achieve all the marks available . The question specifically asked you to offset the loss in 2005/06 using carry back loss relief and then to use the loss against gains in the same year. Thus this is what you must do. The examiner (see comments below) will not give you marks if you do something else!

Examiner's comments. In part (a) there were a number of major problems. First, gains were almost always included in income. Secondly, candidates did not set off the loss in the manner as instructed quite clearly in the question. Part (b) was also answered badly with very few candidates appreciating the alternative loss relief claims or why these alternatives were not beneficial.

Marking scheme

			Marks
(a)	Trading income	1	
	Carry forward loss relief	1	
	Property business income	2	
	BSI	½	
	PA	1	
	Capital gains	1½	
	Capital losses	3	
	Capital gains trading loss relief	1	
	Annual exemption	1	
			12

(b)

General income claim 2006/07	1
Capital gain 2006/07	1
Carry forward loss relief	1
	$\frac{3}{15}$

(a)

	2005/06 £	2006/07 £	2007/08 £
Trading profit	8,800	0	8,600
Less Carry forward loss relief (W1)	0	0	(3,000)
	8,800	0	5,600
Property business income (W2)	0	2,400	2,800
BSI	600	400	500
	9,400	2,800	8,900
Less carry back loss relief (W1)	(9,400)	0	0
	0	2,800	8,900
Less personal allowance	0	(2,800)	(5,225)
Taxable income	0	0	3,675

	2005/06 £	2006/07 £	2007/08 £
Capital gains	16,100	7,800	14,900
Less current capital loss	(2,000)	(7,800)	(4,000)
trading loss	(14,100)	0	0
capital loss b/f (9,000 – 7,800)	0	0	(1,200)
Chargeable gains	0	0	9,700
Less annual exemption	0	0	(9,200)
Chargeable gains	0	0	500

Workings

1   *Loss relief memorandum*

	£
Trading loss 2006/07	26,500
Less Claim in 2005/06 against income	(9,400)
Claim in 2005/06 against gains (16,100 – 2,000)	(14,100)
Claim in 2007/08 (balance)	(3,000)
	0

2   *Property business loss*

The loss of £600 in 2005/06 is carried forward against property business income in 2006/07, giving a net figure of £(3,000 – 600) = £2,400.

(b)   A claim could have been made for current year loss relief in 2006/07 as well as (or instead of) the claim for 2005/06, but the income for that year would be covered by the personal allowance.

For 2006/07, there were no net gains so no claim could be made.

The whole loss could have been carried forward for relief against trading income in 2007/08, but this would have delayed loss relief and would not have fully relieved the loss.

57 Oscar Thomson

> **Text references.** Chapter 6 covers property income.
>
> **Top tips.** Set out the net income for each property and then bring them together as a total amount of property business income.
>
> **Easy marks.** The deduction of agent's commission, advertising for tenants and legal fees were easy marks.

Marking scheme

	Marks
Property A	
Rent receivable 6.4.07 to 5.6.07	½
Rent receivable 6.10.07 to 5.4.08	½
Lease premium taxable as property business income	1
Agent's commission	½
Advertising	½
No deduction for capital expenditure	½
Property B	
Rent receivable	½
No deduction for rent received late	½
Impairment loss (irrecoverable rent)	½
Agent's commission	½
Property C	
Rent receivable	½
Agent's commission	½
Legal fees	½
Repairs	½
Loan interest	½
Furnished room	
Rent a room relief	1
Total property income for 2007/08	1
	10

	£	£
Property A		
Rent receivable 6 April 2007 to 5 June 2007		
2/12 × £12,000	2,000	
Rent receivable 6 October 2007 to 5 April 2008		
6/12 × £8,000	4,000	

Lease premium

	£		
Premium paid	5,000		
Less: 2% × (10 − 1) x £5,000	(900)		
Taxable as property income		4,100	
Less: agent's commission		(750)	
advertising for new tenants		(100)	
new kitchen units (Note 1)		(0)	9,250

Property B		
Rent receivable 6 April 2007 to 5 April 2008	18,000	
Less: impairment loss (Note 2)		
March 2008 1/12 x £18,000	(1,500)	
agent's commission	(800)	15,700

Property C		
Rent receivable 6 July 2007 – 5 April 2008		
9/12 × £6,000	4,500	
Less: agent's commission	(600)	
legal fees on lease agreement	(150)	
repairs	(1,500)	
loan interest	(2,500)	(250)

Furnished room		
Rental less than £4,250 so rent-a-room relief applies		0
Property business income 2007/08		24,700

Notes

1 The new kitchen units are a capital expense and so not deductible.

2 The rent due on 6 February 2008 is taxable in 2007/08 as it is receivable in that tax year, even though it is not received until after the end of the tax year.

ACCA

Paper F6

Taxation (United Kingdom)

Mock Examination 2

Question Paper	
Time allowed	
Reading and Planning	**15 minutes**
Writing	**3 hours**
ALL FIVE questions are compulsory and MUST be attempted.	

During the reading and planning time only the question paper may be annotated.

DO NOT OPEN THIS PAPER UNTIL YOU ARE READY TO START UNDER EXAMINATION CONDITIONS

ALL FIVE questions are compulsory and MUST be attempted

58 Darren Radhill

(a)   Darren Radhill is 40 and Sales Manager for a multi-national company.

For the year 2007/08 he earned a salary of £45,000 from which tax of £12,390 was deducted.

He lives in a house purchased by his employer for £295,000 in 2003, the annual value of which is £3,500. The house was furnished by the company at a cost of £7,500 and Darren pays his employer rent of £1,000 per month.

On 6 October 2007 his employer provided him with an interest free loan of £10,000. At 5 April 2008 the balance outstanding on the loan was £8,000.

In April 2007, Darren had inherited a house on the death of his grandfather and decided to let it as furnished accommodation. The property was in very poor condition and required work to make it habitable. The income and expenses passing through the bank account opened for the property for 2007/08 were:

	£
Rent received	18,000
Land registry fees on transfer	100
Structural repairs to make property habitable	2,500
Water rates	600
Agents booking fees	1,800
Cleaner	1,260

He always claims wear and tear allowance.

In March 2008 Darren received net interest of £2,000 from his UK bank account. During 2007/08 he also received UK dividend income of £450 (net).

Darren's employer does not provide a pension scheme so Darren pays an annual premium of £4,680 (net) into a personal pension scheme. In December 2007 he made a payment of £780 to a registered charity under Gift Aid.

Assume that the official rate of interest for 2007/08 is 6.25%.

Required

(i)   Calculate Darren's net assessable income and tax payable for 2007/08.   **(15 marks)**

(ii)   State the date by which Darren must submit his tax return. Outline the penalties that will apply if he does not submit the return on time.   **(5 marks)**

(b)   Denzil Dyer has been a self-employed printer since 2004. He has recently registered for value added tax (VAT).

Denzil's sales consist of printed leaflets, which are standard rated. He sells to both VAT registered customers and to non-VAT registered customers.

For a typical printing contract, Denzil receives a 10% deposit at the time that the customer makes the order. The order normally takes fourteen days to complete, and Denzil issues the sales invoice three to five days after completion. Some customers pay immediately upon receiving the sales invoice, but many do not pay for up to two months.

Customers making an order of more than £500 are given a discount of 5% from the normal selling price. Denzil also offers a discount of 2·5% of the amount payable to those customers that pay within one month of the date of the sales invoice.

All of Denzil's printing supplies are purchased from a VAT registered supplier. He pays by credit card and receives a VAT invoice. However, Denzil also purchases various office supplies by cash without receiving any invoices.

Denzil does not use the annual accounting scheme, the cash accounting scheme or the flat rate scheme.

Required:

(i) Advise Denzil as to when he should account for the output VAT relating to a typical standard rated printing supply. **(4 marks)**

(ii) Explain the VAT implications of the two types of discount that Denzil gives or offers to his customers. **(3 marks)**

(iii) Advise Denzil of the conditions that will have to be met in order for him to recover input VAT. You are not expected to list those goods and services for which input VAT is non-recoverable. **(3 marks)**

(Total = 30 marks)

59 Helium Ltd (BTX 12/04)

Helium Ltd is a UK resident company. It owns 40% of the ordinary share capital of Argon Ltd and 5% of the ordinary share capital of Boron Ltd. Both of these companies are incorporated overseas, and the directors of each company hold their board meetings overseas. Helium Ltd sells imported electrical equipment that has been manufactured by Argon Ltd and Boron Ltd.

The following information is available for Helium Ltd for the year ended 31 March 2008:

Trading income

The trading profit is £100,000. This figure is before taking account of capital allowances.

Industrial building

Helium Ltd had a new factory constructed on 1 July 2007 at a cost of £380,000. The factory was immediately brought into industrial use.

The cost was made up as follows:

	£
Land	50,000
Site preparation	12,500
Professional fees	10,000
Offices	68,000
Staff canteen	32,000
Factory	207,500
	380,000

Plant and machinery

Helium Ltd purchased the following assets in respect of the year ended 31 March 2008:

		£
15 April 2007	Machinery	38,750
13 September 2007	Van	23,840
10 October 2007	Motor car	14,500

The motor car was purchased for one of the company's directors who will use the car 45% for business purposes. The tax written down value of the general pool at 1 April 2007 was £72,455. Helium Ltd is a medium-sized company for capital allowances purposes.

Loan interest received

Loan interest of £7,500 was received on 30 September 2007, and £7,500 on 31 March 2008. There were no accruals at the year end. The loan was made for non-trading purposes.

Dividends received

Helium Ltd received gross dividends from its overseas investments, Argon Ltd and Boron Ltd, of £90,000 and £10,000 respectively during this year. The company also received dividends of £13,500 from Carbon plc, an unconnected UK company. This figure was the actual cash amount received.

Charitable donations

Helium Ltd made donations to charity of £30,000 under the Gift Aid scheme during the period.

The results of Argon Ltd and Boron Ltd for the year ended 31 March 2008 were as follows:

	Argon Ltd		Boron Ltd	
	£	£	£	£
Trading profit		400,000		250,000
Corporation tax		(100,000)		(25,000)
Distributable profits		300,000		225,000
Dividends paid				
Net	225,000		180,000	
Withholding tax	–		20,000	
		(225,000)		(200,000)
Retained profits		75,000		25,000

All of the above figures are in pounds Sterling.

Required

Calculate Helium Ltd's corporation tax liability for the year ended 31 March 2008. **(25 marks)**

60 Rotate Ltd (BTX 06/07)

You are a trainee accountant and your manager has asked for your help in advising three unconnected corporate clients that have each sold freehold factories.

Rotate Ltd

On 2 September 2007 Rotate Ltd sold a freehold factory for £470,000. The indexed cost of the factory on that date was £240,100. On 8 August 2007 Rotate Ltd had purchased a replacement freehold factory for £415,000.

Spin Ltd

On 14 November 2007 Spin Ltd sold a freehold factory for £360,000. The indexed cost of the factory on that date was £333,200. On 5 January 2008 Spin Ltd purchased a replacement leasehold factory, with a lease period of 15 years, for £394,000.

Turn Ltd

On 22 December 2007 Turn Ltd sold a freehold factory for £290,000. The indexed cost of the factory on that date was £230,000. 80% of this factory had been used in a manufacturing business run by Turn Ltd. However, the remaining 20% of this factory has never been used for business purposes. On 18 January 2008 Turn Ltd purchased a replacement freehold factory for £340,000.

Other information

(1)   Unless otherwise stated, each of the factories has always been used for business purposes.

(2)   Where possible, Rotate Ltd, Spin Ltd and Turn Ltd have all elected to hold over the gain arising on the disposal of their respective freehold factories under the rollover relief (replacement of business assets) rules.

Required

(a)   State the conditions that must be complied with in order that rollover relief can be claimed. You are not expected to list the categories of asset that qualify for rollover relief.   **(3 marks)**

(b)   Advise Rotate Ltd, Spin Ltd and Turn Ltd of the rollover relief available on the disposal of their respective freehold factories. Your answer should include:

   (1)   Calculations of the capital gains immediately chargeable, and

   (2)   An explanation of the future tax implications arising from the gains that have been deferred.

                                                                                                              (12 marks)

Twirl Ltd disposed of the following assets in its accounting period ended 31 December 2007:

15 August 2007:   Antique chair for £4,000 acquired for £7,800 in July 2004.

30 December 2007: 2 hectares of land held as investment for £40,000. The original plot of 5 acres was acquired in May 2005 for £27,000. The remaining 3 acres were valued at £50,000 in December 2007.

Required

(c)   Calculate the net chargeable gains to be included in Twirl Ltd's profits liable to corporation tax for the year ended 31 December 2007.   **(5 marks)**

   Assume the following RPIs

July 2004	186.8
May 2005	192.0
August 2007	207.3
December 2007	210.1

                                                                                                    (Total = 20 marks)

61 Duke and Earl (BTX 06/07)

Duke and Earl Upper-Crust, aged 44, are twin brothers.

Duke is employed by the High-Brow Bank plc as a financial adviser. During the tax year 2007/08 Duke was paid a gross salary of £120,000. He also received a bonus of £40,000 on 15 March 2008. On 31 March 2008 Duke made a contribution of £85,000 (gross) into a personal pension scheme. He is not a member of High-Brow Bank plc's occupational pension scheme.

Earl is self-employed as a financial consultant. His trading profit for the year ended 5 April 2008 was £34,000. On 31 March 2008 Earl made a contribution of £40,000 (gross) into a personal pension scheme.

Neither Duke nor Earl has any other income.

Required:

(a)   Calculate Duke and Earl's income tax liabilities for the tax year 2007/08, together with the actual net of tax amounts that Duke and Earl will have paid to their personal pension companies.   **(8 marks)**

(b)   Advise Duke and Earl of the maximum additional amounts that they could have contributed into personal pension schemes for the tax year 2007/08, whether or not such additional contributions would have qualified for tax relief, and the date by which any qualifying contributions would have had to have been paid.

(4 marks)

(c) Explain the effect of the pension scheme annual allowance limit of £225,000, and the tax implications if contributions are made in excess of this limit. **(3 marks)**

(Total = 15 marks)

62 Anne, Bryn and Cathy (BTX 6/07)

(a) Anne and Bryn commenced in partnership on 1 July 2005 preparing accounts to 30 June. Cathy joined as a partner on 1 July 2006, and Bryn resigned as a partner on 30 June 2007. Profits have always been shared equally. The partnership's trading profits were as follows:

	£
Year ended 30 June 2006	51,600
Year ended 30 June 2007	79,200

Required:

Calculate the trading income assessments of Anne for the tax year 2005/06, Cathy for the tax year 2006/07 and Bryn for the tax year 2007/08. **(6 marks)**

(b) Darcy and Emma commenced in partnership on 6 April 1998, preparing accounts to 5 April. Frank joined as a partner on 6 April 2007, and Darcy resigned as a partner on 5 April 2008. For the year ended 5 April 2008 the partnership made a trading loss.

Frank was in employment prior to becoming a partner on 6 April 2007. Apart from this, none of the partners has any other income or capital gains.

Required:

State the possible ways in which Darcy, Emma and Frank can relieve their share of the trading loss for the year ended 5 April 2008. **(4 marks)**

(Total = 10 marks)

Answers

**DO NOT TURN THIS PAGE UNTIL YOU HAVE
COMPLETED THE MOCK EXAM**

A plan of attack

What's the worst thing you could be doing right now if this was the actual exam paper? Sharpening your pencil? Wondering how to celebrate the end of the exam in about 3 hours time? Panicking, flapping and generally getting in a right old state?

Well, they're all pretty bad, so turn back to the paper and let's sort out a **plan of attack**!

First things first

You have fifteen minutes of reading time. Spend this looking carefully through the questions and deciding the order in which you will attempt them. As a general rule you should attempt the questions that you find easiest first and leave the hardest until last. Depending on how confident you are we recommend that you follow one of the following two options:

Option 1 (if you're thinking 'Help!')

If you're a bit worried about the paper, do the questions in the order of how well you think you can answer them. You may find the shorter questions less daunting than the longer questions. Alternatively, you may feel better prepared for questions 58 and 59 and wish to start there.

- **Question 58** part (a) is on standard income tax topics. Make sure you make a good attempt at the administrative aspects in part (ii). Part (b) is about VAT and you must make a good attempt at it as well as the first two parts.

- **Question 59** was a corporation tax computation. Use the standard corporation tax proforma in this answer.

- **Question 60** dealt with relief for replacement of business assets, chattels and part disposals. Make sure you attempt all parts.

- **Question 61** tested your knowledge of the tax relief on pensions. But there were also easy marks on straightforward income tax computations.

- **Question 62** was on partnerships and loss relief. Again, a good attempt at both parts is necessary.

Lastly, what you mustn't forget is that you have to **answer all the questions on the paper. They are all compulsory**. Do not miss out any question or you will seriously affect your chance of passing.

Option 2 (if you're thinking 'It's a doddle')

It never pays to be over confident but if you're reasonably confident about the exam then it is best to work through the questions sequentially starting with question 58.

No matter how many times we remind you....

Always, always **allocate your time** according to the marks for the question in total and then according to the parts of the question. And **always, always follow the requirements** exactly. Did you state the date by which the taxpayer must submit his tax return in Question 58 part (a)(i). This was an easy mark.

You've got spare time at the end of the exam.....?

If you have allocated your time properly then you **shouldn't have time on your hands** at the end of the exam. But if you find yourself with five or ten minutes to spare, check over your work to make sure that there are no silly arithmetical errors.

Forget about it!

And don't worry if you found the paper difficult. More than likely other candidates will too. If this were the real thing you would need to **forget** the exam the minute you leave the exam hall and **think about the next one**. Or, if it's the last one, **celebrate**!

58 Darren Radhill

Text references. Chapters 3, 4, 5, 6 and 18 for income tax. Chapters 25 and 26 for VAT.

Top tips. Learn the rules for benefits. They are very examinable. Discounts for VAT are a favourite exam topic.

Easy marks. Payment and return submission dates are easy marks. You could even answer that part of the requirement first to ensure you do not forget to answer it.

Marking scheme

				Marks
(a)	(i)	**Income**		
		Salary	½	
		Accommodation – basic charge	½	
		– additional charge	1	
		– deduct rent paid	1	
		– use of furniture	1	
		Beneficial loan	1	
		Property – income	½	
		– expenses	½	
		– disallowed expenses	1	
		– wear and tear	1	
		Other investment income	1	
		PA	½	
		Extend basic rate band – Gift Aid	1	
		– pension	1	
		Tax bands	1½	
		Tax rates	1	
		Deduct tax credits	1	
				15
	(ii)	Return deadlines	2	
		Penalties	3	
				5
(b)	(i)	VAT period	1	
		Basic tax point	1	
		Payment received	1	
		Issue of invoice within 14 days	1	
				4
	(ii)	Large order discount	1	
		Prompt payment discount	2	
				3
	(iii)	Made to taxable person	1	
		Supported by evidence	1	
		Supplied for business purposes	1	
				3
				30

(a)   (i)   **Darren Radhill income tax 2007/08**

	Non-savings £	Savings £	Dividend £
Employment income (W1)	52,031		
Furnished letting (W4)	12,600		
Bank interest (2,000 × 100/80)		2,500	
UK dividends (450 × 100/90)			500
Net income	64,631	2,500	500
Personal allowance	(5,225)		
Taxable income	59,406	2,500	500

		£	£
Income tax			
£2,230 @ 10%			223
£32,370 @ 22%			7,121
£7,000 @ 22% (W5)			1,540
£17,806 @ 40%			7,122
£2,500 @ 40%			1,000
£500 @ 32.5%			163
			17,169
Less tax credits			
Dividends		(50)	
Interest		(500)	
PAYE		(12,390)	
			(12,940)
Tax due			4,229

Workings

1   *Employment income*

	£
Salary	45,000
Accommodation (W2)	6,750
Beneficial loan (W3)	281
	52,031

2   *Accommodation*

	£
Basic charge: annual value	3,500
Less rent paid (total £12,000)	(3,500)
	Nil

Additional charge

	£
Cost	295,000
Less	(75,000)
	220,000

	£
£220,000 @ 6.25%	13,750
Less: Balance of rent paid £(12,000 − 3,500)	(8,500)
Total	5,250

Furniture £7,500 @ 20% = 1,500

Total accommodation benefit £(5,250 + 1,500) = £6,750

3　*Beneficial loan interest*

$$\frac{£(10,000 + 8,000)}{2} = £9,000 \times 6.25\% = £562 \times {}^{6}/_{12} = \underline{£281.}$$

4　*Property income from furnished lettings*

	£	£
Rent received		18,000
Less: expenses (note 2)		
water rates	600	
agents fees	1,800	
cleaner	1,260	
wear and tear £(18,000 − 600) @ 10%	1,740	
		(5,400)
		12,600

Note. Land registry fees and structural repairs are not allowable expenses as they are capital in nature.

5　*Extension of basic rate band*

	£
Pension (£4,680 × 100/78)	6,000
Gift aid (£780 × 100/78)	1,000
	7,000

(ii)　**Tax return submission**

Darren must submit his tax return by 31 January 2009, if he files the return online. If he wants to file a paper return, the return must be submitted by 31 October 2008. If he does file a paper return, he can request HMRC to compute the tax due. If the return is filed online, tax will be calculated automatically.

If Darren does not submit an online return by 31 January 2009 there is an automatic penalty of £100. If the return still has not been submitted by 31 July 2009 a further automatic £100 penalty is charged. Note that these fixed rate penalties are limited to the amount of tax outstanding. If all the tax has been paid by 31 January 2009 there would therefore be no penalty due.

If the return is more than 12 months late, a tax geared penalty will be charged. HMRC may also apply a daily penalty of up to £60 per day if they obtain approval from the commissioners.

(b)　(i)　**Accounting for output VAT**

Output VAT must be accounted for according to the VAT period in which the supply is treated as being made. This is determined by the tax point.

The printing contracts are supplies of services, so the basic tax point for each contract will be the date that it is completed.

Where payment is received before the basic tax point, then this date becomes the actual tax point. The tax point for each 10% deposit is therefore the date that it is received.

If an invoice is issued within 14 days of the basic tax point, the invoice date will usually replace the basic tax point outlined above. This will apply to the balance of the contract price since Denzil issues invoices within three to five days of completion.

(ii)　**Discounts**

Where a discount of 5% is given for an order of more than £500 then output VAT is simply calculated on the revised, discounted, selling price.

As regards the 2·5% discount offered for prompt payment, output VAT is calculated on the selling price less the amount of discount offered.

There is no amendment to the amount of output VAT charged if the customer does not take the discount but instead pays the full selling price.

(iii) **Input VAT**

The supply must be made to Denzil since he is the taxable person making the claim.

The supply must be supported by evidence, and this will normally take the form of a VAT invoice. Denzil will therefore not be able to recover any input VAT in respect of the purchases of office supplies for cash where there is no invoice.

Denzil must use the goods or services supplied for business purposes, although an apportionment can be made where supplies are acquired partly for business purposes and partly for private purposes.

59 Helium Ltd

Text references. Chapters 19 and 20 for PCTCT and CT calculation. Chapter 23 deals with the overseas aspects.

Top tips. Use a columnar approach when working out the double taxation relief for the UK holding company.

Easy marks. The residence of companies should be well known and the examiner has already given a clue about the significance of board meetings. Use of proformas to calculate the UK and overseas PCTCT as well as DTR ensures you do not make mistakes and lose marks.

Examiner's comments. Only a minority of candidates correctly calculated the overseas income dividend and very few appreciated that the Gift Aid payment should be set against UK income.

Marking scheme

		Marks
Trading income		½
IBA	– Land	1
	– Offices	1½
	– Eligible expenditure	1
	– Allowance	1½
PM	– Pool	1½
	– Car	1½
	– 40% FYA	1½
Interest income		1
Overseas income	– Underlying tax	1
	– Argon Ltd dividend	2
	– Boron Ltd dividend	1
Gift Aid		2
FII		1
SCR		1
CT		2
DTR		4
		25

Helium Ltd – CT liability year ended 31 March 2008

	Total £	UK £	Overseas £
Trading income	100,000	100,000	
Less IBAs (W1)	(13,200)		
CAs (W2)	(46,150)	(59,350)	
Taxable trading income	40,650	40,650	
Interest income (accruals basis)	15,000	15,000	
Overseas income			
– Argon Ltd (W3)	120,000		120,000
– Boron Ltd (W4)	10,000		10,000
Total profits	185,650	55,650	130,000
Less Gift Aid donation	(30,000)	(30,000)	–
PCTCT	155,650	25,650	130,000
FII £13,500 × 100/90	15,000		
'Profits'	170,650		
CT @ 20% (N)	31,130	5,130	26,000
Less DTR			
Argon Ltd (W5)	(24,000)		(24,000)
Boron Ltd (W6)	(1,000)		(1,000)
CT liability	6,130	5,130	1,000

Note. Helium Ltd has no associated companies (both Argon Ltd and Boron Ltd do not fall within the definition of over 50% of share capital etc) and so the small companies' rate applies.

Workings

1   *Industrial buildings allowance*

Allowable expenditure:

	£
Site preparation	12,500
Professional fees	10,000
Offices	68,000
Canteen	32,000
Factory	207,500
	330,000

Note. Offices qualify as cost is lower than 25% of £330,000. Land never qualifies for IBAs.

WDA @ 4% × £330,000 = £13,200

2   *Capital allowances on plant and machinery*

	FYA £	Pool £	Car £	Allowances £
TWDV b/f		72,455		
Additions not qualifying for FYAs				
10 October 2007 Car			14,500	
Additions qualifying for FYAs				
15 April 2007 Machine	38,750			
13 September 2007 Van	23,840			
	62,590			
FYA @ 40%	(25,036)			25,036
WDA @ (25%/£3,000)		(18,114)	(3,000)	21,114
Transfer to general pool	(37,554)	37,554		
TWDV c/f/Allowances		91,895	11,500	46,150

3   *Argon Ltd dividend*

	£
Net dividend	225,000
Withholding tax	–
Gross dividend	225,000
Underlying tax £225,000 $\times \dfrac{100,000}{300,000}$	75,000
	300,000

Dividend due to Helium Ltd (40%) = 120,000

4   *Boron Ltd dividend*

Since Helium Ltd does not own at least 10% of the voting shares of Boron Ltd, no relief is available for underlying tax and so it is not taken into account in calculating the gross dividend.

The gross dividend is therefore:

	£
Net dividend	180,000
Withholding tax	20,000
	200,000

Dividend due to Helium Ltd (5%) = 10,000

5   *DTR Argon Ltd dividend*

Overseas tax – £75,000 × 40% = 30,000

UK tax – $\dfrac{120,000}{130,000} \times$ £26,000 = 24,000

Lower amount applies, ie 24,000

6   *DTR Boron Ltd dividend*

Overseas tax – £10,000 × 10% = 1,000

UK tax – $\dfrac{10,000}{130,000} \times$ £26,000 = 2,000

Lower amount applies, ie 1,000

60 Rotate Ltd

Text references. Chapters 13 to 16 deal with the general computation of chargeable gains and Chapter 19 covers the rules for companies.

Top tips. This question tests thoroughly the rollover relief rules. Remember that you always need to calculate the indexed gain first, before you can think about taking advantage of any reliefs.

Easy marks. The calculation of the three indexed gains were easy marks.

Marking scheme

		Marks	
(a)	Period of reinvestment	1	
	Qualifying assets	1	
	Brought into business use	1	
			3
(b)	**Rotate Ltd**		
	Proceeds/Indexed cost	1	
	Rollover relief	1½	
	Base cost	1	
	Spin Ltd		
	Proceeds/Indexed cost	1	
	Rollover relief	1	
	Base cost of depreciating asset not adjusted	1	
	5 January 2018	½	
	Date of sale	½	
	Ceasing to be used for business purposes	½	
	Turn Ltd		
	Proceeds/Indexed cost	1	
	Rollover relief	2	
	Base cost	1	
			12
(c)	Loss on chattel	1	
	Part disposal – cost	1	
	– indexation	1	
	– gain	1	
	Net gains (no AE)	1	
			5
			20

(a) **Conditions for rollover relief**

    (i)   The reinvestment must take place between one year before and three years after the date of disposal of the original asset.

    (ii)   The old and new assets must both be qualifying assets and be used for business purposes.

    (iii) The new asset must be brought into business use at the time that it is acquired.

(b)   **Rotate Ltd**

	£
Proceeds	470,000
Less: Indexed cost	(240,100)
	229,900
Less: Rollover relief (balancing figure)	(174,900)
Chargeable gain	55,000

The gain that remains chargeable is the amount of proceeds received that have not been reinvested in the purchase of the replacement asset, ie £(470,000 – 415,000) = £55,000.

When the replacement factory is ultimately disposed of the base cost will be £240,100 (415,000 – 174,900).

Spin Ltd

	£
Proceeds	360,000
Less: indexed cost	(333,200)
	26,800
Less: rollover relief	(26,800)
Chargeable gain	–

The sale proceeds are fully reinvested, and so the whole of the gain can be rolled over.

The leasehold factory is a depreciating asset, and so the base cost of this factory is not adjusted.

The gain will be held over until the earlier of 5 January 2018 (ten years from the date of acquisition), the date that the factory is disposed of, or the date that the factory ceases to be used for business purposes.

Turn Ltd

	£
Proceeds	290,000
Less: indexed cost	(230,000)
	60,000
Less: rollover relief (balancing figure)	(48,000)
Chargeable gain	12,000

The proportion of the gain relating to non-business use is £12,000 (60,000 x 20%), and this amount does not qualify for rollover relief.

The business proportion of the sale proceeds (290,000 x 80% = 232,000) is fully reinvested, and so the balance of the gain can be rolled over.

When the replacement factory is ultimately disposed of the base cost will be £292,000 (340,000 – 48,000).

(c)   *Antique chair*

	£
Proceeds (deemed)	6,000
Less: cost	(7,800)
Loss	(1,800)

Indexation cannot increase loss.

Part disposal of land

	£
Proceeds	40,000
Less: cost	

$$£27,000 \times \frac{40,000}{40,000 + 50,000}$$ (12,000)

	28,000

Less: indexation allowance

$$\frac{210.1 - 192.0}{192.0} \; (= 0.094) \times £12,000$$ (1,128)

Gain	26,872
Net gains £(26,872 − 1,800)	25,072

61 Duke and Earl

Text references. Chapter 1 covers the income tax computation. Pension contributions are covered in Chapter 5.

Top tips. Tax relief is available on pension contributions up to an amount of 100% of relevant earnings. Personal pension contributions are always paid net of basic rate tax; higher rate relief is given, where appropriate, by extending the basic rate band.

Easy marks. Part (a) required two straightforward income tax computations.

Marking scheme

			Marks
(a)	**Duke Upper-Crust**		
	Employment income	1	
	Personal allowance	½	
	Income tax	2	
	Net contribution	1	
	Earl Upper-Crust		
	Trading profit	½	
	Personal allowance	½	
	Income tax	1	
	Net contribution	1½	
			8
(b)	No restriction regarding contributions	1	
	Tax relief – Duke	1	
	– Earl	1	
	Period of payment	1	
			4
(c)	Effective limit	1	
	40% tax charge	1	
	Cancellation of relief given	1	
			3
			15

(a)   **Duke Upper-Crust – Income tax computation 2007/08**

	£
Employment income (120,000 + 40,000)	160,000
Personal allowance	(5,225)
Taxable income	154,775
Income tax	
£2,230 @ 10%	223
£32,370 @ 22%	7,121
£85,000 @ 22%	18,700
£35,175 @ 40%	14,070
Income tax liability	40,114

All of Duke's pension contribution of £85,000 qualifies for tax relief, so he will have paid £66,300 (78% × £85,000) to his personal pension company.

Earl Upper-Crust – Income tax computation 2007/08

	£
Trading profit	34,000
Personal allowance	(5,225)
Taxable income	28,775
Income tax	
£2,230 @ 10%	223
£26,545 @ 22%	5,840
Income tax liability	6,063

Only £34,000 of Earl's pension contribution of £40,000 qualifies for tax relief, since relief is only available up to the amount of earnings.

The amount of tax relief is £7,480 (£34,000 at 22%), so Earl will have paid £32,520 £(40,000 – 7,480) to his personal pension company.

(b)   There is no restriction regarding the amounts that Duke and Earl could have contributed into a personal pension scheme for 2007/08.

However, tax relief is only available on an amount up to earnings. Therefore, Duke would only receive tax relief on additional pension contributions of up to £75,000 £(160,000 – 85,000).

Earl has already made a pension contribution in excess of his earnings for 2007/08, and so any additional pension contribution would not have qualified for any tax relief.

Pension contributions for 2007/08 would have had to have been paid between 6 April 2007 and 5 April 2008, since it is not possible to carry back contributions.

(c)   Although there is tax relief on pension contributions up to relevant earnings, the annual allowance limit of £225,000 acts as an effective limit.

Any tax relieved contributions in excess of the annual allowance are taxed at the rate of 40% on the individual, with the tax being paid under the self assessment system.

The annual allowance charge therefore cancels out the tax relief that would have been given. There is no charge where contributions have not qualified for tax relief.

62 Anne, Bryn and Cathy

Text references. Basis periods for income tax are covered in Chapter 9, Partnerships are dealt with in Chapter 11.

Top tips. First allocate the profits of each accounting period between the partners, before attempting to apply the opening or closing year rules.

Where there is a change in the profit sharing arrangements during an accounting period, the salary must be pro rated according to the date of the change.

Easy marks. The profit sharing arrangements in part (a) were straightforward.

Marking scheme

			Marks
(a)	Anne	1½	
	Cathy	2	
	Bryn — Overlap relief	1	
	— Trading income assessment	1½	
			6
(b)	Carry forward	1	
	General income 2006/07	1	
	General income 2004/05 to 2006/07	1	
	Terminal loss	1	
			4
			10

(a) **Trading income assessments**

	£
Anne – 2005/06	
Actual: 1.7.05 – 5.4.06	
9/12 × £25,800 (W1) =	19,350
Cathy – 2006/07	
Actual: 1.7.06 – 5.4.07	
9/12 × £26,400 (W1)	19,800
Bryn – 2007/08	
Final year: 12 m/e 30.6.07	26,400
Less: overlap profits (W2)	(19,350)
	7,050

Workings

1 *Allocation of partnership profits*

	Total £	Anne £	Cathy £	Bryn £
Y/e 30.6.06	51,600	25,800		25,800
Y/e 30.6.07	79,200	26,400	26,400	26,400

2   *Overlap profits – Bryn*

2005/06
1.7.05 – 5.4.06
9/12 × £25,800 (W1)   19,350

2006/07
12 m/e 30.6.06   25,800

Overlap profits are therefore £19,350, which are deducted from his taxable profits in the year in which he leaves the partnership.

(b)   (i)   Emma and Frank can carry their share of the loss forward against the first future trading profits arising in the same trade. Darcy cannot as he has resigned and will therefore not have any future trading profits from this trade.

        (ii)   Darcy, Emma and Frank can claim against their general income for 2006/07. None of them has any income for 2007/08, and so a claim will not be made for this year.

        (iii)   Frank can claim against his general income for 2004/05 to 2006/07, earliest year first, being the three tax years prior to the commencement of trading.

        (iv)   Darcy has resigned and so can claim against his trading profits for 2004/05 to 2006/07, latest year first, being the three years prior to the last year of trading.

ACCA

Paper F6

Taxation (United Kingdom)

Mock Examination 3

(December 2007 paper)

Question Paper	
Time allowed	
Reading and Planning	**15 minutes**
Writing	**3 hours**
ALL FIVE questions are compulsory and MUST be attempted.	

During the reading and planning time only the question paper may be annotated.

DO NOT OPEN THIS PAPER UNTIL YOU ARE READY TO START UNDER EXAMINATION CONDITIONS

ALL FIVE questions are compulsory and MUST be attempted

63 Vanessa Serve and Serene Volley

(a)   Vanessa Serve and Serene Volley, aged 32 and 35 years respectively, are sisters. The following information is available for the tax year 2007/08:

Vanessa Serve

(1)   Vanessa is self-employed as a tennis coach. Her tax adjusted trading profit for the year ended 30 June 2007 is £52,400. However, this figure is before taking account of capital allowances.

(2)   The only item of plant and machinery owned by Vanessa is her motor car. This originally cost £16,400, and at 1 July 2006 had a tax written down value of £10,400. During the year ended 30 June 2007 Vanessa drove a total of 20,000 miles, of which 6,000 were for private journeys.

(3)   Vanessa contributed £6,400 (gross) into a personal pension scheme during the tax year 2007/08.

(4)   In addition to her self-employed income, Vanessa received interest of £1,100 from an investment account at the National Savings & Investments Bank during the tax year 2007/08. This was the actual cash amount received.

(5)   Vanessa's payments on account in respect of the tax year 2007/08 totalled £8,460.

Serene Volley

(1)   Serene is employed as a sports journalist by Backhand plc, a newspaper publishing company. During the tax year 2007/08 she was paid a gross annual salary of £26,400. Income tax of £4,790 was deducted from this figure under PAYE.

(2)   Throughout the tax year 2007/08 Backhand plc provided Serene with a petrol powered motor car which has a list price of £16,400. The official CO_2 emission rate for the motor car is 192 grams per kilometre. The company did not provide Serene with any fuel for private journeys.

(3)   Serene contributed 5% of her gross salary of £26,400 into Backhand plc's HM Revenue and Customs' registered occupational pension scheme.

(4)   In addition to her employment income, Serene received interest of £1,200 on the maturity of a savings certificate from the National Savings & Investments Bank during the tax year 2007/08. This was the actual cash amount received.

(5)   Serene did not make any payments on account in respect of the tax year 2007/08.

Required

(i)   Calculate the income tax payable by Vanessa and Serene respectively for the tax year 2007/08.

(11 marks)

(ii)   Calculate the national insurance contributions payable by Vanessa and Serene respectively for the tax year 2007/08.   **(4 marks)**

(iii)   Calculate Vanessa and Serene's respective balancing payments for the tax year 2007/08 and their payments on account, if any, for the tax year 2008/09. You should state the relevant due dates.

(5 marks)

247

(b)   Note that in answering this part of the question you are not expected to take account of any of the information provided in part (a) above.

Unless stated otherwise all of the figures below are exclusive of VAT.

Vanessa Serve is registered for value added tax (VAT), and is in the process of completing her VAT return for the quarter ended 31 March 2008. The following information is available:

(1)   Sales invoices totalling £18,000 were issued in respect of standard rated sales. All of Vanessa's customers are members of the general public.

(2)   During the quarter ended 31 March 2008 Vanessa spent £600 on mobile telephone calls, of which 40% related to private calls.

(3)   On 3 January 2008 Vanessa purchased a motor car for £12,000. On 18 March 2008 £987 was spent on repairs to the motor car. The motor car is used by Vanessa in her business, although approximately 10% of the mileage is for private journeys. Both figures are inclusive of VAT at the standard rate.

(4)   On 29 March 2008 tennis coaching equipment was purchased for £1,760. Vanessa paid for the equipment on this date, but did not take delivery of the equipment or receive an invoice until 3 April 2008. This purchase was standard rated.

(5)   In addition to the above, Vanessa also had other standard rated expenses amounting to £2,200 in the quarter ended 31 March 2008. This figure includes £400 for entertaining customers.

Required

(i)   Calculate the amount of VAT payable by Vanessa for the quarter ended 31 March 2008.   **(5 marks)**

(ii)   Advise Vanessa of the conditions that she must satisfy before being permitted to use the VAT flat rate scheme, and the advantages of joining the scheme. The relevant flat rate scheme percentage for Vanessa's trade as notified by HM Revenue and Customs is 6%.

Note: your answer should be supported by appropriate calculations of the amount of tax saving if Vanessa had used the flat rate scheme to calculate the amount of VAT payable for the quarter ended 31 March 2008.   **(5 marks)**

(Total = 30 marks)

64 Sofa Ltd

(a)   Sofa Ltd is a manufacturer of furniture. The company's summarised profit and loss account for the year ended 31 March 2008 is as follows:

	£	£
Gross profit		272,300
Operating expenses		
Depreciation	87,100	
Professional fees (note 1)	19,900	
Repairs and renewals (note 2)	22,800	
Other expenses (note 3)	364,000	(493,800)
Operating loss		(221,500)
Profit from sale of fixed assets		
Disposal of shares (note 4)		4,300
Income from investments		
Bank interest (note 5)		8,400
		(208,800)
Interest payable (note 6)		(31,200)
Loss before taxation		(240,000)

Notes

1. *Professional fees*

   Professional fees are as follows:

	£
Accountancy and audit fee	3,400
Legal fees in connection with the issue of share capital	7,800
Legal fees in connection with the renewal of a ten year property lease	2,900
Legal fees in connection with the issue of debentures (see note 6)	5,800
	19,900

2. *Repairs and renewals*

   The figure of £22,800 for repairs and renewals includes £9,700 for constructing a new wall around the company's premises and £3,900 for repairing the wall of an office building after it was damaged by a lorry. The remaining expenses are all fully allowable.

3. *Other expenses*

   The figure of £364,000 for other expenses includes £1,360 for entertaining suppliers; £700 for entertaining employees; £370 for counselling services provided to an employee who was made redundant; and a fine of £420 for infringing health and safety regulations. The remaining expenses are all fully allowable.

4. *Profit on disposal of shares*

   The profit on the disposal of shares of £4,300 is in respect of a shareholding that was sold on 29 October 2007.

5. *Bank interest received*

   The bank interest was received on 31 March 2008. The bank deposits are held for non-trading purposes.

6. *Interest payable*

   Sofa Ltd raised a debenture loan on 1 July 2007, and this was used for trading purposes. Interest of £20,800 was paid on 31 December 2007, and £10,400 was accrued at 31 March 2008.

7. *Plant and machinery*

   On 1 April 2007 the tax written down values of plant and machinery were as follows:

	£
General pool	16,700
Expensive motor car	16,400

   The following transactions took place during the year ended 31 March 2008:

		Cost/proceeds £
12 May 2007	Purchased equipment	11,400
8 June 2007	Sold the expensive motor car	(17,800)
8 June 2007	Purchased motor car (1)	22,200
2 August 2007	Purchased motor car (2)	10,900
19 October 2007	Purchased motor car (3)	13,800
8 January 2008	Sold a lorry	(7,600)
18 January 2008	Sold motor car (2)	(8,800)
10 February 2008	Purchased a second-hand freehold office building	280,000

Motor car (3) purchased on 19 October 2007 for £13,800 is a low emission motor car (CO2 emission rate of less than 120 grams per kilometre). The expensive motor car sold on 8 June 2007 for £17,800 originally cost £26,800. The lorry sold on 8 January 2008 for £7,600 originally cost £24,400.

The cost of the second-hand office building purchased on 10 February 2008 for £280,000 includes fixtures qualifying as plant and machinery. These fixtures originally cost £44,800, and at the date of sale had a market value of £12,600 and a written down value of £9,400. Sofa Ltd and the vendor of the office building have made a joint election regarding the sale price of the fixtures to enable Sofa Ltd to claim the maximum possible amount of capital allowances in respect of them.

Sofa Ltd is a medium-sized company as defined by the Companies Acts.

8.   *Purchase of factory*

On 1 July 2007 Sofa Ltd purchased a second-hand factory. The factory was originally constructed at a cost of £475,262 (including £158,000 for the land and £68,000 for a showroom). The construction of the factory was completed on 1 October 2002, and it was first brought into use on 1 January 2003. The factory has always been used for industrial purposes. The original owner made up accounts to 31 December each year.

Required

Calculate Sofa Ltd's tax adjusted trading loss for the year ended 31 March 2008.

Note. Your answer should commence with the loss before taxation figure of £240,000. You should assume that the company claims the maximum available capital allowances.   **(20 marks)**

(b)   Sofa Ltd has three subsidiary companies:

Settee Ltd

Sofa Ltd owns 100% of the ordinary share capital of Settee Ltd. For the year ended 30 June 2007 Settee Ltd had profits chargeable to corporation tax of £240,000, and for the year ended 30 June 2008 will have profits chargeable to corporation tax of £90,000.

Couch Ltd

Sofa Ltd owns 60% of the ordinary share capital of Couch Ltd. For the year ended 31 March 2008 Couch Ltd had profits chargeable to corporation tax of £64,000.

Futon Ltd

Sofa Ltd owns 80% of the ordinary share capital of Futon Ltd. Futon Ltd commenced trading on 1 January 2008, and for the three-month period ended 31 March 2008 had profits chargeable to corporation tax of £60,000.

Required

Advise Sofa Ltd as to the maximum amount of group relief that can potentially be claimed by each of its three subsidiary companies in respect of its trading loss for the year ended 31 March 2008.

For the purposes of answering this part of the question, you should assume that Sofa Ltd's tax adjusted trading loss for the year ended 31 March 2008 is £200,000.   **(5 marks)**

(Total = 25 marks)

65 David and Angela Brook

David and Angela Brook are a married couple. They disposed of the following assets during the tax year 2007/08:

Jointly owned property

(1)   On 29 July 2007 David and Angela sold a classic Ferrari motor car for £34,400. The motor car had been purchased on 17 January 2000 for £27,200.

(2)   On 30 September 2007 David and Angela sold a house for £393,900. The house had been purchased on 1 October 1986 for £86,000. David and Angela occupied the house as their main residence from the date of purchase until 31 March 1990.

The house was then unoccupied between 1 April 1990 and 31 December 1993 due to Angela being required by her employer to work elsewhere in the United Kingdom.

From 1 January 1994 until 31 December 2001 David and Angela again occupied the house as their main residence. The house was then unoccupied until it was sold on 30 September 2007.

Throughout the period 1 October 1986 to 30 September 2007 David and Angela did not have any other main residence. The indexation factor from October 1986 to April 1998 is 0.650.

David Brook

(1)   On 18 April 2007 David sold an antique table for £5,600. The antique table had been purchased on 27 May 2005 for £3,200.

(2)   On 5 May 2007 David transferred his entire shareholding of 20,000 £1 ordinary shares in Bend Ltd, an unquoted trading company, to Angela. On that date the shares were valued at £64,000. David's shareholding had been purchased on 21 June 2005 for £48,000.

(3)   On 14 February 2008 David made a gift of 15,000 £1 ordinary shares in Galatico plc to his son. On that date the shares were quoted on the Stock Exchange at £2.90 – £3.10. David had originally purchased 8,000 shares in Galatico plc on 15 June 2006 for £17,600, and he purchased a further 12,000 shares on 24 August 2006 for £21,600. David's total shareholding was less than 1% of Galatico plc's issued share capital.

Angela Brook

(1)   On 5 May 2007 Angela sold an antique clock for £7,200. The antique clock had been purchased on 14 June 2005 for £3,700.

(2)   On 7 July 2007 Angela sold 15,000 of the 20,000 £1 ordinary shares in Bend Ltd that had been transferred to her from David. The sale proceeds were £62,400.

Angela has taxable income of £40,000 for the tax year 2007/08. David does not have any taxable income.

Required

Compute David and Angela's respective capital gains tax liabilities for the tax year 2007/08.   **(20 marks)**

66 Edmond Brick

Edmond Brick owns four properties which are let out. The following information relates to the tax year 2007/08:

Property one

This is a freehold house that qualifies as a trade under the furnished holiday letting rules. The property was purchased on 6 April 2007. During the tax year 2007/08 the property was let for eighteen weeks at £370 per week. Edmond spent £5,700 on furniture and kitchen equipment during April 2007. Due to a serious flood £7,400 was spent on repairs during November 2007. The damage was not covered by insurance. The other expenditure on this property for the tax year 2007/08 amounted to £2,710, and this is all allowable.

Property two

This is a freehold house that is let out furnished. The property was let throughout the tax year 2007/08 at a monthly rent of £575, payable in advance. During the tax year 2007/08 Edmond paid council tax of £1,200 and insurance of £340 in respect of this property. He claims the wear and tear allowance for this property.

Property three

This is a freehold house that is let out unfurnished. The property was purchased on 6 April 2007, and it was empty until 30 June 2007. It was then let from 1 July 2007 to 31 January 2008 at a monthly rent of £710, payable in advance. On 31 January 2008 the tenant left owing three months rent which Edmond was unable to recover. The property was not re-let before 5 April 2008. During the tax year 2007/08 Edmond paid insurance of £290 for this property and spent £670 on advertising for tenants. He also paid loan interest of £6,700 in respect of a loan that was taken out to purchase this property.

Property four

This is a leasehold office building that is let out unfurnished. Edmond pays an annual rent of £6,800 for this property, but did not pay a premium when he acquired it. On 6 April 2007 the property was sub-let to a tenant, with Edmond receiving a premium of £15,000 for the grant of a five-year lease. He also received the annual rent of £4,600 which was payable in advance. During the tax year 2007/08 Edmond paid insurance of £360 in respect of this property.

Furnished room

During the tax year 2007/08 Edmond rented out one furnished room of his main residence. During the year he received rent of £5,040, and incurred allowable expenditure of £1,140 in respect of the room. Edmond always computes the taxable income for the furnished room on the most favourable basis.

Required

(a)   State the income tax advantages of property one being treated as a trade under the furnished holiday letting rules.   **(3 marks)**

(b)   Calculate Edmond's furnished holiday letting loss in respect of property one for the tax year 2007/08.
                                                                                             (3 marks)

(c)   Calculate Edmond's property business profit in respect of the other three properties and the furnished room for the tax year 2007/08.   **(9 marks)**

(Total = 15 marks)

67 Samantha Fabrique

Samantha Fabrique has been a self-employed manufacturer of clothing since 1995. She has the following gross income and chargeable gains for the tax years 2004/05 to 2007/08:

	2004/05	2005/06	2006/07	2007/08
	£	£	£	£
Trading profit/(loss)	6,290	51,600	(84,000)	12,390
Building society interest	–	2,100	3,800	1,500
Chargeable gains/(loss)	19,200	23,300	(3,400)	12,600

The chargeable gains are stated after taking account of indexation, but before taking account of loss relief and the annual exemption. No taper relief is available.

Required

(a)   State the factors that will influence an individual's choice of loss relief claims.   **(3 marks)**

(b)   Calculate Samantha's taxable income and taxable gains for each of the tax years 2004/05, 2005/06, 2006/07 and 2007/08 on the assumption that she relieves the trading loss of £84,000 for the tax year 2006/07 on the most favourable basis.

You should assume that the tax allowances for the tax year 2007/08 apply throughout.   **(7 marks)**

(Total = 10 marks)

Answers

**DO NOT TURN THIS PAGE UNTIL YOU HAVE
COMPLETED THE MOCK EXAM**

A plan of attack

What's the worst thing you could be doing right now if this was the actual exam paper? Sharpening your pencil? Wondering how to celebrate the end of the exam in about 3 hours time? Panicking, flapping and generally getting in a right old state?

Well, they're all pretty bad, so turn back to the paper and let's sort out a **plan of attack**!

First things first

You have fifteen minutes of reading time. Spend this looking carefully through the questions and deciding the order in which you will attempt them. As a general rule you should attempt the questions that you find easiest first and leave the hardest until last. Depending on how confident you are we recommend that you follow one of the following two options:

Option 1 (if you're thinking 'Help!')

If you're a bit worried about the paper, do the questions in the order of how well you think you can answer them. You may find the shorter questions less daunting than the longer questions. Alternatively, you may feel better prepared for questions 63 and 64 and wish to start there.

- **Question 63** part (a) tested income tax and national insurance contributions for a self-employed individual and an employed individual. It also covered self-assessment administration. Part (b) tested value added tax. This would have been a good question to start with as it covered topics you should have been familiar with and the computations (especially in part (b)) were not too lengthy.

- **Question 64** was about corporation tax. Part (a) was an adjustment of profits question with capital allowances and industrial buildings allowance. Part (b) could have been tackled separately and you might have wanted to do this part first before getting involved with the computations in part (a).

- **Question 65** dealt with capital gains tax for individuals. This was quite a lengthy computational question so you would have had to watch closely your time limit of 36 minutes for the 20 marks available.

- **Question 66** covered all aspects of property income. There were some trickier technical points here, but you should have been able to secure a reasonable pass on the more basic computations. Again, watch the time limit and move on to another question if you exceed it.

- **Question 67** was about trading losses for an individual. If you were happy with this area, it would have been a good place to start because this 10 mark question could easily have been answered in 18 minutes.

Lastly, what you mustn't forget is that you have to **answer all the questions on the paper. They are all compulsory**. Do not miss out any question or you will seriously affect your chance of passing.

Option 2 (if you're thinking 'It's a doddle')

It never pays to be over confident but if you're reasonably confident about the exam then it is best to work through the questions sequentially starting with question 63.

No matter how many times we remind you....

Always, always **allocate your time** according to the marks for the question in total and then according to the parts of the question. And **always, always follow the requirements** exactly. Did you state the due dates in Question 63(a)(iii)? These were easy marks and you should make sure that you get them.

You've got spare time at the end of the exam.....?

If you have allocated your time properly then you **shouldn't have time on your hands** at the end of the exam. But if you find yourself with five or ten minutes to spare, check over your work to make sure that there are no silly arithmetical errors.

Forget about it!

And don't worry if you found the paper difficult. More than likely other candidates will too. If this were the real thing you would need to **forget** the exam the minute you leave the exam hall and **think about the next one**. Or, if it's the last one, **celebrate**!

63 Vanessa Serve and Serene Volley

Text references. Chapter 2 deals with taxable income and computation of income tax. Chapter 5 covers pensions. Look in Chapters 8 and 9 for computation of trading income and capital allowances. Chapters 3 and 4 cover employment income. Chapter 12 deals with national insurance contributions. Chapter 18 covers self assessment. Value added tax is dealt with in Chapters 25 and 26.

Top tips. You should use the standard layout for income tax computations, separating out the different types of income. Note that part (b) on VAT could be tackled without reference to part (a) and you might have wanted to start on part (b).

Easy marks. The calculation of the national insurance contributions in part (a)(ii) were easy marks. You should also have known the due dates in part (a)(iii).

Marking scheme

			Marks	
(a)	(i)	*Vanessa Serve*		
		Trading profit	½	
		Capital allowances	1½	
		NS&I bank interest	1	
		Personal allowance	½	
		Extension of basic rate band	1	
		Income tax payable	1	
		Serene Volley		
		Salary	½	
		Pension contribution	1	
		Car benefit	1½	
		NS&I certificate interest – exempt	½	
		Personal allowance	½	
		Income tax liability	1	
		Income tax suffered at source	½	
				11
	(ii)	*Vanessa Serve*		
		Class 2 NICs	1	
		Class 4 NICs	1½	
		Serene Volley		
		Class 1 NICs	1½	
				4
	(iii)	*Vanessa Serve*		
		Balancing payment	1	
		Due date	½	
		Payments on account	1	
		Due dates	½	
		Serene Volley		
		Balancing payment	½	
		Due date	½	
		No payment on account required	1	
				5

(b) (i)   *Output tax*

Sales	½
Input tax	
Telephone	1
Car purchase	½
Car repairs	1
Equipment	1
Other expenses	1
	5

(ii) Fixed percentage scheme limits   2
      Simplified administration   1
      VAT saving   2

	5
	30

(a) (i)   **Vanessa Serve – income tax**

	Non-savings income £	Savings income £	Total £
Trading profit	52,400		
Less: capital allowance (W1)	(1,820)		
Taxable trading income	50,580		
NS&I bank interest (gross)		1,100	
Net income	50,580	1,100	51,680
Less: personal allowance	(5,225)		
Taxable income	45,355	1,100	46,455

Tax

	£
£2,230 × 10%	223
£32,370 × 22%	7,121
£6,400 × 22% (extended band for pension)	1,408
£4,355 × 40%	1,742
£1,100 × 40%	440
Income tax liability/payable	10,934

Working 1

	Car £	Allowance £
TWDV b/f	10,400	
Less WDA @ 25%	(2,600) × 14/20	1,820
TWDV c/f	7,800	

Serene Volley – income tax

	Non-savings income
	£
Salary	26,400
Less: pension contribution	(1,320)
	25,080
Car benefit (W2)	4,100
Net income	29,180
Less: personal allowance	(5,225)
Taxable income	23,955

Working 2

Car benefit percentage
190 – 140 = 50 ÷ 5 = 10 +15 = 25%

£16,400 x 25%   £4,100

Note
The interest on the NS&I savings certificates is exempt from income tax.

Tax

	£
£2,230 × 10%	223
£21,725 × 22%	4,780
Income tax liability	5,003
Less: PAYE	(4,790)
Income tax payable	213

(ii) **Vanessa Serve – national insurance contributions**

	£	£
Class 2 NICs		
52 × £2.20		114
Class 4 NICs		
£(34,840 – 5,225) = 29,615 × 8%	2,369	
£(50,580 – 34,840) = 15,740 × 1%	157	2,526
Total NICs		2,640

Serene Volley – national insurance contributions

	£
Class 1 NICs	
£(26,400 – 5,225) = 21,175 × 11%	£2,329

(iii) **Vanessa Serve – balancing payment and payments on account**
Balancing payment 2007/08

	£
Income tax and Class 4 payable £(10,934 + 2,526)	13,460
Less: payments on account	(8,460)
Income tax due on 31 January 2009	5,000

Payments on account 2008/09

Due 31 January 2009 £13,460 ÷ 2	£6,730
Due 31 July 2009 £13,460 ÷ 2	£6,730

Serene Volley – balancing payment and payments on account
Balancing payment 2007/08

Income tax due 31 January 2009	£213

Payments on account 2008/09

No payment on account required for as income tax due for previous tax year is below £500 *de minimis* limit

(b) (i) **Vanessa Serve – value added tax payable**

		£	£
Output tax			
Sales:	£18,000 × 17.5%		3,150
Input tax			
Telephone:	£600 × 17.5% × 60% (note 1)	63	
Car purchase (note 2)		0	
Car repairs:	£987 × 7/47 (note 3)	147	
Equipment:	£1,760 × 17.5% (note 4)	308	
Other expenses:	£(2,200 – 400) x 17.5% (note 5)	315	(833)
VAT payable for quarter ending 31 March 2008			2,317

Notes

1 Only the business element of telephone use is recoverable.

2 No input tax can be recovered on a car not exclusively used for business purposes.

3 The whole of the input tax on the car repairs is recoverable because there is some business use of the car.

4 The input tax on the equipment is recoverable in this VAT period because the actual tax point is 29 March 2008 when payment was made.

5 No input tax is recoverable on business entertaining.

(ii) To join the flat rate scheme, Vanessa's business must have:

- a tax exclusive annual taxable turnover of up to £150,000; and

- a tax exclusive annual total turnover, including the value of exempt and/or other non-taxable income, of up to £187,500.

The main advantage of using the scheme is the simplification of VAT administration. Since Vanessa does not have VAT registered customers, she would not have to issue VAT invoices. Also she would not have to record purchase invoices.

There may also be a VAT saving by using the flat rate scheme. For example, if Vanessa had used the scheme in the quarter to 31 March 2008, her VAT liability would have been:

Output tax

£(18,000 + 3,150) = £21,150 x 6%	£1,269
This is a saving of £(2,317 – 1,269)	£1,048

64 Sofa Ltd

> **Text references.** Chapter 19 deals with adjustment of profit for companies. Chapter 22 covers groups.
>
> **Top tips.** Make sure you read the information given in the question very carefully. You were told the figure to start your adjustment of profit. The examiner also gave a clue in part (b) about the figure that you should have ended up with for part (a).
>
> **Easy marks.** The capital allowances computation was straightforward if you used the standard format. The items to be disallowed should also have been well-known.

Marking scheme

		Marks
(a)	*Adjustment to profit*	
	Loss before taxation	½
	Depreciation	½
	Accountancy fees	½
	Legal fees – share capital	½
	Legal fees – renewal of short lease	½
	Legal fees – loan relationship	½
	New wall	½
	Repair to existing wall	½
	Business entertaining	½
	Staff entertaining	½
	Redundancy counselling	½
	Health and safety fine	½
	Profit on sale of shares	½
	Bank interest receiveable	½
	Debenture interest payable	1
	Capital allowances on P&M	
	TWDVs b/f	½
	Additions not qualifying for FYA	1
	Disposals	1
	Balancing charge on car	½
	WDAs	1
	Additions qualifying for FYA: equipment	½
	fixtures	½
	low emission car	½
	FYA @ 40%	½
	FYA @ 100%	½
	TWDVs c/f	½
	Allowances	1
	Industrial buildings allowance	
	Eligible expenditure	1
	Showroom	1
	Residue before sale	1
	25 year life	½
	WDA	½
		20

(b)   *Settee Ltd*

Availability of group relief	½	
Corresponding period 1	1	
Corresponding period 2	1	
Couch Ltd		
No group relief – not in 75% group	1	
Futon Ltd		
Availability of group relief	½	
Corresponding period	1	
		$\frac{5}{25}$

(a)   **Sofa Ltd – tax adjusted trading loss**

	£	£
Loss before taxation		(240,000)
Add: depreciation	87,100	
professional fees (note 1): share capital	7,800	
repairs and renewals (note 2): new wall	9,700	
other expenses (note 3): business entertaining	1,360	
fine	420	106,380
		(133,620)
Less: profit on sale of shares	4,300	
bank interest – taxed as interest income	8,400	
CAs on plant and machinery (W1)	40,680	
IBAs (W2)	13,000	(66,380)
Tax adjusted trading loss		(200,000)

Notes

1   The legal fees related to the renewal of a short lease (less than 50 years) are allowable. The cost of obtaining loan finance is allowable as a trading expense under the loan relationship rules as the loan was used for trading purposes.

2   The cost of the new wall is not allowable because it is a capital expense. The repair to the existing wall is allowable as a revenue expense.

3   Business entertaining is not allowable. Staff entertaining is allowable. Counselling on redundancy is specifically allowable. The health and safety fine is not allowable.

Workings

1   *Capital allowances on plant and machinery*

	FYA £	Pool £	Exp. car (1) £	Exp. car (2) £	Allowances £
TWDV b/f		16,700	16,400		
Additions not qualifying for FYA					
8.6.07 Car				22,200	
2.8.07 Car		10,900			
		27,600			
Disposals					
8.7.07 Car			(17,800)		
Balancing charge			(1,400)		(1,400)
8.1.08 Lorry		(7,600)			
18.1.08 Car		(8,800)			
		11,200			
WDA @ 25%		(2,800)			2,800
WDA max				(3,000)	3,000
Additions qualifying for FYA					
12.5.07 Equipment	11,400				
10.2.08 Fixtures (N1)	44,800				
	56,200				
Less: FYA @ 40% (note 2)	(22,480)	33,720			22,480
19.10.07 Car	13,800				
Less: FYA @ 100%	(13,800)	0			13,800
TWDV c/f		42,120		19,200	
Allowances					40,680

Notes

1   The sale price put on the fixtures can be an amount up their original cost. Since it has been agreed that Sofa Ltd is to obtain maximum capital allowances on the fixtures, the election must have been the maximum amount possible.

2   FYAs are available at 40% since the question states that Sofa Ltd is a medium sized company.

2   *Industrial buildings allowance*

	£
Original cost	475,262
Less: cost of land	(158,000)
Eligible expenditure (note)	317,262
Less: WDAs given to original owner	
y/e 31.12.03 to y/e 31.12.06 = 4 years	
£317,262 × 4 x 4%	(50,762)
Residue before sale	266,500

Note

The cost of the showroom is allowable because it is less than 25% of the eligible cost (£317,262 x 25% = £79,316).

Date brought into use	1 January 2003
Tax life ends	31 December 2027
Date of purchase	1 July 2007

Number of years of tax relief remaining at purchase is 20½ years.

WDA is $\dfrac{£266,500}{20\frac{1}{2}}$ = £13,000

(b) **Settee Ltd**

Group relief is available between Sofa Ltd and Settee Ltd because they are part of a 75% group.

Group relief applies to corresponding accounting periods.

Corresponding period 1 (1 April 2007 to 30 June 2007)
Loss of Sofa Ltd
3/12 x £200,000 £50,000

Profit of Settee Ltd
3/12 × £240,000 £60,000

Maximum group relief is lower of these two figures ie £50,000

Corresponding period 2 (1 July 2007 to 31 March 2008)
Loss of Sofa Ltd
9/12 × £200,000 £150,000

Profit of Settee Ltd
9/12 x £90,000 £67,500

Maximum group relief is lower of these two figures ie £67,500

Couch Ltd

There is no group relief available between Sofa Ltd and Couch Ltd because they are not members of a 75% group as Couch Ltd is only a 60% subsidiary.

Futon Ltd

Group relief is available between Sofa Ltd and Futon Ltd because they are part of a 75% group.

Corresponding period (1 January 2008 to 31 March 2008)
Loss of Sofa Ltd
3/12 x £200,000 £50,000

Profit of Futon Ltd £60,000

Maximum group relief is lower of these two figures ie £50,000

65 David and Angela Brook

Text references. Chapter 13 deals with general computation of chargeable gains and transfers between spouses are in Chapter 14. Chattels and Principal Private Residence relief are in Chapter 15. Shares are covered in Chapter 17.

Top tips. Work through the disposals in order and then bring them together in a summary for each taxpayer. Don't forget that you need to compute the capital gains tax liabilities, not just state the taxable gains.

Easy marks. The calculation of the gains before applying reliefs should have gained easy marks. Use of the annual exemption and calculation of the tax payable were also straightforward.

Marking scheme

		Marks
Jointly owned property		
Car – exempt		½
House:	Proceeds	½
	Cost	½
	Indexation	1
	PPR exemption period	2½
	Calculation of exemption	1
	Taper relief	1
David Brook		
Antique table – exempt		1
Bend Ltd – no gain, no loss disposal		½
Galatico plc:	Deemed proceeds	1
	Cost	2
Half share in house		½
Annual exemption		½
Capital gains tax		1
Angela Brook		
Antique clock – marginal relief		2
Bend Ltd:	Proceeds	½
	Cost	1
	Taper relief	1½
Half share in house		½
Annual exemption		½
Capital gains tax		½
		20

Jointly owned property

Car
Exempt asset

House

	£
Proceeds	393,900
Less: cost	(86,000)
	307,900
Less: indexation allowance £86,000 × 0.650	(55,900)
	252,000

Less: PPR relief (W1)

$£252,000 × \dfrac{219}{252}$ (219,000)

Gain before taper relief	33,000

Non business asset

Ownership period 6.4.98 to 30.9.07 = 9 years plus additional year = 10 years

Workings

1			Exempt months	Chargeable months
1.10.86 – 31.3.90	Actual occupation		42	
1.4.90 – 31.12.93	Up to 4 years working elsewhere		45	
1.1.94 – 31.12.01	Actual occupation		96	
1.1.02 – 30.9.04	Not occupied			33
1.10.04 – 30.9.07	Last 3 years		36	
Total months			219	33

David Brook – capital gains tax payable

Antique table
Exempt gain – non-wasting chattel sold for £6,000 or less

Bend Ltd
No gain, no loss transfer to spouse

Base cost for Angela £48,000

Galatico plc shares
Post 6.4.98 acquisitions – disposal on a last in, first out basis

24.8.06 acquisition

	£
Market value 12,000 x £2.95 (W2)	35,400
Less: cost	(21,600)
Gain before taper relief	13,800

Non business asset
Ownership period 24.8.06 to 14.2.08 = 1 year

15.6.06 acquisition

	£
Market value 3,000 x £2.95 (W2)	8,850
Less: cost $£17,600 × \dfrac{3,000}{8,000}$	(6,600)
Gain before taper relief	2,250

Non business asset
Ownership period 15.6.06 to 14.2.08 = 1 year

2   Quoted share valuation

£2.90 + ¼ £(3.10 – 2.90)

	Non business asset (10 years) £	Non business asset (less than 3 years) £2.95 £	Total £
½ share in house	16,500		
Galatico plc			
24.8.06 acquisition		13,800	
15.6.06 acquisition		2,250	
Gains before taper relief	16,500	16,050	
Taper relief percentage	60%	100%	
Gains after taper relief	9,900	16,050	25,950
Less: annual exemption			(9,200)
Taxable gains			16,750

Capital gains tax		
£2,230 × 10%		223
£(16,750 – 2,230) = £14,520 × 20%		2,904
Capital gains tax liability for David		3,127

Angela Brook – capital gains tax payable

Antique clock

Non-wasting chattel subject to marginal relief

	£
Proceeds	7,200
Less: cost	(3,700)
Gain	3,500
Gain cannot exceed £(7,200 – 6,000) = £1,200 × 5/3	2,000

Non-business asset
Ownership period 14.6.05 to 5.5.07 = 1 year

Bend Ltd shares

	£
Proceeds	62,400
Less: cost	
£48,000 × $\dfrac{15,000}{20,000}$	(36,000)
Gain before taper relief	26,400

Business asset (unquoted trading company)
Ownership period (runs from David's acquisition) 21.6.05 to 7.7.07 = 2 years

Summary

	Business asset (2+ years) £	Non business asset (10 years) £	Non business asset (less than 3 years) £	Total £
Bend Ltd shares	26,400			
½ share in house		16,500		
Antique clock			2,000	
Gains before taper relief	26,400	16,500	2,000	
Taper relief percentage	25%	60%	100%	
Gains after taper relief	6,600	9,900	2,000	18,500
Less: annual exemption				(9,200)
Taxable gains				9,300
CGT liability £9,300 × 40%				3,720

66 Edmond Brick

Text references. Chapter 6 deals with property income.

Top tips. Remember that property income is pooled to give a single profit or loss. However, if someone has furnished holiday lettings and other lettings, two sets of accounts have to be drawn up as if there were two separate UK property businesses. This is so that profits and losses treated as trade profits and losses can be identified. The examiner has helpfully structured this question so that you were required to make such separate calculations.

Easy marks. Deduction of expenses such as council tax, insurance and advertising were easy marks.

Marking scheme

			Marks
(a)	Availability of capital allowances	1	
	Trading loss relief	1	
	Relevant earnings for pension purposes	1	
			3
(b)	Rent receiveable	½	
	Repairs	1	
	Other expenses	½	
	Capital allowances	1	
			3

(c)   *Property two*

Rent receiveable		½
Council tax		½
Insurance		½
Wear and tear allowance		1
Property three		
Rent receiveable		½
Insurance		½
Advertising		½
Impairment loss		½
Loan interest		½
Property four		
Lease premium		1
Rent receiveable		½
Insurance		½
Rent paid		½
Room		
Rent received		½
Rent a room relief		1

$$\frac{9}{15}$$

(a)   The income tax advantages of Property one being treated as a trade under the furnished holiday letting rules are:

(i)   Capital allowances are available on furniture instead of the 10% wear and tear allowance.

(ii)   Loss relief is available against general income instead of just against property business income.

(iii)   The income qualifies as relevant earnings for pension relief purposes.

(b)   **Property one**

	£
Rent receivable £370 × 18	6,660
Less: repairs	(7,400)
other allowable expenditure	(2,710)
capital allowances	
£5,700 × 50% (FYA)	(2,850)
Loss	(6,300)

(c)   **Property two**

	£	£
Rent receivable £575 × 12	6,900	
Less: council tax	(1,200)	
insurance	(340)	
wear and tear allowance		
10% × £(6,900 − 1,200)	(570)	
Profit		4,790

Property three

	£	£
Rent receivable £710 × 7	4,970	
Less: insurance	(290)	
advertising	(670)	
impairment loss £710 × 3	(2,130)	
loan interest	(6,700)	
Loss		(4,820)

Property four

Premium taxable as property business income (W)	13,800	
Rent receiveable	4,600	
	18,400	
Less: insurance	(360)	
rent payable	(6,800)	
		11,240
Furnished Room		
Rent receiveable	5,040	
Less: rent a room relief (note)	(4,250)	
Profit		790
Property business profit		12,000

Working

	£
Premium paid	15,000
Less: 2% × (5-1) × £15,000	(1,200)
Taxable as property business income	13,800

Note

Claiming rent a room relief in respect of the furnished room £(5,040 − 4,250) = £790 is more beneficial than the normal basis of assessment £(5,040 − 1,140) = £3,900.

67 Samantha Fabrique

Text references. Chapter 10 deals with trading losses.

Top tips. You should use the standard layout for losses: set up the columns and lines required and then slot in the numbers. A loss memorandum is also useful as a double check that you have used the losses correctly.

Easy marks. There were easy marks for setting out the trading income and gains stated in the question and using the personal allowance and annual exemption.

Marking scheme

			Marks
(a)	Rate of tax	1	
	Timing of relief	1	
	Waste of personal allowance/annual exemption	1	
			3
(b)	Trading income	½	
	Trading loss relief carried forward	1	
	Building society interest	½	
	Trading loss relief against general income	1	
	Personal allowance	½	
	Gains	½	
	Capital loss relief carried forward	1	
	Trading loss relief against gains	1	
	Annual exemption	1	7
			10

(a) Factors that will influence an individual's choice of loss relief claim are:

(i) The rate of income tax or capital gains tax at which relief will be obtained, with preference being given to income or capital gains charged at the higher rate of 40%.

(ii) The timing of the relief obtained, with a claim against general income/capital gains of the current year or preceding year resulting in earlier relief than a carry forward claim against future trading profits.

(iii) The extent to which the income tax personal allowance and the capital gains tax annual exemption will be wasted by using a claim against general income/capital gains.

(b) **Samantha Fabrique – taxable income**

	2004/05 £	2005/06 £	2006/07 £	2007/08 £
Trading income	6,290	51,600	0	12,390
Less: trading loss relief carried forward	(0)	(0)	(0)	(7,000)
	6,290	51,600	0	5,390
Building society interest	0	2,100	3,800	1,500
	6,290	53,700	3,800	6,890
Less: trading loss relief against general income (N)	(0)	(53,700)	(0)	(0)
Net income	6,290	0	3,800	6,890
Less: personal allowance	(5,225)	(0)	(3,800)	(5,225)
Taxable income	1,065	0	0	1,665

Samantha Frabrique – taxable gains

	2004/05 £	2005/06 £	2006/07 £	2007/08 £
Gains	19,200	23,300	0	12,600
Less: trading loss relief against gains (note)	(0)	(23,300)	(0)	(0)
	19,200	0	0	12,600
Less: capital loss carried forward	(0)	(0)	(0)	(3,400)
	19,200	0	0	9,200
Less: personal allowance	(9,200)	(0)	(0)	(9,200)
Taxable gains	10,000	0	0	0

Note

Loss relief has been claimed against general income and gains for 2005/06 since this gives relief at the earliest date and at the highest rate of tax. No claim should be made to set the loss against general income in 2006/07 since this is already covered by the personal allowance for that year.

Trading loss memorandum

	£
Loss 2006/07	84,000
Less: used 2005/06 (income)	(53,700)
used 2005/06 (gains)	(23,300)
Available for c/f	7,000
Less: used 2007/08	(7,000)
Loss unused	0

Tax tables

The following tax rates and allowances are to be used in answering the questions

Income tax

Starting rate	£1 – £2,230	10%
Basic rate	£2,231 – £34,600	22%
Higher rate	£34,601 and above	40%

Personal allowances

	£
	£
Personal allowance	5,225
Personal allowance aged 65 to 74	7,550
Personal allowance aged 75 and over	7,690
Income limit for age-related allowances	20,900

Car benefit percentage

The base level of CO_2 emissions is 140 grams per kilometre.

Car fuel benefit

The base figure for calculating the car fuel benefit is £14,400.

Pension scheme limits

Annual allowance	£225,000

The maximum contribution that can qualify for tax relief without any earnings is £3,600.

Capital allowances

	%
Plant and machinery	
Writing down allowance	25
First year allowance – plant and machinery	40
– low emission motor cars (CO_2 emissions less than 120 g/km)	100

For small businesses only: the rate of plant and machinery first-year allowance is 50% for the period from 1 April 2006 to 31 March 2008 (6 April 2006 and 5 April 2008 for unincorporated businesses).

Long-life assets

Writing-down allowance	6

Industrial buildings

Writing-down allowance	4

Corporation tax

Financial year	2005	2006	2007
Small companies (SC) rate	19%	19%	20%
Full rate	30%	30%	30%
Lower limit	£30,000	£300,000	£300,000
Upper limit	£1,500,000	£1,500,000	£1,500,000
Marginal relief fraction:	11/400	11/400	1/40

Marginal relief

$(M – P) \times I/P \times$ marginal relief fraction

Value Added Tax

Registration limit	£64,000
Deregistration limit	£62,000

Capital gains tax: annual exemption

Individuals £9,200

Capital gains tax: taper relief

The percentage of the gain chargeable is as follows:

Complete years after 5 April 1998 for which asset held	Gains on business assets (%)	Gains on non-business assets (%)
0	100	100
1	50	100
2	25	100
3	25	95
4	25	90
5	25	85
6	25	80
7	25	75
8	25	70
9	25	65
10	25	60

National insurance (not contracted-out rates)

		%
Class 1 employee	£1 – £5,225 per year	Nil
	£5,226 – £34,840 per year	11.0
	£34,841 and above per year	1.0
Class 1 employer	£1 – £5,225 per year	Nil
	£5,226 and above per year	12.8
Class 1A		12.8
Class 2	£2.20 per week	
Class 4	£1 – £5,225 per year	Nil
	£5,226 – £34,840 per year	8.0
	£34,841 and above per year	1.0

Rates of Interest

Official rate of interest	6.25%
Rate of interest on underpaid tax	7.5% (assumed)
Rate of interest on overpaid tax	3.0% (assumed)

Calculations and workings need only be made to the nearest £.

All apportionments may be made to the nearest month.

All workings should be shown.

Review Form & Free Prize Draw – Paper F6 Taxation (1/08)

All original review forms from the entire BPP range, completed with genuine comments, will be entered into one of two draws on 31 July 2008 and 31 January 2009. The names on the first four forms picked out on each occasion will be sent a cheque for £50.

Name: _____   Address: _____

_____

_____

How have you used this Kit?
(Tick one box only)

☐ Home study (book only)

☐ On a course: college _____

☐ With 'correspondence' package

☐ Other _____

Why did you decide to purchase this Kit?
(Tick one box only)

☐ Have used the complementary Study text

☐ Have used other BPP products in the past

☐ Recommendation by friend/colleague

☐ Recommendation by a lecturer at college

☐ Saw advertising

☐ Other _____

During the past six months do you recall seeing/receiving any of the following?
(Tick as many boxes as are relevant)

☐ Our advertisement in *Student Accountant*

☐ Our advertisement in *Pass*

☐ Our advertisement in *PQ*

☐ Our brochure with a letter through the post

☐ Our website www.bpp.com

Which (if any) aspects of our advertising do you find useful?
(Tick as many boxes as are relevant)

☐ Prices and publication dates of new editions

☐ Information on product content

☐ Facility to order books off-the-page

☐ None of the above

Which BPP products have you used?

Text	☐	Success CD	☐	Learn Online	☐
Kit	☑	i-Learn	☐	Home Study Package	☐
Passcard	☐	i-Pass	☐	Home Study PLUS	☐

Your ratings, comments and suggestions would be appreciated on the following areas.

	Very useful	Useful	Not useful
Passing ACCA exams	☐	☐	☐
Passing F6	☐	☐	☐
Planning your question practice	☐	☐	☐
Questions	☐	☐	☐
Top Tips etc in answers	☐	☐	☐
Content and structure of answers	☐	☐	☐
'Plan of attack' in mock exams	☐	☐	☐
Mock exam answers	☐	☐	☐

Overall opinion of this Kit	Excellent ☐	Good ☐	Adequate ☐	Poor ☐

Do you intend to continue using BPP products?   Yes ☐   No ☐

The BPP author of this edition can be e-mailed at: suedexter@bpp.com

Please return this form to: Lesley Buick, ACCA Publishing Manager, BPP Learning Media Ltd, FREEPOST, London, W12 8BR

Review Form & Free Prize Draw (continued)

TELL US WHAT YOU THINK

Please note any further comments and suggestions/errors below.

Free Prize Draw Rules

1   Closing date for 31 July 2008 draw is 30 June 2008. Closing date for 31 January 2009 draw is 31 December 2008.

2   Restricted to entries with UK and Eire addresses only. BPP employees, their families and business associates are excluded.

3   No purchase necessary. Entry forms are available upon request from BPP Learning Media Ltd. No more than one entry per title, per person. Draw restricted to persons aged 16 and over.

4   Winners will be notified by post and receive their cheques not later than 6 weeks after the relevant draw date.

5   The decision of the promoter in all matters is final and binding. No correspondence will be entered into.